'With its immense detail, valuable information and lovely photography, this is for those who take their food and wine extremely seriously . . .' — **The Age**

'One of the most elegant and articulate travel and cookbooks . . .' — **Daily Telegraph**

'Acclaimed chef Dansereau takes you on an insider's tour of France and Italy, visiting the best restaurants, food and wine producers and hotels in both countries. As well as making you drool with desire, it's full of tips for when you're over there.' — **New Woman**

'. . . laced with history, recipes and anecdotes' — **Vogue Living**

'Passion shines through each page of Food & Friends . . .' — **Winehunter Magazine**

'The photography is splendidly, evocatively personal, and it's matched only by the persuasive, easy authority of the writing' — **Oyster Magazine**

'Food & Friends is about generosity, expertise and quality. Most of all it's about a passion for food.' — **Blue Magazine**

Serge Dansereau is the chef and co-owner of The Bathers Pavilion in Balmoral, Sydney. Born into a French-Canadian family, he pursued a career of excellence in the hospitality industry, winning the position of executive chef at The Regent, Sydney, at the extraordinarily young age of twenty-seven. Serge is most well known in Australia for his support of small producers and for his commitment to using the finest of ingredients.

Serge is married to Yvette Eunson and together they live in Balmoral with their young daughter, Céleste.

FOOD &

A chef's journey through France & Italy

FRIENDS

Serge Dansereau

HarperCollins*Publishers*

I would like to dedicate this book to:

My parents, who instilled in me respect for others
and dedication to work;

Klaus, my first chef, who taught me by selfless example
and devotion;

Ted, who gave me a unique chance and kept me ever-focused;

Yvette, *ma raison de vivre joyeusement.*

HarperCollins*Publishers*

First published in Australia in 1998
This new edition published in 2000
Reprinted in 2000
by HarperCollins*Publishers* Pty Limited
ABN 36 009 913 517
A member of the HarperCollins*Publishers* (Australia) Pty Limited Group
http://www.harpercollins.com.au

HarperCollins*Publishers*

25 Ryde Road, Pymble, Sydney NSW 2073, Australia
31 View Road, Glenfield, Auckland 10, New Zealand
77–85 Fulham Palace Road, London W6 8JB, United Kingdom
Hazelton Lanes, 55 Avenue Road, Suite 2900, Toronto, Ontario M5R 3L2
and 1995 Markham Road, Scarborough, Ontario M1B 5M8 Canada
10 East 53rd Street, New York NY 10022, USA

National Library of Australia Cataloguing-in-Publication data:

Dansereau, Serge, 1956– .
Food and friends: a chef's journey through France & Italy.
ISBN 0 7322 6446 4.
1. Cookery, Italian. 2. Cookery, French. 3. Cooks — Italy.
4. Cooks — France. 5. Italy — Description and travel.
6. France — Description and travel. I. Title.
641.50944

Designed by Katie Mitchell, HarperCollins Design Studio
Typeset in Giovanni 9.5/16
Printed in Australia by Griffin Press on 70 gsm Ensobelle
7 6 5 4 3 2   00 01 02 03

CONTENTS

Preface

When the time came to revise *Food & Friends* for a new edition, my first thought was that maybe it was time to create a reading version of my book. This might sound strange, but at approximately one kilogram, the original version did not make for easy bedtime reading.

I loved the original format, the quality of the paper, the layout and the way it showcased so many of the photographs that I took during my travels. Despite the success of the first version (it even won the Julia Child Cookbook Award for Best Design), after a while I felt that people loved the book more for the pictures and the accessibility it offered to parts of the text rather than the whole story. The question I guess most authors ask themselves is, do people read the text? In the case of cookbooks the question is a very valid one, as pictures of gorgeous food can be satisfaction enough.

I worked for nearly one year on the original manuscript, reliving my travels, my encounters with the food artisans and wine makers of France and Italy, researching the history and the development of specific products. All of this went in to a rich and rambling text that was politely pruned back by my editor. A third of my original text did not go into the book.

This second version allowed me to include some previously unpublished text, but mostly it makes the book accessible and easier to read.

If this book can reach more young chefs who need to be inspired as I was inspired by my travels, if it can reach food lovers, people afraid to cook or in need of a reason to cook, or weary travellers who seek a dream and a goal to reach, then I will be delighted with this new version of *Food & Friends*.

S.D.

Acknowledgments

While planning our primary travel schedule, Yvette and I were the beneficiaries of recommendations from friends and food colleagues. Our thanks go to Deeta Colvin, who represents some of the great houses of France, and Simon Johnson, who made many of the bookings in Italy; and to Qantas, who helped us with our travel arrangements and provided valuable support.

In France I have to thank Ken Hom; Lionel Poilâne; Jacques Vernier; Monsieur Rouzaud, the owner of Champagne Louis Roederer; Philippe Heusch of Georges Bruck; Paul Haeberlin; Jacques Lameloise; Georges Blanc; Anne Willan and her husband Mark at Château du Feÿ; Philippe Frick from Domaine Laroche; Jean-Claude Monteil; Dominique Hériard-Dubreuil, President of Rémy Martin, and Jason Bowden; Pierre-Jean Pébeyre and his father Jacques; Max, my friend in Monaco; and Alain Ducasse, who opened his kitchens to me in Paris and Monaco.

In Italy my profound thanks go to Fausto, the concierge at the Hotel Splendido in Portofino; to Vincenzo Finizola, general manager of the Four Seasons Hotel, Milan; to Elisabetta Bastianello; Jean Salvadore at the Villa d'Este; Dr Roberto Corradi; Gabriele Ferron at Pila Vecia; Natale Rusconi and his team at the

Cipriani Hotel in Venice; my life-long friend Annie Feolde from Enoteca Ristorante Pinchiorri; Roberto Guldener and the two Majas; Allegra Antinori at Castello della Sala; Maria Possenti; Carlo and Carla Latini; Marina Colonna; and Diane Seed.

Back in Australia I need to generously thank all my staff who have supported me during different periods over the past fifteen years; specifically I need to thank Elaine Kwok for her help, as well as Nichan Chahinian, Andrew Price, Udo Maik, Terence Rego, Richard Allsop and many other chefs in the kitchen, but above all and with great respect I thank Ron Coleman, my loyal, hardworking and talented assistant, a chef who understands flavour like no one else.

I would like to acknowledge the team at HarperCollins who worked on the first edition of *Food & Friends*, and now on this new paperback travel edition of the book.

And, finally, to my darling Yvette, who had to suffer two months of constant travel, little sleep, fast driving, interminable meals and my manic energy, only to come back to Australia to constantly support me and keep me focused to produce this book—to her I give my deepest thanks, love and appreciation.

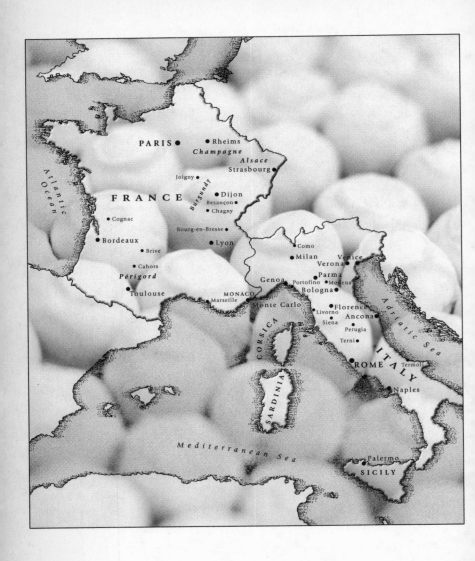

PROLOGUE

*I*t was 7.00 am and I had been up since the first rays of the sun appeared on this Parisian dawn. The excitement of meeting Lionel Poilâne had been keeping me awake since the early hours of the morning—that and the prospect of tasting a slice of oak-fired, heavy-crusted bread fresh from the oven of the most famous baker in the world.

Monsieur Poilâne, whom I had met once before on a memorable visit to Paris some years ago, engendered in me a sense of awe on account of his dedication to the preservation of his craft and the authenticity of his product. His *pain au levain* (sourdough bread loaf) was known the world over and could be sampled by people fortunate enough to live in or visit France, and by those in Tokyo, London and New York who were to able to purchase the fresh, air-freighted bread.

Lionel and I had arranged to meet for breakfast in his *boulangerie* on rue du Cherche-Midi, but as usual I was early. To delay my arrival I decided to stop at a café-bar and have a *jus de pamplemousse* (grapefruit juice).

It is always fascinating to watch the parade of life early in the morning, but never more so than on the first morning of one's visit to a city like Paris. My wife Yvette and I had arrived in France only the night before, and the excitement of being in the most beautiful city in the world had brightened our eyes. We were looking forward to wandering the streets of Paris, making discovery after discovery in dusty music shops, second-hand bookshops, tiny bistros that never made it into any guide, intriguing museums and indescribable food shops. For us, this vacation was long overdue. In my ten years of work as executive chef at the Regent Hotel in Sydney, I had scarcely taken a break. Now, during the quieter winter season at the hotel, I could finally afford to take two whole months off. Our itinerary was busy—our schedule had become increasingly challenging as overseas friends insisted that we visit their local producers or eat at their favourite restaurants—but we were looking forward to enjoying every minute of this holiday.

As I sat sipping my juice, I reflected on the fact that this tour was always going to be unique. It was to be a once-in-a-lifetime event, a rare opportunity to view, experience, discuss and learn not only about the quality of the products sampled, but also about the importance of the men and women who created them. We were in the privileged position of being able to go behind the scenes to look at some of the best restaurants, food and wine producers and hotels in France and Italy. So many friends had offered to open their doors, homes and hearts to us to help us make our journey a rare experience. We were grateful, and we were excited.

But on this first morning of our holiday, in April 1997, when the first tiny buds were sprouting on the chestnut trees along the Champs Élysées, Yvette had decided to put off the start of what we both knew would be a demanding trip and enjoy the luxury of an extra few hours in bed. We were staying in the apartment of my friend Ken Hom, the talented chef, writer and television presenter whom I first met more than ten years ago at the launch of his *East*

Meets West cookbook. Ken was not in town at the time of our visit, but he had generously lent us his apartment, located in a quiet cul-de-sac at the foot of the historic Montmartre hill and close to many of the city's finer restaurants, food stores and street markets. For Yvette, however, the delights of Paris could wait: a sleep-in was her first priority.

And so, having left my wife amongst a pile of duvets, her only valediction being the request that I bring her back a fresh croissant, I had wandered out of the apartment and into a crisp spring morning, ready to take on the day.

Sitting in the café, I smiled at the sight of the *garçon* being considerately distant with his customers. He was giving them the space deemed necessary in the morning; chatting, after all, could be kept for the inevitable afternoon return visit. Fresh beer kegs were being delivered to the café, and this prompted me to return to the subject that had never been far from my thoughts: bread. I remembered reading somewhere that Lionel described his bread as 'solid beer'. My mouth started watering at the thought of what lay in store for me.

I looked at my watch. It was still a little before the appointed time, but I decided to pay my visit to Lionel Poilâne anyway. I had only to stroll over to the next street, the fashionable rue du Cherche-Midi, and I had arrived at the *boulangerie*.

The shop was small and it struck me as very rustic for a *quartier* that is now characterised by all that is sleek and modern. Customers were already queuing up. The sight reminded me of an article I had read some time ago, telling of how, during the Cold War, pictures of the famous queues at Boulangerie Poilâne were used in Moscow to illustrate the failure of the capitalist system to feed its people. Little could the recipients of such propaganda have known that the people photographed were actually lining up for a luxury product! To me, the sight of the queue merely illustrated the failure of most other bakeries to provide a product that the public wished to eat.

The smell and the warmth were the first things to accost my senses. As I was ushered into the back room, where most of Monsieur Poilâne's visitors are met, I felt like a pilgrim entering St Peter's to be received by the highest authority. Looking around, I gained a sense of Monsieur Poilâne's respect for the past. His rustic table and chairs were practical and appropriate, with no compromise to modernity. The walls were covered with paintings of beautiful breads that artists over the years had exchanged for Poilâne's product.

I did not have to wait long for Monsieur Poilâne to appear and greet me. He remembered me from years ago on my first visit to Paris—a remarkable thing, considering the number of people he must have met through his work. Lionel Poilâne is fond of saying that he likes to recognise the bakers out of his customers in the shop. Sometimes, in the middle of a tour, a visitor has admitted to being a baker, and Lionel has responded that he didn't need to be told that: the person's heavy hands, red eyes and the pallor brought about by working all night long in a bakery were dead give-aways.

Lionel has always been generous towards his own colleagues, or to people who show a genuine interest in bread. He sees himself as a preserver of a unique product, a product that is nearly as old as the human race itself. The ability to cultivate wheat has often been cited as one of the reasons why humans became established in permanent settlements. Lionel explained to me that some of the very first technological inventions were created to aid the harvesting and milling of grains. A grain, he added, stored an enormous amount of information about our past, like a sort of DNA of our heritage.

Lionel took me to the *fournil*, or bakehouse. For me, standing there marked a moment that is difficult to describe. Some places have a huge impact on your life, and this was such a place for me. It was like a revelation, a religious experience, not so much because the *fournil* was old and historic but because it represented an attitude—a belief that you can make your mark in the world if you focus and believe strongly enough in your product. This feeling, which I first experienced when I visited Monsieur Poilâne years ago, was now even stronger. I understood and further appreciated his achievement.

The *boulangers* on duty were starting up the ovens to prepare for the next batch of bread. The force of the roaring fires was so intense that I thought they must have been fuelled by compressed gas. I was wrong. The intensity of the heat, Lionel told me, was created by the specific design of the building, which created the necessary conditions for a very strong updraught.

The role of the baker is critical, as at Boulangerie Poilâne no standard recipe is provided and no scales or measuring instruments are at hand. As the vagaries of bread preparation are too great to be encapsulated in written instructions, bakers are the best, indeed *only*, means of achieving perfect bread. They have to read the elements: humidity, outside temperature, storms. They have to read the condition of the ingredients: flour temperature and composition, strength of the fermentation. And then there are the exterior factors, like room and oven temperature, and the size of *la pétrie* (the dough), that have to be taken into consideration. These factors must all be judged and balanced to create a bread that will represent the product of the house. No two batches will ever be identical, and this is because of the personalities of the different bakers employed by Poilâne, and the varying conditions of the *pétrie*.

The first step for the bakers at Boulangerie Poilâne is to prepare the *pétrie*. The difference between what we consider normal bread and Poilâne's sourdough is natural fermentation, or wild fermentation, to provide the raising agent. This is called *fermentation au levain* and is quite unlike the more predictable and controllable industrial yeast. In Poilâne's case, the *levain* (leaven) is created by keeping a small amount of dough from the previous batch to be introduced into the new *pétrie* as the starting mixture. This link with each batch does not guarantee consistency of texture, but it does ensure a similarity of taste.

Once the baker has his four ingredients at the ready—leaven, flour, salt and water—the *pétrissage* (mixing) begins by using an electric mixer, the only concession to modernity in the *fournil*. The introduction of the electric mixer was highly controversial in the bread-making community at the time, as it was seen as a way to reduce the number of bakers a firm would employ. Fierce debates (quite common in French society) were held to resist its introduction. In most cases it was introduced in secret after proving that it did not affect the quality of the bread. One can only imagine how exhausting it must have been to make a *fournée* (batch) when bakers used to mix everything by hand. Lionel could remember doing this during many frustrating nights in the 1960s, a time of frequent power cuts.

The next stage for Lionel's bakers is the resting of the dough. This is accomplished while the *pâtière* (raw dough) is covered by cloths to protect it against the draughts that feed the oven, and placed near the heat source of the oven to help in the development of the leaven. After the dough has increased by one third in volume, the sensitive work really begins. The dough, which now weighs over 100 kilograms (220 pounds), needs to be divided into lots of precisely 2100 grams (4½ pounds)—mostly without using scales. Monsieur Poilâne told me that 'a dough precisely weighed is a dough with an unnatural feel.'

The separate pieces of dough are then allowed to rise in *panetons entoilés* (cloth-lined wicker baskets) covered with heavy cloths. When judged ready they are floured and marked with the traditional Poilâne pattern of four slashes forming a square.

The most rewarding stage of the process comes next: the *enfournage*, where, with a quick action of the baker's wrist, the dough is loaded on the *pelle* (paddle) and the oven filled as fast as possible. This takes up to twenty minutes. Water is sometimes sprayed to help the bread avoid premature drying and to give the loaves a thicker crust. The loaves are ready when most of the moisture has evaporated and the dough is cooked to a crisp, darkish colour.

The *défournage* is an exercise in juggling: the less contact the baker's hands have with the hot bread, the fewer burns the baker will suffer. It was quite an event to see loaves flying and being caught by the skilful bakers who loaded them into the cooling racks. For the bakers at Boulangerie Poilâne, the most annoying part of the breadmaking process is the transporting of the heavy loaves to the resting room, one floor up, through the only exit—a dreaded, narrow staircase. In the resting room more moisture is leached out in the now fogged-up room, where the bread waits for only a few minutes before it is distributed to the discerning customers of Paris.

After my tour of the *fournil* I was taken back to Lionel's *atelier* (meeting room) where we were to have breakfast together. I certainly didn't complain, as my appetite had been well and truly stimulated by the aroma of the freshly baked bread. A basket of pastries arrived with a great heap of sliced and toasted sourdough bread. Apart from the bread, the most famous item in Poilâne's shop has to be the delicious apple tarts ... or is it the thick and heavy raisin bread ... or the shortbread biscuits ... or perhaps the flaky, light and crispy croissants ... ? Whatever the case, my own favourite was the rich and decadent *pain au chocolat*. The *tartines* (bread slices) were buttered by Lionel and offered with beautiful wild honey, *confitures de fruits* (fruit jam) and fragrant tea. Lionel had a traditional *café au lait*. His voice changed to a soft melody when he took a call from his young daughter, but strengthened imperiously to call Marie Thérèse, his assistant, when he needed to change an appointment. There was no doubt Lionel was used to directing a large organisation with strong leadership. In bliss I continued eating my pastries, glad to be free of those responsibilities that I had so recently left behind in Sydney.

Before departing I visited Monsieur Poilâne's suite-like offices, located on the floors above the bakery. Here the ordering, finance, payroll and all other facets of this multimillion-dollar business took place. It was also here that Lionel kept his incredible collection of antiquarian books on bread. His profound attachment to the past, combined with a keen interest in the present, was revealed by the scope of his interests and the artefacts thereof: aviation, pedagogy, astronomy, art, science, modernism, gastronomy—nothing escaped this man's interest. Never had I met a more intellectual and articulate man with such gentle generosity. I left, physically and intellectually replenished.

If I had derived so much pleasure and knowledge from just one morning, how much more lay in store for me in the days and weeks ahead, I wondered?

PARIS ON A PLATE

O*ne of the joys of Paris is to see and be tempted by the* incredible array of fresh produce offered in the many picturesque market streets of the city. If you have access to a kitchen you can be blessed with the experience of cooking with some of the best products in the world. Luckily for Yvette and I, not only did Ken have a very well-equipped and functional kitchen, but he also lived near one of the best market streets in Paris: rue Lepic.

To visit this street and to see the variety of products on offer is an exhilarating experience. For me, it proved to be very difficult to choose anything at all, as everything seemed so appealing. In the end I purchased enough for three meals, thinking I bought only for one.

Most market streets have a great variety of merchants: butchers, fishmongers, cheese sellers and greengrocers. There is often also a chocolate shop, a wine merchant, a delicatessen and a mini market (groceries), not to forget the all-essential bakery and pastry shop. During our one-week stay in Paris, Yvette and I took our time to establish our preferred suppliers. Several visits were necessary to find which ones specialised in a particular product and could provide us with the freshest and best quality available.

It took us time to get used to the Parisian fridge, where space is very restricted—unlike the average Australian or American model.

In Paris you really need to purchase small quantities on a daily basis and try only to think ahead one or two meals at a time instead of stocking up for the whole week. This has several advantages: it encourages buying fresh food; it forces you to shop for and understand quality; and it helps you to build a menu with a view to seasonal availability. The best and most ideal method for preparing a menu, we discovered, was to select a central item around which to build a balanced and seasonal menu that was both to our taste and appropriate to the occasion.

Every day we ventured to the market street of rue Lepic and selected food for an upcoming breakfast or dinner—lunch mostly being taken outside at a café or with a friend at a brasserie.

At the top of the street was the Boulangerie D. Perrat—Boulanger-Confiseur-Glacier-Pâtissier. The building stood proudly at the corner with rue des Abbesses. The *gâteaux* (cakes) and *viennoiserie* (pastries) were displayed in the windows in so visually tempting a fashion that it was not hard to imagine hundreds of Parisian households gorging themselves on these great concoctions daily. A small car pulled up in front of the shop and opened its boot to reveal a mountain of freshly baked *baguettes*, *demis* and *ficelles* (breads) that quickly sold to customers like us. We could not resist the thin, crusty *ficelle* and decided that it would be part of our dinner—ideal for the oysters that we planned to buy. I knew I would have to come back over the next few days to try the *brioche Danoise* (Danish pastries) and my favourite, the delicious *pain au chocolat* that smelled so good. I made a mental note to pick up some of those early the following morning when they were sure to be very fresh.

At Poissonnerie de la Butte at the top of rue Lepic we inspected all the new arrivals from the coasts of France and other more distant destinations. We saw *palourdes* (clams) of an enormous size, *homards* (lobsters) from Brittany, *lotte* (monkfish), *Saint-Pierre* (John Dory, smaller in size compared to those found in Australia), *moules de Couchot* (black mussels), *thon* (tuna) from Spain, *fines de claire* (oysters kept fresh in a basket of seaweed), *rougets* (red mullet—a small fish prized by all French chefs), *langoustines* (scampi), *bigorneaux* (winkles), the exotic *bulots* (whelks) and *amande-de-mer* (shellfish), as well as *coquilles Saint-Jacques* (scallops) in their shells packed in wooden baskets, and many other fish that could only inspire visions of great recipes. I selected sixteen oysters of different sizes and planned to prepare them for us in two ways: fresh and steamed, with maybe some ginger and rice vinegar.

We then passed the simply named shop, Fleuriste, which was full of fresh flowers from all over Europe (and maybe Australia too—I saw native flowers that grow around Sydney). The array of flowers was quite astonishing. For Parisians, shopping is not complete without bringing home at least one bunch of beautiful, scented flowers.

At the next shop, Boucherie Chevaline, we admired the display but purchased no products. On display were cuts of horse meat such as *filet de cheval* (horse steak), *jambon de cheval* (horse ham), and *rillettes* (coarse patés) made of horse meat, a dish which was once prized by the Parisians and still has a loyal following. At one time the meat was highly recommended by French doctors for people with certain allergies. Today it is mostly older people who indulge in its consumption. Some ardent lovers will tell you that it is better than beef and that it is the only meat to use if you wish to have a true steak tartare. Horse meat does not differ that much in taste from beef. It is somewhat leaner, however, and has a texture not dissimilar to venison.

Our next stop was at an impressive cheese shop, M. Catherine, Fromager, which also sold milk, cream and butter. Great mounds of regional butter comprised the central display. We were able to sample three butters before selecting one *mi-salé* (lightly salted) type from Brittany, as well as purchasing some *fromage frais* for our dessert. It was very difficult not to be tempted by several of the perfectly matured cheeses, including a Bleu d'Avergne, a Fourme d'Ambert, a Comté and many *fromages fermiers de chèvre* (fresh goat's milk cheeses) displayed rustically on straw. Fortunately, we both knew that our eyes were bigger than our stomachs, so it was time to move on. We would be back soon enough.

At Pierre L'Ecuyier the spit was working feverishly to produce perfectly roasted chickens, and not far away, at La Poularde, another group of men in white aprons were busy trying to attract customers with basted pheasants, quails and golden chickens. I made a mental note to return here as well.

Not to be outdone in the quantity of produce on sale, and certainly not in the variety on display, another shop, Magasin de Tripe, was offering to its customers every tripe product imaginable, from *paté de tripe à la mode de Caen* to ready-to-cook tripe. It was also displaying offal products like *pieds de veau blanchit* (blanched calves' feet), *langue-de-boeuf* (ox tongue), *rognon* (kidney), *foie de veau* (calves' liver), *coeur de boeuf* (ox heart), *foie de porc* (pigs' liver), *cervelle de veau* (calves' brains), *coeur d'agneau* (lambs' heart) and black chicken feet. If you ever thought that only the Chinese ate offal, you need to think again and include the French!

Our next stop was at Boucherie Centrale Lepic. I was immediately overwhelmed by the enormous choice of meat, game and offal available in the store. Here I could select from *lapin de garenne* (wild rabbit), *bécasse* (woodcock), *veau de lait* (milk-fed veal), *queue de boeuf* (oxtail), *foie gras frais* (fattened fresh goose liver), *agneau pré salé* (saltbush lamb), *canette des Landes* (Landes duckling), *jarrets de veau* (veal shank), *poulet de Bresse* (Bresse chicken) and many other products to make any chef stare with eyes full of passion. I selected some *pigeonneaux* (squabs) and salted lard, which I planned to braise with some Savoy cabbage.

We moved on next door to the vegetable shop, Aux Quatre Saisons. Again, one could only be delighted by the array of fresh produce on display. I found first my *choux de Savoie* (the very green, leafy cabbages that are difficult to find in Australia), then I selected some large waxy potatoes from Normandy with the intention of turning them into small *rösti* (crisp potato cakes). For dessert I bought some beautiful strawberries that came from the south-west of France and had a divine perfume. I eyed other produce with a view to my next visit—like the fragrant fennel, tiny cherries, dark-red rhubarb, white asparagus, mini melons, green beans from Kenya and the just-delivered tomatoes still attached to their green vines. I left suitably thrilled by this shop and looked forward to savouring more of its treasures over the next week.

Yvette and I had a quick and curious look next door in the *traiteur* shop. This local catering shop offered us canapés, salads, pâtés, terrines or a full buffet for the home. One of my uncles, my mother's sister's husband, was French-born and he had owned a *traiteur* shop. He eventually established himself in Montreal, working for large, prestigious hotels. It was due to him that I became a chef.

The modern *traiteurs* of Paris are expert at preparing a whole festive menu for small or large groups. They produce *saumon à la Parisienne* (whole, poached, decorated salmon), *pâté de foie* (pork and chicken liver pâté) and the *foie gras terrine* so prized by the French people. Salads of every description are made here, as well as meals ready to be taken home and reheated. The *traiteur* shop is a paradise for busy people—certainly a superior alternative to the fast food restaurants springing up everywhere around the world. Here you can find *Pieds de porc panés* (crumbed pigs' feet), *Poitrine de veau cuite* (cooked veal shoulder), *Poireaux vinaigrette* (leeks in vinegar dressing), *Champignons à la Grecque* (mushrooms in the Greek style), *Salsifis braisé* (braised salsify), *Moules à la crème* (mussels in cream sauce), *Oreilles de porc cuites* (cooked pigs' ears) or a *quiche* with a simple potato salad.

Down the street we discovered Taffa, a newly established *traiteur* business. It provided a blend of Chinese and French food culture: traditional oriental food was displayed, in the form of a modern *yum cha* selection, but the shopfront was set up in the manner of a traditional *traiteur*. At Taffa I saw superb *dim sum*, *siumae*, scallops with seasoned salt, shrimps with pepper, and prawn ravioli. In the conservative food world of Paris, it was heartening to see succulent-looking food that showed a true interest in oriental flavours.

The last stop on any Parisian's shopping route is normally for the heavier items, like water and wine. Each neighbourhood has several wine merchants but you can also find wine in the grocery stores. I wanted two wines, one that could go with the oysters, and a light burgundy for the squab. I selected an Entre-Deux-Mers, a crisp white wine from Bordeaux that goes well with shellfish, and a Côte-Rôtie for the pigeon. With all our senses stimulated from our visit to the market of rue Lepic, we made our way back to Ken's apartment to prepare a meal with products that, individually, would tempt any food lover and, combined, were to become a mouth-watering finale to an exciting day.

Our dessert, a simple dish of strawberries and *fromage frais*, was so fresh and delicious that I was inspired to make a fondue of strawberries and rhubarb for the following evening's dessert. So the next morning I was up early, buying the necessary ingredients for the fondue, and for a creamy ice-cream to serve up with the fruit. The fragrance of vanilla heated gently in milk soon had Yvette eager to join me in the delicious task of preparing the ice-cream. This is the recipe we used.

Rhubarb and Strawberry Fondue with Vanilla Ice-cream

For the ice-cream:

275 ml (9 fl oz) milk
1 vanilla pod, split
3 eggs
1 egg yolk
75 g (3 oz) caster sugar
300 ml (9½ fl oz) fresh cream

Heat the milk and vanilla pod in a saucepan over low heat until steaming. Remove from the stove. Allow to infuse for 8 minutes. Strain. Whisk eggs and yolk with the caster sugar until light and fluffy. Pour in a little of the hot milk and whisk well, then whisk egg mixture back into the milk. Stir constantly over low heat for 3 minutes, until slightly thickened. Remove from the stove and plunge the base of the pan into cold water. Allow to cool.

Whip the cream until it holds soft peaks. Gradually stir into the custard. Pour into an ice-cream maker or, failing this, turn into a plastic container and freeze for 12 hours. If it becomes icy, put in a food processor, quickly blend and return to the freezer for 2 hours.

For the fondue:

750 g (1¾ lb) rhubarb
500 g (1 lb) strawberries
800 ml (25 fl oz) water
720 g (25 oz) pure brown cane sugar cubes
3 vanilla bean pods, split
100 ml (3 fl oz) sparkling wine

Preheat the oven to 160°C (325°F).

Scrape the rhubarb stalks, removing any fibrous thread, and cut into 4 cm (1½ in) lengths. Arrange them in a baking dish. Wash, dry and hull the strawberries. Cut in half and place them in a separate serving dish.

Put water, sugar cubes and vanilla pods into a pan and bring to the boil, stirring until the sugar has dissolved. Boil the syrup, without stirring, for 3 minutes over gentle heat. Remove from the heat and add the sparkling wine. Pour half of this hot liquid over the prepared rhubarb. Cover the dish with a lid or foil and bake for 25 minutes or until rhubarb is tender. Allow to cool.

Pour the remaining hot syrup over the strawberries. Allow to cool.

To assemble:

Either cut the ice-cream into a large 8 cm x 8 cm x 8 cm (3 in) square or scoop with an ice-cream spoon and arrange on plates with the rhubarb and strawberry fondue and a touch of syrup.

(Serves 8)

While our ice-cream cooled in the freezer, Yvette and I set out for another day of exploring.

Paris can offer you anything, but for the itinerant visitor one of the best things it offers is the opportunity to shop for the very best that is associated with food. Yvette and I did not take a shopping list with us but we did enjoy purchasing odd bits and pieces— a book, a casserole dish, a product or a special tool that only seemed to be available in Paris.

To any chef who visits Paris, a pilgrimage to the 180-year-old E. Dehillerin is an absolute must. The exterior of the shop, located on the corner of rues Coquillière and Jean-Jacques Rousseau in the first *arrondissement*, can never prepare you for the astonishing range of merchandise to be found inside. This is nirvana for chefs who have the ambition of one day opening their own restaurants. I had never seen such an eclectic kitchen shop, full of utensils and devices that could have belonged to the time of the famous chef Carême.

When we entered E. Dehillerin we had to quickly decide whether to remain upstairs to browse among the thousands of small tools and moulds, or go downstairs. We decided to go downstairs first. Walking down the old wooden staircase we were greeted by the sight of pots and pans of every conceivable shape, of every available metal finish and for every possible use. The traditional beaten copper pans were all proudly displayed here. Copper is close to being an ideal metal for cooking with, as it conducts heat quickly and evenly when put on the stove. It also has the desirable property of losing heat very rapidly if removed from the heat source. Full copper pans are still sold, but because of the reaction certain foods have with the metal they are often lined with either tin or—if money is no object—silver. These days stainless steel is the most popular material, as it is a good conductor, does not react with any food and is easy to clean.

The *batterie de cuisine* at E. Dehillerin came in several metal combinations, the most impressive being the *cuivre extra fort martelé*, a very thick pan made of copper beaten into a rugged exterior and lined with tin. We found the most traditional casserole dishes here: *braisière rectangulaire* (a rectangular braising pan), *poissonière* (to cook whole salmon), *sauteuse évasée* (a wide sauté pan), *marmite traiteur* (a large stock pot), *bassine à ragoût* (a large stewing pan), and an unusual casserole dish called *pomme-anna cuivre*, a double-sided pan used to cook *pomme-anna*, which is a thin layering of potato that requires cooking on both sides.

Still on the ground floor we passed by the tall asparagus cooker, the *soufflé casserole* and the tiny pots that are used to serve sauce at the table. They looked impressive all lined up next to each other beside the ladles used to pour flaming alcohol at the table, *passoires à légumes* (vegetable colanders), *plaques à rôtir* (roasting trays) and bowls of copper for the beating of egg whites, or of stainless steel for the mixing of salads.

Our exploration of the downstairs section exhausted, we went back upstairs to examine the more expensive equipment, like the *presse à canard* (duck press), the cast-iron pots—plain or enamelled for ease of cleaning and better presentation—and all the other essential kitchen items, from knives and *coupe-volaille* (poultry scissors) to docket-holders, moulds, piping bags, *pâté en croûte* moulds, chocolate moulds, *bombe* moulds for ice-cream, cake rings, *croque-en-bouche* forms (the pyramidal cones used in cake construction), charlotte tins (angle-sided cake tins with handles), snail dishes and porcelain services. If an item existed, it could be found at E. Dehillerin.

I left this shop hoping that the inventory would never change, and that it would continue to support the small artisans of France—the copper makers, wood carvers, silversmiths, metal forgers, or any of the dying trades that have been making *batterie de cuisine* since before the turn of the century.

Wandering on further, we soon arrived at place de la Madeleine. I had been looking forward to revisiting this street, for here were some of the best shops a food-lover could wish to see.

First we stopped at No. 6 place de la Madeleine and entered the doors of a well-stocked shop called Maille. Established in 1747, Maille was world-famous for its mustards. Amongst the range of products on offer was *moutarde de Dijon*, the famous hot mustard. The shop also stocked countless vinegars and a huge range of condiments and *cornichons* (pickled gherkins), ready for the table to accompany any dish of the French repertoire.

Undeniably the most famous shop on place de la Madeleine is Fauchon, which requires several buildings to accommodate its enormous range of products. Auguste Fauchon, the man responsible for this institution, originally came from his native Normandy in 1886 to start selling fruit and vegetables from a barrow in place de la Madeleine. He eventually succeeded in buying a small corner shop, which traded so well that, in time, he acquired two more shops on this famous square. Fauchon had a talent for sourcing unusual and exclusive produce, from preserves to exotic fruit and vegetables. To this day the selection of tropical fruits is so marvellous that it is observed with awe by even the most fastidious Parisians.

As Yvette and I peered in through the windows of the Pâtisserie Fauchon, with its displays of sumptuous cakes, we could only wonder at the organisation and commitment behind Fauchon's quest to offer products of quality. Elegant *croque-en-bouche* vied for our attention with *Saint-Honoré, tarte au citron, gâteau à l'ananas, gâteaux mousse à la pistache* or *mousse à la vanille, fraisier* and every cake that has ever been conceived in every shape possible. However, these represented only a small temptation compared with the store's other offerings, like its glazed or candied fruit, the *pâté de fruit*, the *amandines, macarons*, shortbread biscuits flavoured with vanilla or rose petals, a hundred types of handmade chocolates, or the *petits fours* ready to be taken home to finish a meal. I could not resist buying a *baguette* for our dinner and some *pain au chocolat* to eat on the spot. Next door was the groceries section, and here, as with the pâtisserie, the range was astounding. We walked through the whole store admiring the merchandise, starting in the cocktail section with its nuts, olives and crackers, then to the *conserve de légumes* section and on to teas, honeys, mustards, sauces, maple syrup, sugared biscuits, mushrooms, vinegars, oils and fruit juices, all either in beautiful jars with the Fauchon label or under their own brand names if the products have an established history.

The best section for me was the *plat cuisinier* (cooked meals), all set in their rustic-looking jars. The care taken in selecting the ingredients and cooking them was reflected in the price. Still, so nice were they that I decided to buy one for our evening meal. The only problem was in deciding which one. I could choose from *Civet de lièvre* (jugged hare), *Cassoulet de confit de canard* (rustic bean and duck stew), *Poulet Basquaise* (chicken in tomato, green pepper and garlic sauce), *Boeuf Beaujolais* (braised beef with Beaujolais wine), *Tripe de Caen* (tripe stew), *Poulet en gelée* (chicken in aspic), *Salmis de palombe* (casserole of wood pigeon), *Petit salé de lentille verte* (salted pork belly with green lentils), *Pot au feu* (beef and vegetable stew), or *Caille au choux* (quail with cabbage). I finally decided on the *Boeuf Beaujolais* and, with my crusty baguette, I was determined that we would feast, despite the fact that the jar looked so good it was tempting to take it back to Sydney and eat it in the middle of winter.

Exhausted from all the walking we had done and the great many sights we had taken in, Yvette and I stopped at L'Écluse at 15 place de la Madeleine. As we seated ourselves at the bar of this wine bistro, the bartender, on seeing our parcels, knew we needed a drink. He brought us a perfectly aged Château Daussault 1987 St Émilion, which had the great nose of the *terroir*, delicate and refined. We drank it with a plate of *saucisson sec* (dried sausage).

Finally, as a last quick stop, we could not resist a peek at Maison de la Truffe, where truffled dishes like *Terrine de foie gras truffé, Oeuf en gelée au jus de truffé, Cuisse de canard truffé* and every imaginable tinned truffled product were on display.

Eating the finest produce in the setting of a private apartment can be a more intimate and rewarding way to spend time in a city than staying in a hotel and eating at restaurants. At the end of our day, replenished by our *Boeuf Beaujolais* and strawberry and rhubarb fondue, not to mention the smoothest of vanilla ice-creams, Yvette and I felt blessed—blessed to be in Paris, and blessed by the friendship of Ken Hom, whose generosity had enabled us to be enriched by unforgettable experiences like this.

ENOUGH AND THEN SOME MORE

I *love chocolate in every form, from the mundane to the noble.* When I visit a restaurant I only give the dessert menu a cursory glance, as I always know I will choose the chocolate dessert. I love *pain au chocolat* for breakfast, *mousse au chocolat* for lunch, a serious chocolate cake for dessert at dinner and a chocolate bar before I go to bed. I have considered going into therapy but I am afraid I will be told to cut down. My wife would love me to stop eating so much chocolate, but as I do not have a weight problem she does not have a strong case for me to do so. Also, she thinks it is not worth making me miserable. I have always been like this, or at least since the time I was able to purchase my own chocolate.

What a joy, then, when Ken Hom rang to tell me that one of the best chocolate shops in Paris, run by Denise Acabo, was near his apartment at L'Étoile D'Or on rue Fontaine. I planned and schemed for my visit to the shop to coincide with my afternoon craving.

The *chocolaterie* and *confiserie*, situated on a street of music merchants, struck me as an anomaly in a place where an extensive array of shops existed to sell, rent and repair instruments for every style of music performed in the city. A big red awning offered no doubt as to the location of the shop—that and the sweet aroma that wafted out onto the street each time a customer entered or left the shop.

Denise Acabo was easily spotted. Ken had warned me of the proprietor's eccentricity, and so I was not surprised to see a vivacious woman with schoolgirl braids behind the desk. Denise's shop was similar to that of an old-fashioned apothecary, with antique shelving and bevelled mirrors artfully displaying a range of exquisite, enticing chocolates. Wooden drawers, left discreetly open to reveal their treasures, were carefully stocked with finely manufactured chocolates from the best *chocolatiers* of France.

Denise is one of the greatest advocates of the chocolates of France. She displays and sells all the best brands and has a thorough knowledge of each chocolate's intensity, unctuosity and characteristic flavour. The selection she stocks includes chocolate from Pralus of Roanne near Lyon, which was created by Auguste Pralus early this century and continued by his son François. This family of experts even roast their own cocoa beans, obtained from Central and South America, to produce an exquisite chocolate *couverture* (coating chocolate).

While I was in Denise's shop I saw the divine Conquistador chocolate, made by Bernard Dufoux and named for its composition of caramel, pistachios, sugared orange, flamed raisins and a trickling of roasted almonds and hazelnuts. There were also chocolates by Christian Bochard, a *maître chocolatier* based in Grenoble, including his speciality, a mandarin *confit* dipped in chocolate and perfumed with Grand Marnier. The products of André Boyer, a 100-year-old house based in the small town of Sault-de-Vaucluse in Provence, were also represented. There the great-grandfather of André Boyer, Ernest Boyer, opened a small shop in 1887, producing the very best nougat. He was considered a *maître nougatier* because of his great expertise in handling the best Provence lavender honey and the regional almonds to prepare an irresistible nougat confection that has been appreciated by connoisseurs ever since.

Denise disclosed the name of her favourite product—Bernachon, a rare and precious chocolate. Bernachon is prepared in Lyon by Jean-Jacques Bernachon, who is married to the daughter of world-famous chef Paul Bocuse. The Bernachon family is one of the very few *chocolatiers* of France still making their own chocolates to a very particular and exacting method. They select their cocoa beans from particular growers and plantations around the world to ensure that they use the best beans available. They know and nurture their growers as chefs nurture their own small suppliers. I sampled some of the aromatic chocolate and had to agree with Denise that it was a treasure of complexity.

One of the large houses committed to producing a great chocolate—which is used in many pastry shops throughout France, and is the one I use for my own desserts—is Valrhona. It has a large range of strengths and varieties and combines a glorious silkiness with an aristocratic taste—an 'adults-only' chocolate with deep, murky and typically French bitterness that stimulates your tastebuds like no other product. Valrhona's very stylish packaging has set a new standard of presentation and has created in an eager clientele a new demand for beautifully wrapped, exquisite tasting chocolates. To make a gift of a small box of Guanaja Valrhona chocolate is to help define a new level of style and taste.

I left Denise's shop with a small but precious supply of Bernachon and Valrhona chocolate that I intended to give away during my travels. Yvette detected an ulterior motive and gently removed my supply from my possession, promising to ensure its salvation until our next stop. I had to admit that it was in safer hands than my own.

When in Paris years ago, I had made plans to have dinner with a good friend at Joël Robuchon's restaurant. Unfortunately, my friend Max could not make it from Monte Carlo and I ended up cancelling my reservation. Since the closure of Robuchon's restaurant in 1996 I have deeply regretted my decision not to go. This is reinforced every time I read his name in a food article, see his books on my bookshelf or someone tells me how a Robuchon meal was the best meal of their life.

When the food world first heard the rumour that Joël Robuchon was retiring at the peak of his career, nobody could quite believe it was true. How could such a leading chef be lost to future generations? How could the restaurant survive Joël Robuchon's departure? Who would replace a chef of his impeccable reputation? Eventually I heard that Alain Ducasse from Le Louis XV in Monaco was heading to Paris to take over the stoves at the avenue Raymond Poincaré. Amazing news. I could not believe that Ducasse would leave the famous restaurant that had made his reputation. However, I soon learnt that Alain Ducasse was actually keeping his Michelin three-star restaurant in Monaco and was intending to travel between the two locations. Even if this could have been perceived by food critics as overconfidence, his incredible energy and commitment made him the person who could accomplish this culinary feat.

After overcoming the incredible difficulties allied with replacing a favourite of Paris such as Joël Robuchon, Ducasse has now been accepted by Parisians in much the same as was the pyramid in the Musée du Louvre. He is acknowledged as an integral part of creative Paris.

Yvette and I were ushered into the foyer of the grand bourgeois townhouse that houses Monsieur Ducasse's Parisian restaurant. The room was furnished with well-padded sofas and classic wood mouldings. Our view took in the sumptuous club bar and cigar room, where we were to be met by the personal assistant of Monsieur Ducasse, Luca Allegri.

I had made contact with Alain Ducasse well before the start of our European trip. My hope was that I might be allowed to spend a little time in his kitchen, observing the service. However, Monsieur Ducasse had kindly suggested that Yvette and I should have a meal in the restaurant before taking a tour of the kitchens. So here we were, ready to enjoy the offerings of one of Paris's finest restaurants.

Soon a young and gracious man introduced himself to us. Luca is from a famous Italian family with a history of working in hotels on the Italian Riviera. Luca's father, an impressive *chef concierge* at the Splendido in Portofino, whom we were to meet later on our journey, probably had something to do with placing Luca in the hands of Monsieur Ducasse.

After the arrangements had been made—Luca had wisely suggested we take the tour of the kitchens on a different night so as to enable us to enjoy the meal without interruption—we were led through the gallery to a luxurious, wood-panelled lift, which took us up to the dining room. I felt that I had been transported to a different world, a world of luxury, dedication, quality and total refinement. Sculptures made by the best silversmiths of

France adorned the tables. There were contemporary bronze figurines with heads of forks and spoons, a whimsical little touch that, along with the canvases, *trompe l'oeils* and incredible *boiseries* (wood panelling) of Renaissance, Dutch and Louis XV inspiration, created an inimitable restaurant.

We were seated and draped with impeccable napkins of pure cotton that felt like they had just been unwrapped for the service. The cutlery was set prong down, in the formal French manner, to display the family crest on the back of the silver. *Bouchées* (savoury bites) were served by polished waiters, and a crisp warm *feuilletée* (pastry) of spinach was irreproachable and delicious.

An exemplary touch was created by the arrival of the bread. The tiny baguette of sourdough bread was so beautiful and simple that I committed it to memory before I started to eat it. If this were not sufficient, the butter was presented: two giant slabs of at least a half-pound of the whitest and creamiest butter I had ever seen, one unsalted and one lightly salted. This announced an exceptional meal. I had never tasted bread or butter so good. It was an absolutely unique and pure food sensation, and it reminded me of the reason for my trip to France. Food of this quality created a gastronomic benchmark in my mind that would help me search for or develop products of similar quality in Australia.

I was advised by Denis Courtade, the very personable *chef de salle*, that a menu had been selected for us. We readily accepted this generous offer without qualification.

We started with incredible *bourgeoises*, asparagus grown by Robert Blanc in Villelaure. They were large and white, with gentle green tips that had barely felt the strength of the sun; they were poached in a *bouillon de volaille* (chicken stock), then lightly pan-roasted, touched with a fine dust of parmesan and braised in a *cocotte* (a small braising dish) to retain their incredible flavour. The tiny morels scattered on the plate were glazed with a *velouté* of these unique mushrooms that complemented the flavour of the melting asparagus. What delight!

The next course was one of the best dishes I have ever eaten, a marriage of texture, delicacy and researched elegance that will last me a lifetime. A central *royale* (custard) of *foie gras* perfumed with truffle provided the softness for the gently braised Brittany lobster medallions, which had been simmered in a *coulis* of shellfish. The final element came to the table in a *soupière* (tureen). It was a skilfully refined *velouté* of lobster, tomato, fennel and shallot, deglazed successively with cognac, white wine and *fond blanc* (light stock), and perfumed with peel of cèpe mushroom and pungent dry morel mushroom. It was pure bliss, a soup full of complementary flavours and delicate textures. Any lingering doubts about Monsieur Ducasse's status disappeared with the last drop of my soup.

Around us people were starting to warm up, fuelled perhaps by the quality of the very impressive cellar which, I was told, contained over 40 000 bottles with vintages dating back to 1916 and coming directly from the reserves of the famous châteaux of France.

Next came an intensely distinctive dish—one which, I had been told, was the talk of all Paris—that blended the influences of Italy and northern France. A home-made rigatoni-style semi-dried pasta, handmade and rolled around a piece of dowel to provide its shape, was served with a delicious morel truffled cream, garnished with gently simmered chicken combs and kidneys and impeccable veal sweetbreads. Maybe this dish was the reason why customers were asked of any possible allergies before the start of the meal—a polite way to assess whether they have any offal aversions. Sometimes I feel blessed that I was raised with a French background so I can eat and enjoy the weirdest items that anyone can cook, from any part of the carcass of an animal. It was a magnificent dish.

If this were not enough for lunch, the *pièce de résistance* was still being prepared for us. No meal in France can be regarded as superb unless there is a *foie gras* course designed into it. It seems that this is the dish that will separate the true leaders of gastronomic France from the mere followers. The unspoken belief is that no one in the world can prepare *foie gras* like the French do. I would agree with this except for the fact that *foie gras* is not readily available to chefs outside of France.

Monsieur Ducasse's *foie gras* was so rich and powerful that you could not but relish its exclusivity. We ate a whole duck *foie gras*, braised in a sauce of marinated apple and raisin in old Oporto that was sealed with bread dough in a glass *cocotte* and gently cooked in the oven. In the past, for something very special, the raisins were replaced with the grapes of the famous Château d'Yquem, a practice that was proving difficult nowadays, considering the strictly limited availability of this famous wine. Here we had a fantastic dish that redefined simplicity in respect of the cooking method and the power of rich ingredients.

By now Yvette had eaten as much as she could. I surprised myself by not refusing some cheese from the impeccable selection on offer. I let the expertise of the *garçon* help me make a small plate and we settled on a Beaufort, a ripe Munster, a three-year-old Tomme de Brebis and an excellent Chèvre de L'Ariège, a truly pleasant and satisfying range that I slowly savoured with the balance of the simple St Joseph Rouge 1994 made by Bernard Faurie.

We finished with some fine handmade chocolates accompanied by exquisite mocha coffee. I had to pass on the offer of one of the fifty different types of cigars at the bar, an offer that was not refused by the six young English gourmets lunching next to our table (this seems to be a new fashion that the London gents have taken up with quite astonishing gusto). There was also a fine selection of vintage cognacs and armagnacs at the bar, dating back to 1918—tempting, but in the end I chose a private reserve from Monsieur Ducasse's selection.

Now I can only think back in amazement at our huge appetites. This was a memorable meal of enormous significance in my gastronomic life.

On the following night Yvette and I returned to avenue Raymond Poincaré to spend our night in Ducasse's kitchen. We were ushered from the reception area to the third level, where Monsieur Ducasse had his offices. Luca, his trusted assistant, was making sure that the visit was to our liking. We were shown to Monsieur Ducasse's office, where we proceeded to wait for the great chef finish his phone conversation. The size of the desk at which he sat impressed me: it was big, deep, serious and weighty, especially with a dozen or so heavy files stacked high upon it. I suddenly sensed the complexity of operating two world-class restaurants and several other establishments spread over a large area. A chef of Ducasse's standing is also a very busy businessman.

The welcome Monsieur Ducasse gave us was very much imbued with the seriousness that I knew he applied to all of his projects.

Some years ago Alain was the sole survivor of a plane crash in mountainous terrain in France. This experience apparently strengthened his commitment to his craft, and accelerated his hunger for speed and his abhorrence of unprofessionalism.

We talked on a multitude of subjects and discussed friends we had in common until it was time for Yvette and I to move to the kitchen for our night of observation.

The first sight of the kitchen, with its gleaming stoves, incredible copper pots, expensive casseroles, elegant plates and handcrafted silver, told me that I had arrived in a peerless world. I wished I could have shown my Sydney chefs this kitchen. I was astonished when I observed the huge brigade of over twenty young chefs who all looked as though they had been drilled into a Parisian detachment of the Foreign Legion. This would have to be the finest kitchen I had ever seen—so clean, sleek and stunningly designed that it screamed great food. An incredibly impressive black and gold hand-fabricated Molteni stove was set up in a typical island fashion to allow access from all sides. The emphasis was clearly on conventional cooking technique, not new-age cooking equipment. Technology was reserved for a video system and screens which enabled faultless service from stove to table. These screens were scrutinised frequently and intently by the *chef de cuisine*, whose name was Laurent.

In this kitchen Laurent was the undisputed king. As the conductor, controller and guardian of Monsieur Ducasse's cuisine, he tasted every sauce, scrutinised every item and tested every piece of meat to ensure proper cooking. Not one item of food left the kitchen without his approval. While I was there, waiters brought butter, salads, cold appetisers and desserts to him to inspect. They stood to attention until he had given the nod of assent.

In Sydney I have forty chefs in my brigade, whom I try to supervise with compassion and understanding. In Paris, however, the style is very much more authoritarian. There were harsh words, frayed nerves, yelling and constant domineering—after all, this was France, and traditions had to be upheld!

TO MARKET, TO MARKET

*I*t *was with some apprehension that I found myself standing on* boulevard de Clichy in Pigalle, Paris's number one sex strip, at four in the morning. The rendezvous was to meet Jean-Marie Pollet, export manager for Boiron, a large manufacturer of fruit purée. I stood outside the Moulin Rouge, peering at the passing cars. Around me the neon lights of the sex shops, adult cinemas and nightclubs blinked lewdly at the lingering customers. A dark sedan cruised slowly to the kerbside. Jean-Marie emerged, his face partially covered by hat and scarf. We exchanged a few words and hastily departed in his car; anyone observing us could have been forgiven for thinking our intentions were less than honourable. Once safely ensconced in the warmth of his car we travelled south for thirty minutes to reach our much-anticipated destination, the renowned Rungis Market.

This is the largest fresh-produce market in Europe. It covers 232 hectares (573 acres), contains over 630 wholesalers, 1540 food-related enterprises, 430 producer-sellers and 420 service businesses—in all, a total of over 13 000 employees. The market, which was relocated in 1969 from Les Halles Centrales in the middle of Paris to a distant suburb to the south of the city, is a city in itself. It contains administration offices, doctors, dentists, banks, a post office, a fire brigade, police, travel agents and hairdressers, as well as over one hundred local bars and restaurants that service the workers and public inside the environs of the market.

The amount of business conducted through the market is staggering: 2 050 000 tonnes (2 017 200 tons) of food products, 4 490 000 boxes of cut flowers and over 15 million pot plants are traded annually. Approximately 20 500 buyers ply their trade daily. There are five general sectors of trade at the market: seafood and freshwater products; meat products; fruit and vegetables; dairy, egg, prepared food and catering products; and horticultural products.

We travelled through a huge car park filled with vans, semitrailers and vehicles of every description to reach the market produce. The fish and seafood pavilion, which indicated its presence by the unmistakeable odour of fresh fish, was our first destination. I felt at home in this pavilion and was filled with an excitement similar to the one I experience visiting our own seafood market in Sydney. Like a Parisian lady in search of a trophy to add to her collection of designer clothes, I felt I was on the hunt for the best seafood on earth in one of the best markets of the world.

Fresh fish and seafood arrive from all over the world to the Rungis Market. Wholesalers specialise in specific types of seafood, from freshwater fish to oysters, seafood or shellfish. There were even two competing snail wholesalers doing business in this unique land mollusc. I saw live lobsters from Canada, their giant claws firmly taped, sacks of clams, turbot from Brittany, periwinkles, oysters in pretty baskets, Norwegian salmon, local trout, octopus from Italy, sea urchins and mussels from Spain, cod from Denmark, skate wings from the US, huge halibuts, pike, fresh sturgeon and a vast array of small fish displayed with incredible artistry in their small wooden boxes. The variety and volume of produce was staggering.

The atmosphere was subdued, but one could feel the serious business of buying and selling simmering beneath the surface. The produce was handled carefully and with respect. When I stopped to admire some fresh scallops from Brittany, the famous *coquilles Saint-Jacques*, the wholesaler proceeded to open two or three by hand so I could more closely examine them for quality and freshness. Only recently have we seen scallops sold on the shell in Australia and the US. I remember when, as a youngster, I first saw a whole fresh scallop. It was a defining moment; the realness of the shell with its sea aroma was unforgettable.

The oyster stalls were next. There were flat or Belons oysters, rock or Portuguese oysters and the more common Pacific oysters, some coming from the river basins of Marennes, Belon and Arcachon. Approximately 25 000 tonnes (24 600 tons) of these molluscs are sold each year at Rungis.

I moved on to the fish: fresh trout, fresh sardines, cod, pike, John Dory, salted Spanish cod, halibut from Canada. There were also crates of fresh frogs' legs, dressed on skewers, from Turkey. One of the oddities of this market was that five wholesalers were competing for the sale of parsley and lemons only. Their total business turnover exceeded 10 million French francs per year.

Walking around a market with seafood of this quality and range could only reinforce in me the total joy I experience in being a chef. For me, it provided inspiration and a sense of purpose. Despite the cold, Jean-Marie Pollet and I walked around the fish market one more time. We were enraptured and overwhelmed by the abundance, the variety, the colour and the smell—the clean briny scent of the fresh ocean. With one last lingering glance we headed back out into the cold early morning and on to the next market.

In 1974, just five years after the relocation of the fish market, the abattoirs and meat wholesalers were also transferred from Les Halles Centrales to Rungis. The new facilities were exemplary. The system, I could see, was geared for high volume and to provide space for the display of all the carcasses up for sale. This meant that the area the meat market covered was enormous and the various products had be housed in several huge buildings. A quick verbal sketch from Jean-Marie had the market mapped out for me: two buildings were reserved for beef and veal, another two were for pork, one was for poultry and feather game, and another was for offal. A further scattering of buildings indicated the places where butchery, storage and sales were conducted. The cleanliness and the smooth running of the operation was instantly apparent to me.

I found it quite confronting to contemplate the great quantity of meat Parisians consume. The *chevreaux* (tiny young goats) were in season and I wondered who would purchase such tender young animals. I asked and found out that the Portuguese and Italians were fond of this meat. *Chevreaux* are really a by-product of goat cheese production, being the excess of young goats that the farmers do not need to keep. What we would consider exotic is, in this case, ingrained in the historical ways that many French communities live and eat.

Pork is the basis for a large range of dishes in France, such as *terrine*, ham and sausages, so it was not surprising to discover that the Rungis Market handles more pork than beef. Coming from the French part of Canada, where pork is such an essential staple, I could easily understand how the cold climate had dictated the consumption of a fatty meat to provide the calories needed to survive in the harsh climate. Despite this, I was astonished by the volume of trade I witnessed.

Other buildings in the meat market housed the suppliers of veal, beef and mutton. In the winter season, Jean-Marie told me, game such as hare, wild boar, venison and birds could be purchased here. I saw the delicious milk-fed veal of France and Holland, as well as the season's spring lamb and the *pré-salé* lamb which hails from the saltbush pasture of the coast of the north of France.

It was easy to view the poultry of France in all their splendour here. There were *poulet Landais* from south-west France, *poulet noir de Challans* (a black-footed chicken from the Vendée region), guinea fowl, pigeon, quail, pheasant, *canard de Barberie*, *crépinette* sausage, *magret de canard* (breast of duck), *foie gras* in all its forms, corn-fed chicken and the famous *poularde de Bresse*. Most birds still had their heads intact—and in some cases their tail feathers too—which gave one the eerie feeling of being watched by thousands of eyes.

By now we were hungry and so we headed into one of the cafés where we fortified ourselves with fresh crusty *tartine au beurre*, *pain au chocolat* and crispy light croissants washed down with strong espresso. With the sun rising in the cool morning air and our stomachs full, we were renewed and inspired. We now felt ready to take on anything—even the tremendous fruit and vegetables market.

Most of the locals ride bicycles through the great produce halls, deftly dodging forklifts and pallets piled high with produce. As I wandered through the aisles they whistled politely at me when I was in their path and called *'Bonjour'* cheerily to their fellow workers. I got the feeling that it was difficult to be grumpy while riding a bicycle.

It was springtime and the first of the season's strawberries from Périgord were here, nestled next to baby green beans from Morocco, raspberries from Chile, beans from Kenya, Savoy cabbages, Jerusalem artichokes, rhubarb, little tomatoes on the vine from Ardèche, prepared *bouquet garni* for the busy kitchen, and so many other fresh products.

There was an abundance of fresh stone fruits from Spain and southern Italy, the first areas in Europe to produce summer crops. The opening of border trading within Europe has allowed a great amount of food to be imported into France, which in turn has created a certain amount of resentment from the French farmers. Every year now you see French growers dumping their crops of strawberries or oranges in front of their municipal or departmental offices to protest about the difficulties they have in competing with lower-cost producers from the countries to the south. However, while their grievances are valid, French customers undoubtedly benefit from the cheaper prices and increased variety of products available to them.

Likewise, the French are not short on choice when it comes to cheeses and dairy products. Upon entering the halls of the dairy market, the sheer quantity and variety of cheese on sale struck me as nothing short of staggering. A market like this could only exist in France, I reflected. I walked the entire building with my mouth open, looking at cheeses that I recognised from culinary literature but had never seen before.

Hordes of buyers were descending on their favourite stalls to examine, smell, feel and maybe even taste the various cheeses that were on offer. Each merchant carried a small array of cheese provided by a select few producers. One might specialise, say, in cheese from the Jura or Normandy, or maybe in ageing Beaufort or Cantal, or in goat cheese from the Rouergue region. I walked around eyeing the Reblochon, huge Compté, Parmesan, Brie de Meaux and many others that I would have loved to sample. The array of goat cheeses was infinite, and the form and presentation of each cheese so telling about the character of the region it had come from. This was a true indication of the diversity of France and its products.

We moved next to an enormous circular market where many organisations and institutions pick up groceries and pre-prepared food. The diversity of buyers was fascinating: I noticed a group of nuns in their habits, chefs in their whites, burly buyers who belonged to a chain of take-away shops, and many other types of people roaming the alleys that provided all imaginable catering needs. Here also could be found all the wholesale groceries required to operate a kitchen: *pâtés*, *terrines*, *confit*, *cassoulet*, beef *daube*, whole poached salmon already decorated *à la Parisienne*, sausages and *crépinettes* of every description, smoked fish, caviars, *foie gras*, sauces and stocks in huge buckets, alcohol, wines, wild mushrooms, spices, marinated fruits, butter. To be able to purchase so many special products in one location in Australia would be fabulous, and I have to admit I was envious in the extreme.

We had just one more market to visit before our morning came to an end—the flower market. Nothing could have prepared me for the kaleidoscope of colour and variety contained here. But it was not just the cut flowers pavilion that impressed me; in two huge, temperature-controlled buildings I saw pot plants of every description, in sizes ranging from small house pots to huge street trees. Jean-Marie gave me some figures to marvel at: the annual turnover at the flower market was an astonishing two billion French francs, in exchange for which Parisians beautified their homes and gardens with 36 million bunches of flowers, 18 million pot plants and more than half a million greenhouse trees. I purchased a few bunches of flowers to give to friends back in Paris and knew my contribution to the turnover to be just a drop in the ocean.

Before we parted, Jean-Marie insisted that I sample some of the top-quality lines of concentrated fruit purées he was in charge of exporting. His company, Boiron, was situated at Rungis chiefly for its easy access to the berries and other fruits. My favourite concentrate was the *cassis purée*, a deeply flavoursome temptation of powerful berry syrup, ready to be used in the sauces or desserts prepared by the great pastry chefs of the world. I thanked my generous guide for his morning's tour and said goodbye before turning my feet away from the Rungis Markets and back towards the centre of Paris.

The day had turned out to be a very cold one, but I warmed myself with the thought that my visit would stay ingrained in my memory as one of the most marvellous experiences of my Parisian sojourn.

Yvette and I had been in Paris for just five days now and our experiences had been nothing less than exhilarating. On the following day we would be leaving Paris for Burgundy, and while we felt sorry to have to go, we knew we had enjoyed sights and tastes that few visitors to the city would have the privilege to experience. Food and friendship had fed our bodies and hearts— the generosity and enthusiasm of everyone we had encountered had both gratified and delighted us.

Only one more engagement remained to be fulfilled before leaving Paris, and little did either of us suspect what a rewarding one it would be.

On meeting Jacques Vernier I was immediately infected by his contagious enthusiasm and fascination for cheese and cheese making. After visiting the enormous dairy section at Rungis Market, I thought it might be difficult to get excited over a single cheese shop. But Jacques Vernier's *fromagerie* and its beautiful cheese had a profound impact on me. The sight of Munster, Beaufort, Reblochon, St Marcellin, Époisses, Coulommiers and so many other cheeses coming from as far away as Sardinia and Corsica, all displayed like miniature landscapes of the countries of their origins, was more exquisite to me than the jewellery stores in Place Vendôme.

The role of the *affineur* (cheese merchant) is barely understood outside of the borders of Europe. The task of the *affineur* is to select and purchase the best cheeses of the season and then, in a controlled atmosphere, carefully age them until they reach perfect maturation. The recommendations of *affineurs* as to which cheese is in perfect condition and which is the best cheese to purchase at a particular moment are eagerly sought after by customers. The *affineur*'s expertise can make all the difference between choosing a good cheese and a great cheese.

In Paris every food street has several *affineurs* or *fromagers* catering for the neighbourhood. Jacques Vernier's shop, La Fromagerie Boursault, located in the fourteenth *arrondissement*, caters for a loyal clientele of dedicated cheese lovers, mostly workers and tradespeople. The shop used to be the showcase for the famous house of Boursault cheese, created by Monsieur Jacques Boursault. Jacques Vernier bought the shop several years ago after the departure of its namesake. The shop has retained the name Boursault, even though it is now well associated with Jacques Vernier.

Today La Fromagerie Boursault specialises in the small, unique houses that produce outstanding cheeses in modest quantities. Cheese made of *lait cru* (unpasteurised milk) is Jacques's speciality and *raison d'être*. With cheese made from pasteurised milk, Jacques explained to us, the aromas are uniform to the point of not really providing a challenging complexity. If you heat milk, it reduces the bacteria that would otherwise have contributed to making a great cheese. Jacques drew the following analogy about making cheese with pasteurised milk: 'It is like making love to a woman in the same manner over and over again. Eventually no pleasure can be derived from it; what needs to change is not the woman but the method.'

Lait cru, or unpasteurised milk, is more attuned to vagaries of production. Where the milk comes from, the season during which it was made, and the animal's breed and condition will all affect the flavour of the raw product, and these factors in turn will impact on the cheese produced from it. The result is a cheese with regional characteristics instead of a very predictable product. Jacques described the camemberts of Normandy as an example. In the northern part of Normandy, where milk is obtained from cows grazing on saltbush meadows, one can readily taste the garlicky flavour and increased saltiness present in the camembert, whereas in the Bocage area of the southern part of Normandy, a distinct herbal aroma is present in the cheese.

Luckily, France is blessed with great climatic and regional differences, to the advantage of the producers who can achieve individual identity (sometimes even idiosyncrasy) with their products.

After introducing us to Madame Vernier, who presided over the cash register in a charming and proprietary manner, Jacques took us to the heart of his operation: the caves, or maturing rooms. Here the cheeses are kept at the varying temperatures and humidity levels required to help them develop into perfect products. To age cheese in a perfect environment, Jacques advised that you need to be able to control two elements in the ageing room: the cold or temperature, and the humidity. Each cheese requires a different ageing process. A dry Chèvre, for example, needs a temperature of 12 to 14 degrees Celsius (54 to 57 degrees Fahrenheit) and a relatively dry humidity level of 85 per cent. A washed rind, on the other hand, requires a very high humidity level of 98 to 99 per cent with a relatively warm temperature of 14 degrees Celsius (57 degrees Fahrenheit) so as not to dry the cheese out. A higher temperature would speed up the *affinage* of these cheeses, and the opposite would happen if the temperature were lowered.

Jacques explained his role as that of a bridge builder between the cheese maker and the consumer. But he was also seeking to build bridges between countries: at the time we met him, Jacques was sitting on the European Commission in Brussels, looking into the issue of hygiene for the cheese industry. His aim was to limit the restrictions imposed by many countries on the importation of unpasteurised cheese. For him, the danger of losing the right to produce cheese from unpasteurised milk went to the core of the respect and preservation of longstanding traditions, and the quest for flavour.

Of all the people with whom I share a passion for cheese, I found Jacques to be the most committed, ebullient and enlightened enthusiast. Here was a man interested in all facets of his product, from the buying, ageing, storing and displaying of his cheeses to the joy they ultimately gave his customers.

Yvette and I left Jacques Vernier replete with knowledge and carrying a bagful of cheese. That afternoon, I decided, I would make us a gâteau from Jacques's fresh goat cheese. It would be a fitting use for such a fine cheese, and a delicious light meal for Yvette and myself on our last night in Paris.

Goat Cheese and Capsicum Gâteau

a little olive oil
1 large onion, peeled and sliced
6 large fleshy red capsicums, cut into large pieces
2 cloves garlic
6 basil and 6 parsley stems
11 leaves gelatine
600 g (20 oz) fresh goat cheese, room temperature
50 g (2 oz) soft butter
30 g (1½ oz) Olive Tapenade (see page 256)
1 tablespoon chopped parsley
300 ml (11 fl oz) cream

Preheat the oven to 140°C (275°F).

Heat the olive oil in a pan and sauté the onion until soft. Add the capsicums, garlic and herb stems, sauté for a further 10 minutes. Transfer to the oven for 15 minutes or until fully cooked. Allow to cool, discard the herb stems and purée in a food processor. Strain through a fine mesh sieve to remove the skin (alternatively, you could use peeled capsicum to avoid this step) and chill.

Soak 8 leaves of gelatine in cold water and reserve the remaining 3 in another bowl.

Mix the goat cheese with the butter and spread firmly into the base of a 20 cm (8 inch) cake ring that is sitting on a tray lined with wax paper. Brush over the tapenade, sprinkle with parsley and refrigerate.

Whip the cream and gradually add three-quarters of the cold capsicum coulis. Strain the 8 sheets of gelatine and squeeze out water. Melt on low heat for 1 minute, pour into the capsicum–cream mixture and combine delicately. Pour immediately into the cake ring and smooth. Return to the fridge. When set (approx. 30 minutes), melt the remaining 3 gelatine leaves and add to the remaining capsicum coulis. Pour on top of the cake to form the last layer— a beautiful red glaze. Refrigerate for 4 hours.

To assemble:

With a small sharp knife dipped in hot water, cut carefully around the inside of the cake ring. Remove the ring slowly and, using a thin sharp knife dipped in hot water, cut 8 wedges.

Accompany with a crisp green salad of small mixed leaves and blanched asparagus.

(Serves 8 as an entrée)

SPRING IDYLL

*D*espite *the fact that we had researched our destination in* Upper Burgundy, we were still unprepared for the size and beauty of Château du Feÿ. I followed the precise directions that had been given to me to reach the Château: up the winding road, through the forested hills, turn into the private entrance and drive on through a wood full of mossy trees. At last we saw the exquisite wrought-iron gates of the Château's central court. I parked awkwardly, conscious of the glaring anachronism and incongruity of my modern, mass-produced car beside the walls of the historical Château du Feÿ. We had arrived at the home of my friend Anne Willan.

I had always been a fan of Anne's cooking books (one of them, *French Regional Cuisine*, is my all-time favourite cookbook), so it was a great pleasure to finally meet her a few years back when she was in Sydney promoting her *Time Life* series of cookbooks. We worked together back then to develop the menus and produce the food for the launch of the books. The satisfaction we both derived from the experience formed the basis of a special and mutual respect. To be visiting Anne now at her French cooking school, La Varenne, was a real joy.

We were given a noisy welcome by Zigzag the Dalmatian, whose head appeared at one of the many windows of the Château, and Zulu, a rather more decorous Rhodesian Ridgeback.

Mark Cherniavsky, Anne's charming English husband, came out to meet us. Justine, who helped us carry our suitcases upstairs, was a pleasant surprise: she was Anne's personal assistant and she came from Australia. The warmth and spontaneity of our welcome set the tone for our four-day visit at this beautiful seventeenth-century château.

The interior of le Feÿ was just as lovely as the outside. Built in the mid 1600s during the reign of Louis XIII by Nicholas de Baugy, a personal counsellor to the King, the design was typical of the era, with staircases placed in each wing of the house rather than in the centre. With mirrors at either end of the three main rooms, a grand sense of spaciousness was achieved.

For most of its life le Feÿ was the focus of a vast agricultural estate, initially 4700 acres (1904 hectares), falling to 1000 acres (405 hectares) by the 1850s and 100 acres (40.5 hectares) by 1982. Viticulture was the main source of income and there was convenient transport by river barge to Paris. However, with the advent of railways to sunny southern France, and the damage caused by phylloxera in the late 1800s, winemaking became obsolete in the Yonne Valley. Vestiges of the old estate still remained: an avenue of chestnut trees, walnuts and wild hazelnuts; a wine press, pigeon house and cattle barn in states of disrepair; and in the forest, wild boar, hare and bird life.

When Mark and Anne purchased Château du Feÿ in 1982 they intended to use it as a country house. However, its potential as a cooking school soon became apparent and they relocated La Varenne, their Paris-based school, 90 miles south to Burgundy. They now divide their time between La Varenne in summer and autumn, and a second cooking school at Greenbrier Hotel, West Virginia, in winter and spring.

A seemingly idyllic existence comes at a high price for an author and teacher as prolific as Anne. On the day we arrived, Anne flew in to Paris on a direct flight from Washington. She appeared unruffled and uncreased by her journey, but I knew she had to be tired. I could immediately see what makes her so successful in the culinary world. She has endless energy and a no-nonsense manner that is instantly endearing.

After welcoming us, Anne did a rapid-fire debrief with Justine and Mark regarding the upcoming cooking classes. There were many details to be confirmed, as the itinerary for the students was both comprehensive and varied. Hands-on classes were combined with demonstrations by top French chefs, and handouts, recipes and notes were all provided, fully translated from French to English where required. The course also included visits to Michelin one-, two- and three-star restaurants, as well as to the local produce market at Joigny. At times, courses might also include an address by guest cheesemakers, or a mushroom-picking excursion. Students got to experience total immersion in French cuisine and culture.

Justine served our inaugural dinner—a wonderful roast duck, tender and falling off the bone after hours of gentle roasting. I had offered to prepare dinner the following night, but I doubted whether I would be able to match the exquisite simplicity of this meal.

In the morning Yvette and I went for a walk with Mark to observe the various buildings which make up the Château complex. In the field near the Château were apple trees, uncared for but still producing a great number of apples which once would have been used to produce the Calvados (apple brandy) so favoured by the local people.

We strolled through an enormous vegetable garden enclosed by huge stone walls to protect it from nocturnal animals. This was the garden of Monsieur Milbert, the live-in caretaker of the Château, and his pride and joy. Mark told me the story of how, on one occasion during school season when the students had joyfully noticed the first tender shoots of asparagus poking through the dark soil, ideas for recipes and menus were devised to take full advantage of this beautiful vegetable. However, they rose the next morning to find that all the asparagus had disappeared overnight. Milbert could only blame 'the terrible midnight frost' for this sad disappointment.

Mark showed me the pride of the Château and its past lifeline—a huge circular well which goes to unseen depths. I could not imagine the effort required to dig it since it is over 84 metres (275 feet) deep. Today the well is unused. Mark had at one stage contemplated bringing it back to life, as the Château was in dire need of water when he and Anne took it over, but due to the disconcerting and dangerous habit during the last war of dumping ammunition and arms in the well to hide them from the Germans, the risk of an explosion was not worth the danger of draining it. Instead, Mark had to pay to get a water line built from the village.

Across the courtyard stood the old pigeon house, the object of my most intense curiosity. In the past, the privilege of keeping pigeon houses was reserved for the rich landowners; only they could justify breeding birds which could cause terrible ravages to the peasants' fields. Mark was more than willing to take me inside the tower of the pigeon house. We made our way through the storage rooms full of old furniture that smelt of decades of use, through to a very precarious stairwell and up a fragile ladder to emerge in a surprisingly airy and large chamber that used to house a thousand pigeons. When in full use, the simple act of collecting eggs would, I imagined, have been quite an exercise in agility.

We moved on to the old bakery, which was once in constant use to feed the large army of workers tending the vines and manning the great wine press and the circular stone crusher probably used for the production of walnut oil. The wonderful baker's oven still got fired up on occasion, Mark told us, for guest presentations on traditional methods of bread making.

A short walk through the forest took us past beautiful rustic beehives, still producing flowered honey from the nearby acacia. I spotted a rabbit and, in my imagination, saw deer wandering the forest and wild boars feeding on the fallen apples of the nearby fruit trees. I could easily picture this agricultural estate in its heyday, with its productive vineyards, fields and forests.

Later in the morning we visited the local market at Joigny and marvelled at the abundance of produce: first-of-the-season strawberries, semi-dried garlic, haricot beans, radishes, beautiful watercress and lettuces, and bundles of green and white asparagus. The one item that is *de rigueur* for French shoppers is a sturdy wicker basket, which of course we forgot to bring. We were left fumbling with our many purchases for the evening's dinner while locals strolled by, their baskets overflowing with *baguettes*, a piece of Dauphin cheese, perhaps some *pâté de gibier* (game pâté) and invariably a bunch of spring flowers or fresh potted herbs.

I selected a *lapin de garenne*, a wild rabbit that was deliciously plump, and a *carré de veau de lait*, a milk-fed veal loin perfectly trimmed by the butcher. I chose some young leeks and some beautiful tiny *courgettes* (zucchini), and could not resist the minute *grelot* (ball) potatoes. I also selected some fresh field mushrooms and a great Coulommiers cheese aged by Gilbert Parret, the favourite *affineur* of Anne and Mark, who proceeded to trim the edges, something I had never seen before. A block of Normandy butter and some fresh cream from Parret's stall completed my purchases.

Back at the Château I selected some herbs from the garden (without attracting the wrath of M. Milbert!) then headed to the kitchen to start preparing dinner. First I cleaned the rabbit and kept aside its large liver, which would make an ideal addition to a *terrine*, and carved the saddle and legs for braising, keeping the shoulder and breast bones aside for the making of the stock. I prepared my tiny *grelot* potatoes to roast in the oven with some of the duck fat left over from the previous night. The tiny *courgettes* were scrubbed and readied to be blanched and dressed with a touch of the local walnut oil. I then seared the rabbit in one of Anne's impressive heavy pans of the commercial variety.

With the garden herbs—thyme, parsley, savory and bay leaves—I prepared my stock. I doused my seared golden rabbit in the stock, along with some Bourgogne Aligoté, a dry white wine of the region, and put it in the oven for a gentle braising. When all the elements were cooked I finished the sauce by giving it a final straining, then added some fresh cream, a large spoonful of seeded mustard from nearby Dijon and some finely sliced, fresh garden tarragon. The meal was enjoyed by all of us with a local Côte d'Auxerre wine.

Yvette and I relaxed over the next few days, conscious that this was to be one of our longest sojourns in any particular location. We read books from Anne's impressive collection and took rejuvenating walks together. We visited wine cellars and, on one fascinating occasion, a walnut oil press.

France has a long tradition of producing walnut oil. The regions of Quercy and Périgord in particular are known for their production of this sublime oil (if butter is synonymous with northern France and olive oil with the Provence region, then walnut oil is definitely the product of the south-west). But even here in Burgundy one could find walnut oil being produced.

Walnuts are collected between the months of September and October in France. The better walnuts are sold for use in pastries, but, surprisingly, up to half of the first-quality pickings are used in the fabrication of cheese, where the nuts make a popular coating for soft cheeses. The rest of the production is used for the making of the pure, golden walnut oil so prized by the chefs of France.

Later in our trip we visited a factory where the walnuts were cracked and cleaned by hand. This operation was performed throughout the winter months, with several families working together to encourage a higher speed of production. The man's role was to break the nut with a small hammer, called a *maluque*, and the women had the thankless task of individually cleaning each nut or *cernau*. The cleaned nuts were stored in a cool place until required to produce the oil. The whitest and fleshiest nuts were used first to produce a cold-pressed oil, which is by far the best.

We saw the nuts being crushed in an old stone mill, powered by an ancient electric motor driven by a series of continuous leather straps and complicated crankshafts. In the old days, donkeys or horses were used to power the *moulins*.

The rotating stone crushed 30 kilograms (just over 66 pounds) of nuts in twenty minutes, circling continuously until it produced a fine meal. This meal was then heated to extract more oil. The heating was done in a large cauldron which had a rotating blade to prevent the nuts from burning. The smell of the wood fire and of the heating nuts was intoxicating; I couldn't wait for the result of this first press. After about twenty minutes of heating, the meal was placed in a basket. This was fitted over a mechanical press and a pressure of up to 30 tonnes per centimetre (29.5 tons per ¼ inch) applied. Suddenly the first flow of oil appeared—a trickle at first, then an impressive free flow that almost spilled over the rim of the bucket, but was deftly caught in a new bucket by the operator of the press.

Yvette and I left with a flask of the precious oil. We contemplated the best use for it and decided that an antipasto of vegetables would be just the thing to bring out its warm, toasty flavours. We prepared the dish and left the vegetables to marinate for a day before serving it up to friends. The freshness of the ingredients, not least the walnut oil, was appreciated by all.

Antipasto of Vegetables with Walnut Oil

200 ml (6½ fl oz) virgin olive oil
handful of oregano or thyme leaves
handful of basil leaves
sea salt
freshly ground pepper
1 clove garlic
a little walnut oil

2 large red onions, thickly sliced
8 medium-sized field mushrooms, trimmed
2 cloves garlic, sliced
150 ml (5 fl oz) walnut oil
2 large red capsicums

2 large yellow capsicums

4 ripe tomatoes

4 ripe figs

4 baby eggplants

125 g (4 oz) Ligurian olives

For the onions:

Preheat oven to 110°C (225°F). Peel and slice the narrow end of the onions. Cut remainder of onions into 4 thick slices each. Brush with olive oil and grill lightly. Place on a tray and season with sea salt. Drizzle with olive oil and sprinkle with some oregano and the small leaves of basil. Bake for 30 minutes.

For the mushrooms:

Preheat oven to 150°C (300°F). Trim the mushrooms and place on a shallow oven tray with the gills facing up. Sprinkle with oregano or thyme, plus garlic and walnut oil. Cook in the oven for 1 hour, basting frequently. Remove and discard herbs and garlic, then drain excess oil and juices from the mushrooms. Reserve.

For the capsicums:

Reduce the oven temperature to 90°C (190°F). Quarter the capsicums and remove core and seeds. Top and tail so you have flat pieces. Roll in olive oil and dust with sea salt. Scorch the skin under the grill then cook in the oven for 45 minutes. Peel the skin and drizzle with more olive oil. Reserve.

For the tomatoes:

Reduce oven temperature to 50°C (110°F). Blanch and peel the tomatoes. Cut in half and brush with olive oil. Sprinkle with oregano or thyme, basil and sea salt. Leave to dry in the oven for 10 hours. This will greatly intensify their flavour.

For the figs:
Cut the figs in two then roll in olive oil. Place on a tray and leave for 2 hours at room temperature, basting occasionally.

For the eggplants:
Halve eggplants lengthwise and score the flesh in a crisscross pattern. Brush with olive oil, sprinkle with salt and grill for 3 minutes on each side. Place in a shallow tray and sprinkle with a few herbs, salt, pepper and olive oil. Leave to stand overnight.

For the olives:
Wash well and marinate in a little olive oil and oregano.

To assemble:
2 fresh knobs of Mozzarella (Buffalo if possible), sliced
1 handful mâche leaves (or other small leaves)
When your onions, mushrooms, capsicums, tomatoes and olives have marinated for at least a day at room temperature and overnight in the fridge, they will be ready to use. Drain and arrange on your serving plate with other ingredients.

(Serves 8 as an entrée)

Yvette and I departed from La Varenne reluctantly. Our brief stay in this idyllic area, rich in gastronomy and beauty, had given us more than a liking for the tranquillity and richness of château life in Burgundy. We knew we would one day return.

CREAM OF THE CROP

The next stop on our busy tour was to be Chablis. The weather had turned cold and rainy—a blessing for all the farmers, as in the previous few months there had been little rainfall. Talk in the media had been that the government was about to impose a drought tax, so the rain was a blessing for French taxpayers too. The temperature dropped to 5 degrees Celsius, a bone-chilling ordeal for sun-loving Australians.

The village of Chablis was tiny. This surprised me, considering its reputation in the wine world. Our destination was the Obédiencerie, the ninth-century monastery in the centre of Chablis. Guided by the tall steeple of the church, we found our way to the office of Domaine Laroche, where we were received by Philippe Frick, export manager for Domaine Laroche and one-time *sommelier* at Mark Meneau's three-star Michelin restaurant, L'Ésperance, in Vézelay.

The *grand crus* of Domaine Laroche are aged in barrels in the cellar of the Obédiencerie, so named to reflect the desired state of mind of the monks who lived there in respect to their elders at the monastery of Tours. Domaine Laroche is one of the most prestigious *domaines* of Chablis. It sells its wines in most three-star Michelin restaurants in France and also exports to the best hotels and restaurants in the world, from The Savoy in London to The Regent Hong Kong to Charlie Trotter's in Chicago.

Philippe led us to the cellars. The stone floors and low ceilings were redolent of another era, but more inspiring still was the realisation that the relics of Saint Martin, the patron saint of horsemen and also the patron saint of Chablis, were buried here. To say that the wine is blessed could be very close to the truth.

We tasted some magnificent wines: Chablis Premier Cru Les Fourchaumes, a full-bodied, honey wine with hazelnut and a lightly smoked flavour; a Grand Cru Les Blanchots, a very structured wine with mild spiciness, great density and an accented note of wood; and, the pride of Michel Laroche, Réserve de L'Obédiencerie, a showcase wine full of stone-fruit aroma and spice, perfumed with a layered structure of soft tannin and mild blueberry. This last one showed me the incredible finesse of French wines at their very best.

From the cellars we returned to the chilly world outside, to the vineyards of Domaine Laroche. I was struck by the harsh stoniness of the Chablis soil and expressed my amazement that the vines could survive in such conditions. Philippe informed me that grapes, and in this case the Chardonnay grape, actually thrive in difficult soil. The struggle of the roots to find the nutrients necessary for survival makes them grow through several layers of soil, and this helps in imparting different and complex characteristics to the wine. The austere soil is in fact a rich mix of marl and limestone deposits containing millions of fossilised oysters dating back 150 million years. It may be no coincidence that the wine produced here goes well with oysters and other seafood.

The cold had made us hungry so we stopped to have lunch in Auxerre at J. L. Barnabet's, a one-star Michelin restaurant. The glassed-in kitchen was visible on the way through the restaurant.

It was very impressive, carved out of stainless steel and stacked with beautiful copper pots.

We started our meal with a *Vinaigrette de jeune légumes au saumon mariné* (marinated salmon with a vegetable vinaigrette), followed by a beautiful *Lasagne d'écrevisses au persil* (crayfish and parsley lasagne) and a *Longe de veau rôti en blanquette d'asperges* (roast veal and asparagus). We finished our Chablis, a Saint Martin Vieilles Vignes, which certainly matched the quality of some *premier crus*. We feasted on Livarot, Crottin de Chavignol and Chaource cheese before finishing with a *Bourdaloue aux poires Passes-Crassane et au lait d'amande*, a caramelised local pear tart with an almond milk sauce.

The mist had descended on Chablis as we drove away. We travelled along the narrow country roads of the region, past verdant fields and through forests where we saw wild deer leaping, continuing north towards Champagne.

Since I completed cookery school over twenty years ago, my favourite champagne has been Cristal, by Louis Roederer. Its presentation in a clear bottle, protected from light by a shimmering, yellow-tinged paper, has always attracted me. It is a champagne of great finesse, elegant structure and harmonious balance.

When Yvette and I planned to visit Rheims, the champagne house of Louis Roederer became my focus. The Louis Roederer agent in Australia was most helpful in organising my visit. I knew I would be in for an exhausting time because of the consecutive lunches, tastings and dinners that were scheduled. I feared the consequences of overindulgence in the following days, but bravely decided that I should absorb as much information and take in as many experiences as possible.

Our destination was the Grand Hôtel des Templiers, in Rheims. I had previously stayed at Les Crayères, where Gérard Boyer has his famous restaurant, but was looking forward to staying at a new hotel. Murièle, who would be our charming hostess for the next few days, greeted us at the door. During our stay Murièle seemed to be everywhere, at all hours of the day and night. If we left at 7.00 am she was there beforehand with an exquisite breakfast laid out for us. If we arrived back from dinner at midnight she was there to greet us, take our breakfast order, handle any room service request we made and bid us goodnight. She proved to be a delightful hostess who gave service that was both personal and impeccable.

The Grand Hôtel des Templiers, a nineteenth-century former residence, was elegant and private. The decor was quasi neo-Gothic and our large room was romantic in a feminine way. The furnishings were deep rose-pink and gold, the robes were fluffy and even the slippers were too! Yvette was overjoyed. I accepted the situation and refrained from commenting on the pink flowery motifs decorating every piece of soft furnishing.

Our first appointment was lunch at Le Foch restaurant in the centre of Rheims with Christophe Hirondel, exterior relations director of the champagne house Louis Roederer. Christophe proved to be a great introduction to the hospitality of Champagne. His narration—in impeccable English—of the history of the champagne house of Louis Roederer was an absolute delight to hear. No amount of protest could prevent us from being served a rich lunch, and only by selecting judiciously from our menu were we saved. I knew we would be having a formal dinner that evening at the home of Monsieur Rouzaud, the owner of Louis Roederer, and did not wish to overindulge at lunchtime.

Jacky, the cheerful chef-owner, introduced himself. He had only recently taken over the restaurant and Christophe was keen to meet him. After working around France, Jacky said he was happy to settle in Champagne and build a great table to complement the fine champagnes of the region.

The lunch started with a delicious 1990 Brut Louis Roederer followed by a delicate and fragrant rosé. We sampled simple entrées that culminated in a superb *Bar en argile au sel Guérin et câpres*, a perfectly cooked whole bass wrapped in moist clay and slowly baked in the oven until the heat barely reached its centre. The fish was boned and filleted at the table with a skill rarely seen today. A sprinkle of coarse Guérin sea salt and a small drizzle of olive oil made this dish, with an accompaniment of creamy garlic potato, a delight that I will remember as much as the wine. The contrasts of texture—the softness of the fish and the crunchiness of the sea salt—contributed to the success of the dish. A great comment from Christophe added to its poetic description: *'C'est bon quand ça croque sous la dent'*—'it's great when it cracks under your teeth'.

My love of cheese was satisfied by the great selection on offer from the Marne region. The Chaource we tasted was at its prime. The month of May is ideal for this cheese, as it is the season with the best-quality milk. The Chaource is a white mould cheese with a high fat content. Since we were in the north, the land of the smelly cheese, we were treated to a wonderful Maroilles, a cheese of reddish-brown colour with a moist skin that is created by washing it in beer. Aptly named *'Vieux Puant'*, or old stinker, it is an aristocratic cheese that impressed the palates of Philippe Auguste, Louis XI, Charles VI and François I. It is to this day a well-prized cheese. I also sampled a Langres, the famous brother of the Maroilles. It has a washed rind of pyramidal shape and contains a soft centre with a slightly sharp taste hidden under its crust.

We departed, more than replenished with food and buzzing slightly from the two vintages of great champagne we had tasted. The afternoon schedule Christophe had prepared for us included a tour of the cellars of Louis Roederer and, more importantly, a tasting of the full range of the winery's products.

The Champagne district is the most northerly wine area of France. Apart from a few wines called *tranquilles* (still whites) by the locals, all other wines of Champagne are effervescent, made with a second fermentation in the bottle. The reflective and inquisitive Dom Pérignon developed this method, justly called *méthode champenoise*.

Our gracious guide of the cellars was Martine. She spoke beautiful English, tinged with a melodic French accent. She told us much about the process of wine making. The pride and joy of Roederer is their *caves des vins de réserve*, the precious stock of previous vintages used in the creation of future *cuvées* to add finesse and fragrance to the new wine. The huge oak casks are protected from excessive humidity and temperature variation. Even the air quality is monitored, purified and treated to ensure a perfect medium for further ageing and to avoid any chance of contamination. Herein resides the secret of the better champagne houses.

After visiting the bottling plant, where more than two million bottles per year are filled and 18 000 bottles per day can be disgorged, we made our way towards the private cellar of the famous Cristal. This champagne was created by Louis Roederer specifically at the request of Tsar Alexander II in 1876. The story goes that the Tsar stipulated that the wine should be in a clear bottle so that any tampering or poisoning of the contents would be apparent. This resulted in the creation of a very special *cuvée de prestige*. The bottle was made of crystal, hence the name. After the Russian Revolution, Louis Roederer's number-one market collapsed. Today, ironically, Louis Roederer cannot satisfy the huge demand for champagne in that country.

The elegant tasting room we eventually reached was full of historic reminders of the glory of this champagne house. Shards of baccarat crystal from the glasses ritually smashed by the Romanovs (to avoid anyone else using them) were on display. The ensuing tasting was conducted in the peacefulness of this timber-panelled room, a tribute to achievement, history and a superior product. From a refined Blanc de blanc to a superb Brut Vintage, we marvelled at the complexity and depth of such unique wines.

It was 5.30 pm, time to refresh ourselves before our dinner appointment with Monsieur and Madame Rouzaud. We made our way back to the hotel on foot to appreciate the early spring blossom and to absorb the experiences and tastings of the day.

High walls and elaborate wrought-iron gates announced that we had arrived at the residence of Monsieur Rouzaud. Nervously I rang the bell. The gates swung open silently. Suddenly two golden retrievers leapt across the grounds to greet us with all the confidence of being on their own territory. We rang the front door bell and, upon its being opened by a maid, were ushered inside, accompanied by the dogs who immediately bounded up the magnificent staircase towards the loving hand of Madame Rouzaud.

What an image of perfection! Here we were in one of the most impressive *demeures* (residences) in Rheims, which boasted a staircase to make any hotelier envious, with a beautiful woman dressed in a French satin lounge suit stepping down to greet us. A superb collection of paintings and furniture completed the setting.

Madame Rouzaud, or Béatrice as she introduced herself, led us to the *salon particulier*, a stunning sitting room full of books on literature, art and music, together with antiques evidently collected with a discerning eye. Sitting here, awaiting the arrival of Monsieur Rouzaud home from work, we looked out across the manicured gardens at a majestic oak tree standing in the middle of the grounds.

Monsieur Rouzaud arrived home to a warm welcome. Immediately he prepared a magnum of Cristal 1989. The pop of the cork signalled the continuation of a very pleasant day; we toasted the new world, and we were officially welcomed at Louis Roederer.

Dinner was served in the comparatively intimate upstairs dining room rather than the *grand salon* downstairs. *La cuisinière de la maison* (the chef) had prepared a simple menu which began with a Brittany lobster salad with asparagus and tomato *confit* and was followed by a *Filet de bar rôti aux asperges blanches* (fillet of bass roasted with white asparagus).

Monsieur Rouzaud then served a selection of cheese with a Château de Pez 1978, a rich and mellow wine that removed any illusions of my being only an occasional drinker. We finished with a *Feuillantine de framboise fraîche* (raspberry mille-feuille), which was fresh and fragrant.

The evening provided a rare view of a fortunate and dedicated man. We departed, having met a part of a living dynasty unwaveringly committed to the development of a remarkable champagne.

LES CRAYÈRES

Christophe Cappoloni, *the vineyard manager of Louis Roederer,* was to pick us up early in the morning for a tour of the three main regions of Champagne. But first it was breakfast time. This meal was organised for us in the sunroom of our hotel. I marvelled at the breakfast spread Murièle had ready for us—a creamy home-made yoghurt that she had prepared overnight was a delight, followed by orange juice, some new-season Agen strawberries in a light syrup, some *petit fromage de chèvre frais* and gruyère cheese, egg *cocotte*, some home-made apricot and almond jam to complement the delicate brioche, sweet madeleines, croissants, *pain au chocolat* and *pain rôti*, all served with local butter. It was an exquisite start to the day ahead.

Christophe, a dark-eyed Corsican and trained agronomist, is responsible for the health of the vines owned by Louis Roederer. The first stop he took us to was in the Grande Montagne de Reims, near Verzenay in the northernmost region of Champagne. We stopped to observe the damage caused by frost, the primary curse of the growers. Two nights earlier frost had settled on the field and burned one out of every two tiny buds on the vines. These would not produce grapes and would reduce significantly the production of the vine. In the middle of the vineyards, where markers like tombstones define the different owners, we observed a great stretch of land that was scorched to the ground, leaving only bare stumps of vine. Christophe explained that the damage had been caused by a light plane which had run out of fuel and made an emergency landing in the middle of this vineyard. This was an unfortunate occurrence, considering the acres of open field surrounding the region. Growers already have a difficult time growing grapes in one of the most marginal areas of France, and incidents like this make their commitment even more admirable.

We arrived at the press house in Verzenay. La Montagne de Reims produces mainly Pinot Noir, one of the most important elements of the wine that will give, according to Christophe, *la puissance du vin*, the strength in the wine. To avoid the grapes bursting they are pressed as near as possible to the place where they are picked. Workers will first pick over the grapes to remove any unripe or bruised fruit. This is called *l'épluchage*. Only the perfect raisin will be put in the *caques* (wicker baskets or, these days, plastic crates) which will then be loaded for the trip to the *pressoir* (press house). Here the grapes will be pressed into *moût* (unfermented wine), which is then transferred to the wine house where, for the next few months, it will undergo fermentation. This wine in turn will form part of the delicate *assemblage* (blending) of the coming champagne. After pressing all the *moût* or must, the juices will be stored in vats that are clearly identified as to the provenance of the grapes. This is vitally important for the next phase of champagne production, the crucial blending stage.

After observing the press house we made our way to Hautvilliers. This picturesque village, high on the hill, was dotted with a display of finely crafted street signs that stated the chosen trade of the occupants of various houses. Many of these trades, we noticed, were relevant to the production of champagne, which was not surprising considering that Hautvilliers is the site of

Abbaye d'Hautvilliers, the monastery where Dom Pérignon used his tasting ability and the proverbial patience of a monk to produce the first-ever champagne. This result was achieved, after many observations and trials, by locking carbonic gas in the bottle following the second fermentation. He developed an ingenious *muselet* (a twisted metal restraint that grasped the neck of the bottle) to hold the cork and the effervescent gas in place. Previously, bottles had been sealed only with a piece of cloth and a few drops of olive oil. Dom Pérignon became a legend, celebrated by kings and emperors, as well as the European aristocracy who drank his wine to celebrate all joyous occasions.

Leaving the village, we were impressed to learn from Christophe that the whole region boasts over 2500 growers and makers of champagne, and more than 250 wine merchants or *négociants*.

We made our way south towards the Vallée de La Marne, and crossed the Canal de la Marne, where the barges ply their trade, transporting sand and the grain of the region to other destinations. On either side of the river stood vineyards of Pinot Noir. Our destination was Épernay, the door to the vineyards of the Côte des Blancs where all the famous Chardonnays are grown.

The vines growing on the hill of the Côte des Blancs all faced east—for a very particular reason, as Christophe explained. The easterly disposition provided the longer sun exposure necessary for the growing and ripening of the grapes. Christophe also explained that the soil here was a layered mass of chalk and clay and was quite prized for the growing of the white grape. Champagnes made only of Chardonnay from the Côte des Blancs were called a Blanc de blanc and were considered to be wines of great finesse and fragrance.

We drove through the picturesque village of Avize, where some of the best *crus* (growths) come from. On the side of the hill we saw a mass of tiny vineyards. Here, logic did not seem to exist, especially to people like us who were used to the large landholdings of Australia. The bottom of the hill was littered with diesel-fuelled pot-bellied stoves used to try to protect the more exposed lower vineyards from freezing.

Lunchtime arrived. We stopped at Restaurant La Briqueterie, a large, auberge-style restaurant in Vinay, near Épernay, where we continued the tradition in Champagne of drinking wine for any occasion. We chose a Louis Roederer Brut Premier.

The lunch was a procession of satisfying dishes. We started with a rich *brandade* (potato and salt cod purée), a small *tartare* of raw spiced salmon as well as some house-smoked salmon, a good *rillettes* (salmon pâté) enriched with Normandy butter, a side of salmon cooked in olive oil and mixed with its cooking oil and some of the tasty butter of the north. Our next course was a beautiful *Mignon de veau à l'oseille du jardin*, veal served with a creamy sauce based on sorrel from the restaurant's garden. Christophe had selected a *Jambonette de volaille au pleurotte farcie à la Provençale* (chicken leg stuffed with zucchini and sprinkled with a sauté of tiny oyster mushrooms). We all finished with a *cocotte* (tart) of tiny braised figs with caramel and prunes. By now, my intention to resist overindulging in the wine and food of the region was only a vague memory.

Slowly we made our way back to Rheims, driving through the superb forests of the region—full, I was told, of wild boar, pheasant, deer and quail. Here and there we could see people in the woods collecting the wildflowers that would be sold the next day to celebrate the first day of May, an important French holiday that is the occasion for great displays of public pride.

That night we were scheduled for dinner with Frédéric Heidsieck-Vérine, the export director of Louis Roederer, and his wife, Marie-Dominique, to discuss an upcoming dinner we would be holding in our restaurant in Sydney. Yvette and I had a small rest, followed by a quick swim and a shower, and were soon dressed for a gourmet dinner at the restaurant of one of the most well-known chefs of France: Gérard Boyer's Les Crayères.

The Champagne region has never had a strong history of gastronomy, as much of its past has been dominated by the endless warfare that took place in its forests, fields and villages. It took the establishment in Rheims of Gaston Boyer, the father of Gérard Boyer, to create the base for a great restaurant committed to good food in Champagne.

Gaston moved from Paris to Champagne in 1961. At that time the region lacked a great chef of the reputation of Blanc in Burgundy, for example, Bocuse in Lyon, Chapel in Mionnay or Troisgros in Roanne. The great houses of Champagne preferred to entertain and lodge their guests in the privacy of their grand *demeures*, where chefs were hired to provide the elaborate meals enjoyed by the potential buyers. This allowed their movements to remain concealed from the other makers of Champagne's *grandes marques* (famous labels). The captive clientele of the big families of Champagne prevented the gastronomic development in the region as a whole and it took a long time to reverse these secretive ways of the *grandes marques*. When Gaston Boyer opened his first restaurant he served the great bistro dishes so well liked by the people of the region. Slowly the patrons came to savour his *Pieds de porc* (pigs' feet), his *Andouillettes* (pigs'-stomach sausage) and the *Pâtés de campagne*. The slow process of dedication to a good table in Champagne had started.

Les Crayères, the former château of Madame Pommery, is an exquisite hotel in a magnificent setting. The space and beauty of the grounds with their *boisé* (forested paths) is a delight. The scent from the hundred-year-old trees, as well as the herb gardens and flowerbeds, makes the gardens a walk of discovery each time you wander through them.

I have stayed twice at Les Crayères and both visits were memorable for the superb dinners at the restaurant of Gérard Boyer. The name Les Crayères comes from the chalk pits that dot the area. These pits date back more than 2000 years to the Gallo–Roman era. Madame Pommery had the wisdom in 1868 to link the deep vertical pits with tunnels—an ideal environment in which to store her champagne for ageing. Today the tunnels are accessed through a magnificent stone staircase descending to a depth of 30 metres (100 feet). Here, more than twenty million bottles are stored at a constant 11 degrees Celsius (52 degrees Fahrenheit) for years of maturation. Over 18 kilometres (11 miles) of tunnel now link the estate, and each one bears the name of a major capital: Berlin, Amsterdam or London. Some are created to launch the opening of a new market, like Sydney, Rio de Janeiro or Dublin.

The hotel Les Crayères is small and intimate yet has the feel of a grand home. A private residence at the beginning of the century, it is now a hotel boasting nineteen elegant rooms, appointed to an exquisite level of style. The modern welcome and efficient reception betray the lessons Gérard has learned from the hospitality and service of the great hotels of Asia, where he was involved in some unique food promotions. The service is silent, unobtrusive and refined. The French château decor and the sweeping staircase leading to the upper floors, or to the sun-filled bar and restaurant, have all been designed with a careful eye to preserving the tradition of the region.

I remembered vividly, from my trip several years previously, how one clear morning, with the sun rising over the woods, I stood on my balcony and watched a colourful hot air balloon rise majestically towards the sky like a magnificent *soufflé*. Rarely are mornings so unforgettable, yet they are typical at Les Crayères.

We were met for dinner by Frédéric Heidsieck-Vérine and his wife, Marie-Dominique. We started with a glass of champagne from the daily selection, which pleased Frédéric, as it had Roederer NV (Non Vintage) as a choice. Werner, the *maître d'hôtel*, is in charge of the hospitality. A member of the Boyer team for more than twenty-five years, he is an old hand at managing this great restaurant. His German organisational skills certainly free Gérard from having to concern himself with anything other than the task of producing the great food he is known for. Sensing the pleasure Frédéric derives from his dinners, and my pleasure in once again sampling Gérard's food, Werner guided us with his expert knowledge in our selection of our menu for the evening.

As we looked about us, Yvette and I agreed that the splendour of the restaurant was probably without equal in country France. The main dining room where we were seated had *boiseries* (wall panelling) and antique tapestries and was filled with handmade furniture and great silver implements for the table, such as the *aiguières* (elaborate silver and glass carafes). The wall *boiseries* carved by the *ébéniste* (cabinetmaker) of the past were enhanced by great bouquets of freshly cut flowers. The light streaming from the rotunda, as in a conservatory, gave a pleasant glow to the glittering glasses ready to be filled by the wines of the evening. The luxury of the plates, linen and silver announced the distinction of the food to come.

We visited the kitchen with Gérard's *chef de cuisine*, Kerry Voisin, and observed the well-honed skills of an outstanding brigade. The simplicity of Gérard's food has distinct roots in his father's style. He uses a minimum of ingredients prepared with a sure hand, full of talent. The *Salade du Père Maurice*, a classic dish of the house, was executed with true expertise in the handling of the *foie gras*, artichoke and beautiful fresh beans. The presentation and preparation were quite classic, with sauces made of strong reductions, finished with northern butter. A love of leek and truffles is evident throughout the menu. Some more exotic dishes are starting to make their mark too, like the beef served with *poêlée* (pan-fried) vegetables or the fillet of bass with coriander and a thyme-flavoured lemon *confit* in a tagine style. In general, however, the food is a classic combination of true and tried dishes of Gérard's repertoire.

We returned to the bar at the end of our evening to have a refreshing and soothing tea, then finally called an end to an exhausting but exhilarating day.

THE FEAST OF FRANCE

Driving towards Strasbourg to visit one of the families still producing the traditional *foie gras* of Alsace filled me with gustative expectation. It was my first visit to this historic and frequently contested city, a city which was occupied by the Romans, destroyed by the Huns and rebuilt by the Franks, before falling under the sway of the Holy Roman Empire. In 1262 it became a free imperial city. Four hundred years later Louis XIV took and retained possession of it until it passed into the hands of Germany as a result of the Franco–Prussian war. It was returned to France in 1919 at the end of World War I, but was once again occupied by the Germans during World War II. In 1945 it was permanently restored to France. The volatile history of Strasbourg has moulded its people and the culinary style of the region.

We were booked in at the Hôtel des Rohan, in a pedestrian street a short distance from the famous Cathédrale Notre-Dame, a masterpiece of Gothic and Romanesque art and the jewel in Strasbourg's crown. The other glory of Strasbourg, and not just in my opinion, is *Le foie gras* (literally, the fat liver). Its reputation is known throughout the whole of France and it is appreciated by connoisseurs around the world.

I remember the first time I tasted *foie gras*. It was in Montreal at one of the French restaurants I worked for on a part-time basis during my school years. I fell in love with it immediately and, over the years, after many discussions and deep personal deliberations with friends and fellow students, concluded that *foie gras* has to be the ultimate food product in the world. Nothing can compare with its lushness, depth of flavour and unique melt-in-the-mouth quality. Eaten on a special occasion, it is pure self-indulgence.

Yvette and I were interested to observe the preparation, handling and cooking of these special duck and goose livers, and Philippe Heusch, the owner of Georges Bruck Foies Gras de Strasbourg, received us with enthusiasm to show us around his factory and discuss the intricacies of *foie gras*. The firm has been in the hands of the Heusch family since 1902 and, before this, was in the hands of the father-in-law of Philippe's great-grandfather. The enterprise dates back to 1852 and today, handsome Vincent, the son of Philippe Heusch, is being trained to help run this family enterprise.

The name Georges Bruck is seen in the luxury hotels of the world, from the Plaza Athénée in Paris to the Savoy Hotel in London or the Mandarin in Hong Kong. Every year the Queen Mother receives from Georges Bruck two of the traditional *Foie gras en croûte* for her personal consumption.

We entered the immaculate, wall-tiled factory with father and son Heusch, wearing surgeons' white smocks. There was an incredible amount of machinery to help in the processing: I could see autoclaves, steamers, blenders, mixers, giant funnels, cooling racks and gleaming stainless steel tables. Philippe and Vincent showed us the entire process of preparing *foie gras*, beginning with the arrival of the well-chilled liver from the various production centres. The lobes were firm and of perfect sandy colour, with a touch of pink enhancing their creamy glow. The Heuschs explained that ideally a liver should be soft and supple without traces of graininess. Sizes range from 500 to 700 grams (1 to 1½ pounds). Careful selection separates the good livers from inferior ones, which have a tendency to melt to pure fat during the cooking process, thus becoming useless.

The first processing stage was the separation of the two lobes to open and expose the inside of the liver, whereupon the veins and the gall bladder were removed to avoid any bitterness being imparted to the organ. The liver was then re-formed as neatly as possible and prepared for seasoning and processing. We learnt that there are three categories of liver: the first averages 600 grams (about 1½ pounds) and is faultless; the second has small, protruding veins; and the third may be overly large or small. The better ones will be used for all preparations that require whole livers, like *Foie gras entier en gelée* or *Foie gras mi-cuit*, a terrine.

Foies gras are sold in two forms: fresh and preserved. Fresh *foies gras* need to be consumed as near to their purchase date as possible. The most famous is the *Pâté de Strasbourg*, which is baked in a pastry crust. One of the most delicious *foie gras* dishes is the *Foie gras au torchon*, a whole *foie gras* wrapped in a checked kitchen cloth, tied tightly and poached gently to set. It is purchased in its cooking cloth, which helps retain its moisture for a second serving. The best *foie gras* to give as a gift would have to be the *Terrine de foie gras*, sealed in a beautiful hand-painted Strasbourg-style earthenware container. All these *foies gras* are sealed with a protective layering of fat that can be removed at the time of serving.

The *mi-cuit*, or lightly preserved *foies gras*, are the most refined and least-cooked variety of the preserved type. They are steamed and sealed in a plastic pouch at a temperature of 75 degrees

Celsius (167 degrees Fahrenheit) and should last for four weeks. This delicious *foie gras*, served with freshly made toast and accompanied by a glass of champagne or sauterne, is my ultimate pleasure when away from France.

The *semi-conserve*, or half-preserved, is cooked at a higher temperature of 80 degrees Celsius (176 degrees Fahrenheit) and can be kept for up to four months. This method mostly preserves the creaminess and full flavour. Finally, the *foie gras de conserve*, or preserved *foie gras*, is cooked at 100 degrees Celsius (212 degrees Fahrenheit) to sterilise the product. It is tinned and sold throughout the world in delicatessens or specialty food shops. It can be kept on the shelf without refrigeration for several years and actually gains from being aged.

The essential difference between *Le foie gras de Strasbourg* and the *foie gras* from other regions is the addition of spices. Philippe and Vincent would not divulge their recipes, revealing only that they contained at least fifteen spices, the mixtures varying slightly for each preparation. I detected salt, pepper, nutmeg, juniper berries and allspice, but could only guess at the other finely ground spices that imparted a subtle but distinctive flavour to *Le foie gras de Strasbourg*.

Before I left the factory I noticed on the table a tray of peeled, glistening black truffles to be used in the preparation of *Foie gras truffé*. Unfortunately, these days most commercial preparations contain only between 1 and 3 per cent truffles, due to their high cost. The ideal place to enjoy this luxurious combination is at the prestigious restaurants of France, especially those in the south-west region, when truffles are in full season.

We were blessed with a perfect spring day on our drive through La Route des Vins d'Alsace (the Alsace Wine Route), the famous drive that takes you through some of the most unforgettable villages and vineyards of Alsace. The serenity of the meandering road could easily tempt you into hiring a bicycle and riding slowly through the lush undulating *coteaux* (hills) at the foot of the Vosges Mountains. However, I realised that one would have to be very fit to attempt to climb the steep hills that make the route so picturesque, so I wisely decided to continue travelling by car.

Our appointment with Marc Haeberlin in Illhaeusern was scheduled for late afternoon. We slowly made our way to the base of the mountains, dropping further and further behind some testosterone-charged, new red Ferraris coming from nearby Switzerland and Germany. The entire road from Marlenheim to Thann comprises about 180 kilometres (110 miles) of absolute postcard prettiness. We arrived in Saint Hippolyte, where the view uphill is filled with the impressive Château du Haut-Koenigsbourg. This château is the most popular attraction in Alsace. Despite the fact that it has been destroyed several times and rebuilt in a questionable, romantic neo-Gothic style, many people love its feudal look and its creaky rooms of Gothic and Renaissance style. The view, at any rate, is certainly beyond criticism. From the château you look down on the plains of the Rhine Valley and up to the Black Forest and the Alps in the background.

The perfect rows of vines climbing uphill towards the hilltops of the Vosges, across a landscape dotted with ruined medieval castles and the remains of traders' houses, formed an unforgettable panorama. At the fortified villages along the route we could have taken a history lesson, sampled some unique wines in the tasting rooms, or enjoyed a meal at any number of rustic *Winstubs*. If we had had enough time we could have explored some of the nineteen *sentiers viticoles* (small vineyard trails) wending their way through the heart of the grape-growing area and its picturesque villages.

But we had an appointment to meet. We made our way south to the village of Ribeauvillé and then to the admirably well-preserved Riquewihr with its medieval fortifications. The village was lined with tempting shops, busy selling a multitude of Alsatian products, from cookbooks to the earthenware typical of the village. There were food shops offering freshly baked macaroons or meringues, specialities to delight both the eyes and the tastebuds. The *Winstubs* were everywhere, their facades decorated with geranium-filled balconies. Inside they served *choucroute*, a traditional dish of cabbage, potatoes and pork, and other regional specialities.

At last we arrived at Illhaeusern, excited at the prospect of spending an evening in the kitchen with Marc Haeberlin. L'Auberge de L'Ill, Marc's restaurant, is synonymous in France with great food and excellent table service. Situated on the water's edge of the Rivière de L'Ill, which is fed by the springs in the Vosges Mountains, it is an idyllic location.

L'Auberge is run by one of the most close-knit families of any of the three-star restaurants in France. The operation is divided into areas of expertise: Marc leads the kitchen brigade; the cuisine is the responsibility of his father, the renowned Paul Haeberlin; Marc's brother, Jean-Pierre, is the *sommelier* (wine waiter) and is responsible for the service; and Madame Haeberlin, Paul's wife, is in charge of the flowers, the manicured gardens of the *auberge* (inn) and of the nearby hotel run by Danièle, Marc's sister.

L'Arbre Vert, their original restaurant, used to be a typical Alsatian *auberge*, serving regional specialities such as *écrevisse* (freshwater crayfish), *choucroute*, *foie gras*, *confit* and their famous *matelote* (a stew of local fish braised in white wine). The restaurant had a fairly colourful history, owing to the fact that it was situated near the bridge over the River L'Ill. L'Arbre Vert was unfortunately destroyed at the beginning of World War II, not by the German army but by the retreating French, who were destroying the nearby bridges over the river. After the war the family rebuilt their old *auberge* with much improved facilities and in this way demonstrated the seriousness of their ambitions. Their desire was to develop a fine reputation based on the quality of the cellar, the service, the decor and, above all, the quality and consistency of the food. They wanted to create one of the best restaurants in Alsace.

Upon entering the foyer of the *auberge*, Yvette and I instantly felt a warmth which had nothing to do with temperature but everything to do with atmosphere. The place was unpretentious and devoid of the pomposity so apparent in many other restaurants, and yet it was clearly a temple dedicated to good living.

Marc came out to greet us. He was full of nervous energy and an enthusiasm that bespoke of great generosity. I had not expected the appearance of Paul Haeberlin himself, but suddenly the venerable chef was in front of us, shaking our hands. He said very little, which I gathered was due to a hearing difficulty, but his eyes sparkled at the prospect of pleasing more enthusiasts interested in the food of the *auberge*.

Marc showed us around the restaurant and its grounds. Weeping willows created a filter for the spring sun and cast a dappled light over the river. The garden was full of seasonal flowers. As we toured the grounds I noticed a lunch party lingering in a garden setting under some trees. Tiny blossoms were falling like powdery snow onto their table, into their champagne, catching in their hair as they laughed contentedly. It was breathtaking.

We left Marc so that he could attend to his pre-service duties and so that we could visit the recently built Hôtel des Berges, situated on the river next to the restaurant. Marc and Danièle Baumann-Haeberlin created this superb establishment for people who wished to stay and indulge in more than just one meal at the Haeberlin family's restaurant. Marc's affability, good humour, generosity and good looks make him a perfect host for the guests.

To ensure that we got a feel for the village and its surroundings, Marc had insisted that we take the mini tractor and go for a ride in the woods. Since the tractor only had one forward gear, I figured I could handle driving it.

The forest was beautiful. In it lived the game that had featured prominently on the menu of the old L'Arbre Vert, and was still a part of the cuisine served up by Paul and Marc. The thought of food soon had us heading back down the road towards the *auberge*, where a magnificent treat awaited us.

I always feel excited when I enter someone else's kitchen. The rush of activity is invariably surprising, but I feel solidarity with the chef's task, and respect for his domain. I found the Haeberlin kitchen very well set up, like an old, neat workshop that your uncle might have, with all his old tools in perfect working condition. The benches and old silverware were imbued with a sense of accumulated effort and activity. The kitchen felt to me as if it had developed over the years.

We were led to the private salon just off the kitchen where the family spends most of its time between services. Paul was watching the French news on an old television set, his ear close to the speaker to hear the commentary. Jean-Pierre was spread over the comfortable couch, catching a snooze. Madame Haeberlin was knitting a sweater. Marc shared a quick bite with us before the service began. We sipped a 1990 Léon Beyer Riesling 'Les Écaillers' while eating a first course, a *Salade de langoustines et son beignet sur une brandade de morue, vinaigrette de crustacés*, a scampi tail and fritter with a salt cod *brandade* and a shellfish dressing with caviar.

We returned to the kitchen for the service. Everyone seemed at ease with their place and position, from the pastry chef and glass washer to the *sauciers* and others involved in the back-of-house activities. Some of the dishes on the menu had been there since the restaurant's inception—they were the classics of the house. This continuity certainly made for a comfortable and prepared team.

Marc is the *aboyeur* (the order caller) at the pass, taking the commanding position in the kitchen where one controls the inflow of orders and outflow of food. In most other restaurants the *chef de cuisine* handles this role, allowing the chef-owner to focus on creating dishes and ensuring the total quality of the operation. This leaves him the time to greet guests and help in the selection of their menu. Here, Jean-Pierre covered this role with great aplomb, being by far the more voluble and congenial partner when it came to dealing with the clientele.

The orders came in quickly. Marc called them out loudly to be heard by all the chefs. That night, most guests selected from the *menu dégustation* (tasting menu), a blessing and a curse at the same time. A blessing because it helps the kitchen produce consistent food for an unusually large number of people in a short time; a curse because Marc would like people to try the specialities of the house and the classics that have made the reputation of the *auberge*. I also could see that Marc would have liked them to try his newer dishes, those that will define a new generation of classics. Obviously the set price attached to the *dégustation* menu is a real incentive to order from it. It gives the guests the opportunity of sampling several dishes for a reasonable price.

The speed of service increased inexorably towards what, to an outsider, would be regarded as pandemonium; luckily everyone performed his or her duties with speedy efficiency. This kitchen was very amicable yet did not lose sight of its goals, and certainly did not evince the cold efficiency that I'd earlier found in Monsieur Ducasse's kitchen. Staff in this kitchen went about their job as a family, not as a crack commando team watched by an uncompromising sergeant major.

Crumbed *goujonnettes* (fritters of carp), a typical dish of the region, were served as an *amuse-gueule* (appetiser) with a *rémoulade* (mustard mayonnaise) of celeriac. It was surprising for me to see the service staff help themselves to the *goujonnettes* under Marc's eyes. The famous *Terrine de foie gras et sa gelée blonde* (*foie gras* terrine with Madeira jelly) passed us by in a beautiful, rustic handmade pot. Waiters and *sommeliers* were now rushing in all directions to gather stunning antique ice buckets from which to serve the wine, silver platters to carry the plated food, and long-stemmed glasses for the great Alsatian vintages cellared by Jean-Pierre.

Paul appeared in his immaculate whites to check the kitchen. He nodded to the cooks and went straight to the board where all the orders were spiked. A quick glance told him the progress of the evening. For me, seeing such a legend in the kitchen, especially one of his age, was awe-inspiring.

The food rolled before our eyes throughout the night. I checked the service of the desserts in the pastry shop. I tasted several dishes offered by Marc, who insisted we eat them. I did. Yvette struggled to get through the delicious duck breast filled with *foie gras*—not surprising considering we had had a heavy, traditional Alsatian meal at lunch.

Waiters were now starting to come off the floor to polish wineglasses, a sure sign that the service was coming to an end. We saw the last dishes go out, said our final farewell to Paul Haeberlin, who quietly slipped out through the back door into the night, and took our leave, amazed by the restaurant and the Haeberlin family of Illhaeusern.

top left: World-famous *boulanger,*
Lionel Poilâne.

top right: *La pétrie* (dough) at
Boulangerie Poilâne. The *levain*
(leaven) is created by keeping a
small amount of dough from the
previous batch to be introduced
into the new *pétrie* as the starting
mixture.

bottom: Denise Acabo's L'Etoile
d'Or is one of the best chocolate
shops in Paris.

top and bottom:
Service at Alain
Ducasse's restaurant
on avenue de
Raymond Poincaré.

top: The historical Château du Feÿ, where Anne Willan's famous cooking school, La Varenne, is located.

bottom: Goat cheeses maturing in the ageing cellars at Jacques Vernier's *fromagerie*.

right: The beautiful Les Crayères, Rheims, Champagne.

bottom left: Inside the pigeon house at the Château du Feÿ.

bottom right: *Muselets* with Champagne Louis Roederer's distinctive seal.

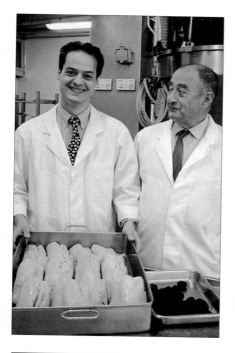

top left: Philippe Heusch of Georges Bruck Foies Gras de Strasbourg, and his son, Vincent.

top right: Marc Haeberlin managing the service at L'Auberge de L'Ill.

bottom: The legendary Paul Haeberlin.

top: Service at Lameloise in Chagny, Burgundy.

bottom: Behind the scenes at Georges Blanc's family restaurant in Burgundy.

top left: Barrels of cognac in an ageing cellar at Rémy Martin, Bordeaux.

top right: Jean-Claude Monteil in his mushroom warehouse in the Corrèze region.

bottom: Black Périgord truffles from the Pébeyre family truffle merchants.

top: Freshly baked bread on offer at La Maison du Caviar in Monaco.

bottom: Delicate work at Alain Ducasse's Louis XV in Monaco.

MERCILESS PLENTY

*J*acques Lameloise was the youngest chef ever to receive three Michelin stars. He humbly admitted this to me on my departure from his wonderful village hotel, Lameloise, in Chagny. During our three-day visit to Chagny, Yvette and I discovered Jacques to be a person with a big heart, a deep sense of hospitality and a self-deprecating manner. We loved our stay at Lameloise.

Pierre Lameloise, Jacques Lameloise's grandfather, worked in some of the greatest houses of the period—the famous Plaza-Athénée Hôtel, the Ledoyen and Lapérouse restaurants—and with such legends of the past as Auguste Escoffier at the Savoy in London. The Hôtel de Commerce, which was built in the sixteenth century, was taken over by Pierre Lameloise in 1920. Situated in Chagny, at the centre of the Côte d'Or and at the convergence of many roads, canals and train lines, the hotel was ideally situated to attract passing trade. The hard work of Pierre was rewarded in 1935 when he received (as his son and grandson would many years later) a coveted Michelin star. Unfortunately he was not to live much longer. With his death, and the interruption of World War II, the hotel fell into a decline. But Pierre's son, Jean, was determined to revive the reputation of the hotel and its table. With his wife, Simone, he worked to regain the reputation his father had established. Soon Jean became famous for dishes like *Quenelles de brochet* (poached pike mousse), *Truite au Montrachet* (trout in white wine) and *Perdreau à la vigneronne* (gently roasted partridge with local grapes). He regained a Michelin star for the hotel in 1951, and in 1960 the Hôtel de Commerce changed its name to Lameloise, to better reflect the nature of the family operation with the restaurant as its focus.

Meanwhile Jean's son, Jacques, was born in the hotel in 1947. He followed the family tradition by going off to Paris to undertake culinary studies and then worked at the better restaurants of France to perfect his skills. He followed in the footsteps of his grandfather to the Savoy Hotel, Ledoyen, and eventually ended up at Lassere in Paris in 1970 to complete his training. After his return to Chagny, and having adjusted to his father's kitchen, he slowly made his contribution while still learning the various skills that bring a more focused and determined approach to food. In 1974 the restaurant achieved its second Michelin star. Due to his continuing commitment to modernising the structure of the enterprise and searching for the best products of Burgundy, and to Jacques's obvious ability, Lameloise received its third Michelin star in 1979.

The kitchen of a chef is normally a good indication of his discipline. When Jacques invited me to spend a night in his kitchen to observe the service, I accepted with delight. Knowing that the last renovation of Lameloise had taken place more than twelve years previously, I was prepared to excuse Jacques for having a somewhat old and worn kitchen. But here the cleanliness, order and state of maintenance was impeccable. Age seemed only to have bettered the place. I was reminded of an insight once offered to me by a chef: if I could improve permanently on only one item a day, he had said, my cuisine would, after time, be judged a great one. Such an insight seemed to be Jacques Lameloise's philosophy.

I spent the next few hours observing a great team in full motion and absorbing lessons: how *foie gras* could be cooked and served in inimitable ways, how to colour a red wine sauce with a small amount of beetroot juice, how to reheat cooked meat with a light induction of steam to avoid drying the flesh.

Towards the end of the service I was ready to retire, but Jacques insisted that Yvette and I attend dinner in the dining room. No amount of protest could deter him. I reluctantly accepted, after agreeing to a maximum of three courses. Little did I know that seven courses were going to be directed our way.

As the impeccable *maître d'hôtel* seated us at a table laid with plates carrying the restaurant logo and superb glass vases etched with the monogram of the restaurant, I couldn't fail to observe that comfort and class had certainly made their mark in Burgundy. The dining room was superb. Its white walls were covered with richly framed paintings, it had great artworks of silver and its vases were full of fresh roses and exotic flowers. The exposed beams and arabesque columns revealed the venerable age of the building. Most tables were illuminated by gorgeous lamps with solid silver bases, which provided intimacy and just the right amount of lighting for the food.

I immediately became suspicious of the size of the meal we were about to consume when a plate of *amuse-gueules* arrived. A beautiful *foie gras* mousse was set on a crescent-shaped crouton on a citrus-cured cube of salmon. As well, a light *feuilletée* of almond and poppy seed with a tiny layer of air-dried beef and *fromage blanc* slices were set in front of us. For purely academic reasons, I sampled them all.

An enormous slab of Achiré butter was deposited on our table with a rustic assortment of home-baked bread. The crust and heavy centre emitted a true sourdough aroma, too tempting to resist. Then a seared lobster tail, served with buttered asparagus and drizzled with a few drops of sweet balsamic vinegar—just enough to enhance the firm but flavoursome flesh of the Normandy lobster—was set in front of us, leaving us no other choice but to devour it with enthusiasm.

I will always remember our next course. It was a seared, thick slice of *foie gras* with a green rhubarb compote, so fine, so acidic, but perfectly balanced with the taste of the liver. It was garnished with an amazing slice of red rhubarb, paper thin, and dried to a featherweight crispness. A red wine reduction sweetened with the juice of beetroot made for a perfect *foie gras* dish.

Two dishes followed, one for each of us, both ravioli. Yvette's was made of Brittany scampi, served with a caviar topping, garnished with fresh chervil and a sauce made with a shellfish and lobster coral-infused *velouté* (velvety white sauce). Jacques crowned the dish with a light froth of egg white that produced a delicious and very balanced dish. My ravioli dish was a long-standing speciality of the house: *Ravioli d'escargots de Bourgogne dans leur bouillon d'ail doux*, which consisted of a wrapped *ragôut* of the large Burgundian snail in a special ravioli dough. Jacques offered me the recipe and was keen for me to try the dish with a triple-blanched garlic sauce combined with a touch of cream and garnished with a green zucchini *julienne*, a small tomato *fondue* and some wilted stalks of Italian parsley. So light and delicious was it that I finished the dish, mopping up the sauce with the scrumptious bread.

I could easily have stopped there, but before we could leave the table another house speciality appeared. I was torn between cursing Jacques and giving him my total admiration. *Compote de queue de boeuf à la purée de pommes de terre et truffes* sat in front of us, glistening with a rich sauce. The oxtail had evidently been braised for hours. It had been boned, shredded and set on top of a creamy circle of mashed potato and topped with simmered black truffle. I gave up any pretence of saving my appetite for another day.

Back in Sydney some months later, I adapted Jacques's delicious beef brisket to suit Australian ingredients, and came up with the following recipe, which uses open field mushrooms in place of the expensive truffles found in France. Still, when the truffle season is on in France, I cannot resist getting some sent over to serve to my guests for a full experience.

Beef Brisket with Mushroom Confit and Potato Purée

For the beef:
1½ kg (3 lb) piece beef brisket
80 ml (3 fl oz) vegetable oil
1 onion, roughly chopped
1 carrot, roughly chopped
1 clove garlic
1 sprig thyme
3 bay leaves
salt and ground pepper
cold water to cover

In a cast-iron or other heavy pot, sear the beef on high heat with the oil until well coloured. Drain excess oil then add the vegetables, garlic, herbs, salt and pepper. Cover with cold water. Braise, covered, in the oven at 175°C (350F) for 3 hours. Allow to cool in the stock. Once cooled, remove the beef brisket and shred into long strands, taking care to remove any fat or gristle.

For the sauce, strain the stock into a saucepan and reduce. If your sauce becomes too thick, add a glass of red wine and cook until you have the right consistency.

Strain with a very fine chinois or sieve.

For the mushrooms:
    8 open field mushrooms, 12 cm (5 in) diameter
    2 sprigs thyme
    2 cloves garlic, sliced
    150 ml (5 fl oz) walnut or olive oil
    salt and ground black pepper

Trim the stalks and flaps of the mushrooms, then with the gills facing up, place on a shallow oven tray. Sprinkle with thyme, garlic and oil. Season, and cook in the oven at 150°C (300°F) for 1 hour, basting frequently. Remove and discard thyme and garlic then drain excess oil and juices from the mushrooms. Put aside.

For the potato purée:
    500 g (16 oz) Desirée potatoes (or any good mashing variety)
    100 g (3½ oz) cold butter, diced
    100 ml (3 fl oz) cream or milk, warmed
    salt and pepper

Drop potatoes into cold salted water, bring to the boil and cook until soft. (If you are using new potatoes, cook them with the skin to avoid an elastic texture; otherwise, peel the potatoes before cooking.) Purée them through a rice presser or a hand masher, do not use an electrical machine.

Add cold butter, mix, then adjust the seasoning. Just before serving gradually add warm cream or milk until you achieve the right consistency. There is no standard recipe for the perfect purée, everything depends on the quality and variety of potato you use and on the time of the year.

To assemble:

In a small pan slowly warm the desired quantity of beef, moistened with a touch of sauce.

To present this dish perfectly, use metal or plastic tubing 9–10 cm (4 in) in diameter and 6 cm (2½ in) high. Place the tube on each mushroom and cut a perfect round shape, using a small sharp knife. Put the ring in the centre of a plate and fill with 2 cm (1 in) of potato purée, top with 3 cm (1½ in) of beef brisket then remove ring and set mushroom on top. Drizzle the sauce around the plate and serve.

(Serves 4 as a main)

To finish our meal at Lameloise, I was guided like a lamb to choose from the impressive selection of aged cheeses set in an immaculate silver and polished wood Christofle trolley. I chose an Époisse, a Sandré and a beautiful washed rind cheese made by the monks of the region.

We declined dessert, but unfortunately the *maitre d'hôtel* came back with a grin on his face and a to-die-for assemblage of chocolate desserts called *Grande assiette du chocolatier*. This had obviously been created by a talented pastry chef who had no regard for the multitude of courses customers could have ingested on their way to the conclusion of a meal at Lameloise. The selection was so good that each tiny dessert needed to be eaten slowly and with thought. Before my dessert was finished, two silver platters full of the most dainty assortment of *petits fours* arrived at the table. What could I do but be polite and sample some of them? I can still remember the taste of the tiny lemon tarts, the light and crispy almond *tuiles* (wafers), the tiny raspberry tarts and the pistachio-studded dried meringue.

We determined to escape the dining room. First, though, I needed to say thank you to Jacques. He appeared, laughing before he reached our table, making light of his exceptional performance. We took the staircase to our room, where Yvette decided to have a herbal tea to appease her conscience. Tea arrived with what else but a completely fresh set of *petits fours*! If I remember correctly, that's when I started sobbing.

We were late to rise the next morning. The abundant hospitality of Jacques Lameloise had left us feeling like two fattened bears ready to sleep away the winter months. But there was no time for luxuries like sleep. Our schedule was relentless: we had to be in the village of Vonnas, just north of Lyon, that afternoon. So with an effort we dragged ourselves out of bed and drove the 100 kilometres through the rural and rustic countryside of Bresse.

Bresse is known for its poultry. Originally the Bresse region produced four types of chicken—black, blue, grey and white—but the white chicken was considered superior, becoming known as the Bressane breed. In 1936 a tribunal was set up to legally define the Bresse region as producer of the Bresse chicken, and in 1957 the French parliament passed a special law to confirm the status of the *Poulet de Bresse* and its official *Appellation D'Origine Contrôlée* (AOC), setting precise conditions and regulations for the growing and marketing of the *Poulet de Bresse*.

It was for more than chickens that we had come to Bresse, however.

Today the village of Vonnas would not be on the map if it were not for the establishment more than one hundred years ago of an inn by the Blanc family. Jean Louis Blanc and his wife were the first to build an *auberge* in Vonnas, a typical farming village where local cattle merchants, buyers from the Lyon market, Burgundian wines wholesalers and *Poulet de Bresse* merchants of the region would congregate after the sales for a drink and a bite to eat. This small *auberge* and great meeting place quickly gained a reputation for its rustic, full-flavoured food.

The running of the kitchen was eventually transferred from 'La Mère Blanc' to her daughter-in-law, Elisa Gervais. Elisa continued the task of feeding the ever-growing clientele, and with her natural talent in the kitchen, inherited from her own mother, easily produced the great buttery dishes and generous servings of what was known as 'women's cooking'. This cooking gained so much in stature that Curnonsky, the Prince of the Gastronomes, wrote in 1933 that Elisa Gervais was 'the finest cook in the world'. Her cuisine was honest cooking, full of simple yet traditional dishes using the varied ingredients of the region. She served the local *Poulet de Bresse*, frogs' legs from the marshes of the nearby Dombes, hand-raised milk-fed veal, special crêpes *Vonnassiennes*, yabby gratin, chicken-liver pâté, *Fricassée* of chicken in cream sauce, and many other ever-popular dishes.

Georges Blanc took over in 1968 from his mother, who had maintained the dishes and traditions that had made the *auberge* such a success. Georges decided to expand the business and to build more rooms to lodge the ever-growing gastronomic tourist trade that came to sample the specialities. Following his upgrading, and resulting from a total commitment to his trade, he was awarded his third Michelin star in 1981.

Yvette and I were to stay in this redoubtable hotel for a night. Our room faced the peaceful Veyle River, where weeping willows cascaded to the water. The river's green banks and casual walkway hid the more touristic aspects of the village, which included a bistro, food boutiques, wine rooms and souvenir shops owned by the Blanc enterprise.

During our visit to the kitchen, which Georges was checking before the service, we were introduced to his long-standing *chef de cuisine*, Patrick, and to Georges's son, Frederick. Frederick is the *saucier*, in charge of all the meat- and sauce-based dishes. His focused eyes and authoritative bearing set him apart from the team as a future leader. We spent some time observing the first dishes being produced by a professional team in a superb kitchen before sitting down with Georges for an aperitif of one of his Domaine wines. While we drank, I admired the eclectic splendour of the bar. The collection of modern paintings adorning the walls was no less extraordinary than the menu cover, with its bold colours and food themes. We were served small appetisers of duck *rillettes* wrapped in blanched spinach and set on a crouton, then a mini ragoût of fresh snails in a vivid green sorrel sauce and a tiny soup cup of potato *velouté*, enriched with a *brunoise* of calves' feet—a wonderful indication of things to come.

The dining room was teeming with waiters and full tables in action. The atmosphere was theatrical, with its coloured fabrics, strong paintings, scattered silver sculpture and a diverse clientele ready for a grand dinner or a birthday to be celebrated. Close to us, a glamorous table of five had their well-groomed dog at their feet.

We started the main meal with beautiful pea ravioli, topped with a Mediterranean melt-down of vegetables enriched in a lemon verbena sauce. This was followed by a favourite of mine, a frog-leg ragoût set around a spinach *timbale* and a rich butter sauce flavoured with dry spices.

Georges sent us two different *Poulet de Bresse* dishes that feature pre-eminently on the menu: a *Poulet de Bresse à la crème façon Grand-Mère Blanc* and a rich *Poulet de Bresse comme au G7 avec gousses d'ail et foie gras*. The first was a dish preserved from Georges's mother's repertoire, and the second a dish created for the leaders of the seven industrial powerhouses of the world at a summit in France. A fitting duo of contrast with strong regional roots.

The meal did not stop when we were full, as we were at the mercy of a system that has no regard for restraint. We followed the main course with a regional *spécialité* of *Crêpes Vonnassiennes*, a corn-based crêpe surrounded by *a filet* of melted butter, and a pre-dessert—a new introduction, designed to aid digestion in preparation for the dessert proper—that I could have done without. Nevertheless, I was ready for the *Chocolat moelleux*, a warm, to-die-for, soft-centred chocolate dessert that could have finished me gracefully, if not for the plethora of *petits fours* that followed. We retired to our room, grateful that our comfortable bed was within walking distance of the dining room.

The next day, after thanking Monsieur Blanc for our excellent evening, we headed (on his recommendation) to the Musée de la Bresse–Domaine des Planons, a typical farm of the Bresse region which has been converted into an educational and historic centre preserving the traditional way of life in Bresse and the farming of the famous *poulets de Bresse*.

We learnt that there are three categories of *Poulet de Bresse*. The *Poulets* (chickens and hens) spend their first five weeks in enclosed heated barns, then roam free range for at least nine weeks before spending their last eight to fifteen days in wooden cages (*épinettes*), living on a diet of enriched food. The final target weight of a *Poulet* varies from 1.5 to 3 kilograms (3 to 6 pounds). The second category is the *Poulardes*: five-to-six-month-old hens that have not attained sexual maturity. These have eleven weeks of ranging freely and a few weeks in the *épinettes*. The third category, the *Chapons* (castrated chicken), is the pride of the *Volaille de Bresse*. Castration is performed at a young age and the *Chapon* grows for nine months afterwards, enjoying twenty-three weeks of liberty and four weeks in the *épinettes*.

Poulardes and *Chapons* are produced only for Christmas and Easter. Christmas is the time of the great tradition of the *Glorieuses*, where the plucked chickens are proudly displayed in a large exhibition attended by hundreds of growers and an appreciative public. Over 2500 *Glorieuses* compete for the famous ribbons, and once the judging has been completed they are put up for sale. The bargaining is intense, as a winning bird is a guaranteed gastronomic feast.

Had I had access to a kitchen I would have cooked one of these wonderful Bresse chickens on the spot, but knowing that we would be on the move for the next several days, I resisted the temptation to buy a bird and instead satisfied myself with dreaming up a dish that would do justice to the rich flavour of the flesh. The following recipe for a steamed free-range chicken with mushroom and sage stuffing is a simple one, but unsurpassable in flavour. It is best enjoyed with boiled potatoes and slow-braised leeks or winter vegetables.

Steamed Chicken with Mushroom and Sage Stuffing

1 free-range chicken, 1.6 kg (3 lb)
40 ml (1 fl oz) olive oil
1 large onion, diced
160 g (5½ oz) mushrooms
½ loaf crusty fresh Italian bread, crumbed in a food processor
100 g (3½ oz) cold butter, diced
1 tablespoon chopped Italian parsley
2 tablespoons chopped sage
salt and pepper

20 g (½ oz) butter, softened
1 leek, cleaned and sliced
1 carrot, peeled and sliced
80 ml (3 fl oz) olive oil
1 bay leaf

Heat the oil and sauté the onion until golden brown, then add mushrooms and cook until dry. Add breadcrumbs and remove from the heat. Add butter, most of the parsley and sage (reserve some of the herbs), stir well and season.

Allow to cool, then stuff the cavity of the chicken. Smear the soft butter on the skin then sprinkle with the reserved chopped herbs on top. Truss the chicken and season.

Preheat oven to 180°C (350°F).

In a small pan, soften the leek and carrot in the olive oil. Cool and place leek and carrot in an oven bag with the chicken and bay leaf. Seal bag well. Place the chicken in a heavy casserole (a heavy cast-iron pot is ideal for this), and tightly cover with the lid. Cook for 1½ hours in the oven or steam in a steamer.

To assemble:
Remove chicken from the pot and allow to rest for 10 minutes before you cut open the oven bag. Portion the chicken, using kitchen scissors, and serve, accompanied by boiled potatoes and winter vegetables.

(Serves 4 as a main)

THE QUALITY OF AGEING

I have always enjoyed a good cognac after dinner. My wife sometimes looks at me with a glint of reproach in her eye but has never attempted to deprive me of this pleasure.

It was, then, with some consternation from Yvette's point of view, and a great deal of eagerness on mine, that we anticipated our arrival in Cognac in the region of Bordeaux.

We had left the Bresse region early that morning to take one of our longest journeys, literally crossing France in a day. We travelled first to Lyon, bypassing one of the great gastronomic cities of the world (we would save it for a return journey, we promised ourselves), crossing the busy Clemont-Ferrand and driving on to the industrial city of Limoges, which has been producing fine porcelain since the late eighteenth century. Finally, with the sun lying low in the west, we reached Cognac.

It is always fascinating to me to learn the history behind the creation of a great product, especially one as remarkable as cognac.

The town of Cognac grew up on the banks of the Charente River during the sixteenth century. The Charentes region, situated on the coast of the Atlantic with the Gironde estuary to the south, was a crossroads for traders, who would come by sea loaded with wood, furs and other merchandise. The northern sailors prized the salt produced in the area on account of it being an essential preserving agent. Wine was sold too, though due to the climate and soil composition, it was mostly thin and undistinguished. Since wine was taxed on volume rather than on its selling price, the Charentais, on the urging of Dutch merchants, started to boil it down. The resulting liquor was later spiced with herbs and diluted with water to be drunk as a strong tonic. The cooked wine was known as *vin brulé*, or in Dutch, *Brandewijn*. This was soon abbreviated to 'brandy', a name that was adopted by the English traders.

Because of changing alliances and ever-constant continental and sea wars, trade in Cognac could be disrupted for long periods. This compelled the producers to store the brandy locally. Over its years of storage, it was discovered that the liquor acquired the tannin taste of the oak barrels in which it was stored. The forced ageing turned the brandy a beautiful amber colour and gave it a great nose and a unique concentration of flavour. To further enhance its quality, a double distillation process was adopted, resulting in a less fiery and more refined liquor. By the early eighteenth century, this exceptional *eau-de-vie* had earned the name Cognac after its port of origin.

With every great product there is always a pioneer at the forefront of its creation. The House of Rémy Martin was founded in 1724 by a visionary whose sons, Paul Rémy and Paul-Émile Rémy, followed in his footsteps. Two hundred years later André Renaud, the manager of this famous house, created the VSOP (very special old pale) system of rating superior cognac. This was achieved at the time of the creation of the Rémy Martin company in 1925. In Sydney I once met Dominique Hériard-Dubreuil, daughter of André Hériard-Dubreuil, who was instrumental in furthering the reputation and the development of the house of Rémy Martin after the retirement of André Renaud. Today Dominique is the president of Rémy Martin.

Yvette and I met up with Jason Bowden, who was to be our guide over the next two days. The refined environment of Rémy Martin Maison Mère, the head office, blended with great architectural modernity, made for a fitting image of what Rémy Martin is today.

In this age of instant communication, speedy transport and constant demand, the concept of ageing for decades is difficult to understand. To put stock away for up to fifty years seems financially unwise, and beyond the patience of most of us. However, the secret of producing superb cognac resides in the capacity to age the great *eaux-de-vie* (literally, water of life) in Limousin oak casks for a very long time and to blend them with consummate art into a superb spirit.

Three grape types are used to produce the wines for the making of cognac: Colombard, Folle Blanche and Ugni Blanc. The grapes are pressed, the stems and seeds are removed and the grape juice is allowed to ferment naturally for a period of between one and two weeks. The resulting wines will be kept on lees (the sediment) until their distillation. The distilling will occur in the *charentais alambics* (the copper stills). The *bouillis* (first distillation) will produce an *eau-de-vie* with a proof of 50 per cent. This process is repeated to produce the *bonne chauffe*, resulting in pure cognac with a much higher proof reading of nearly 70 per cent. These *eaux-de-vie* are then sold to the cognac houses where they will be aged in oak barrels.

Jason took us along the road to the ageing cellars and there, in front of us, the full story revealed itself: forty-two huge stone storage buildings, called *chais*, were spread out in the distance. Over 100 000 kilolitres (22 million gallons) of cognac were contained here, spread over 10 hectares (24 acres). Each of them was covered with the 'Noble' mould, the *Torula Cognaciensis* fungus, which grows like black cottonwool on the exterior walls due to the constant evaporation of alcohol. The fungus was poetically referred to as 'Angel's Share'.

Inside the silent *chais* the unmistakable mould smell rose from the bare earthen floor, mixing with the light vapours of the ageing cognac and the profound aroma of the Limousin oak. Cognac is aged in the small oak barrels made at nearby Merpins by Seguin Moreau, which is the biggest European cooperage operation and is owned by Rémy Martin. Unlike the barrels made for wines, cognac requires a different type of oak. Here pedunculate oak is used for a twofold advantage: its coarser grain helps the necessary alcohol evaporation, and its powerful tannins penetrate into the brandy, which will over time take on a splendid amber colour. The same wood used in the making of wine would impart a harsh and aggressive taste.

Jason explained to us that, over years or decades, cognac oxidises and attains unique characteristics. Skilful blending to achieve the various house styles is then necessary. In this, the role of the cellar master rivals the status of the champagne blenders. The cellar masters are able to use a near infinite variety of stock to produce a constant style by mixing, tasting and ageing the different barrels chosen from their different *chais*, each of which will have individual characteristics of moisture, temperature and maturing potential. Secret codes are then written on all barrels. This well-preserved skill is only divulged to the next generation of blenders.

Our lessons absorbed, Jason thought we were ready for a tasting. We returned to the special tasting room at Rémy Martin.

There in front of us were five tasting glasses filled with different products of the house, accompanied by Volvic mineral water, the most neutral of table waters, and some plain table biscuits to cleanse our palate between tastings.

The glasses used were a novelty for me. Rémy Martin rejects the traditional brandy balloon, preferring to use the small, narrow glasses more commonly associated with sherry, so as not to allow too much of the aroma and flavour to escape. Moreover, Rémy Martin abhors the heating of cognac, either by the warmth of the hands or the more radical flame treatment.

The tasting of cognac involves an even deeper form of ritual than the tasting of wine. The tasting room temperature was set at 18 degrees Celsius (64 degrees Fahrenheit). We first checked the clarity and luminosity of the cognac to test the condition and result of its filtering. Having done this, we evaluated its viscosity by tilting the glass and coating the side by a complete rotation, then putting the glass back in its vertical stance to observe the streaks, legs or tears of cognac as they fell back down. I learned that they should be thick and very straight. We proceeded to our first nosing, holding the glass about 4 centimetres (1½ inches) below the nose without swirling the contents. Here I identified the first cognac, a VSOP, and its aroma of wood vanilla.

The next step was the second nosing. After swirling the glass vigorously, more vanilla and some apricot aromas were released. We then did our *mise en bouche* (tasting), putting a few drops behind the teeth and allowing them to fall onto the tongue to achieve a sort of burning sensation. The idea behind these steps is that, with the mouth and nose prepared for the various aromas and flavours present, the tasting will be much easier on the tongue. The taster's senses will not be shocked by the vapours or heat of the cognac.

Being trained by our first tasting we proceeded to taste the Napoléon, which was smooth, full of warmth and body. We then tasted the XO Special, which had aromas of port, rose, walnut and ripe figs, being of an average age of twenty-two years. We followed with the Extra, a cognac full of chocolate, wood, dried apricot, grapefruit and caramelised pear aromas coming from its slender and stylishly simple bottle. We finished with the ultimate Louis XIII, the pride of Rémy Martin, presented in its unique hand-blown carafe, a replica of a royal flask found on the battlefields of Jarnac in 1569 and later acquired by Paul-Émile Rémy Martin. Louis XIII has become the new benchmark of cognac, being composed of only first *crus* of the Grande Champagne and a blend of over 8000 cognacs made over three generations of cellar masters. This beautiful amber cognac with the aroma of lychees, passionfruit, fig and old cigar box, made it a superb tasting.

Jason had organised a delectable lunch for us with the cellar masters of Rémy Martin in the family's private dining room. We sampled a *Feuilleté d'asperges et de morilles à la ciboulette* (fresh asparagus and wild morels under puff pastry with chives), a *Tournedos de boeuf, sauce bordelaise* (beef fillet with a red wine and bone marrow sauce), and a *Biscuit au caramel et abricot* (caramel and apricot sponge).

We then visited the old country residence of Dominique Hériard-Dubreuil, situated in the middle of the vineyard of the Grande Champagne. The subdued elegance of the summer house belonged to another era. Its beautiful hedges, fruit trees and manicured grounds had an ageless stillness.

Dominique, who had been called away on business, had instructed Jason to take me for a tasting in her astonishing personal cellars, so we made our way to the dark *chai*, the cognac ageing room. Old wine presses, stills and rustic equipment were there, gathering dust, but left in place out of respect for the skills of past workers, now long gone. All that lived on from the past was the slow-maturing cognac in its century-old barrels. The soft earthen floor, the blackened beams and ceiling, the old barrels covered with the webs of the protective spiders that deter destructive insects, all made this an incredible and unique experience.

The visit included one of my most memorable tastings: Jason siphoned for us glasses of Louis XIII directly from Dominique's private stock. Sublime.

From Cognac our next destination was Libourne, a region of Bordeaux, where we were fortunate enough to have an introduction to the Établissements Jean-Pierre Moueix, one of the most famous *négociants* (wine merchants) in the region. What set Établissements Jean-Pierre Moueix apart are the wine holdings they have under their care. Château Pétrus is the most expensive wine in the world and arguably one of the best.

The Établissements Jean-Pierre Moueix is situated on the Quai du Priourat at Libourne. It faces the Dordogne River and in appearance is more like a warehouse than a cellar. Beauty is not a prerequisite, however, as none of the wines are sold directly to the public. Instead they are distributed to companies representing the firm throughout the world, each of which receives a tiny allocation of Pétrus, as well as the chance to purchase other wines of the Libournais region that are either produced or distributed under the care of Établissements Jean-Pierre Moueix.

The Établissements Jean-Pierre Moueix has a long history as *négociants*. The business is a family one, built on a solid foundation first established by Jean-Pierre Moueix in 1937. In those years the wines of the right bank of the rivers Gironde and Dordogne never attracted much attention for their quality. They were seen as wines with little ageing potential. But Jean-Pierre Moueix was instrumental in changing connoisseurs' perceptions of the wines of the St Emilion, Pomerol, Fronsac and Libournais regions so that their reputations now rival some of the other Bordeaux of the left side of the rivers.

As *négociants* the company secured a proportion of many vineyards' production to sell on behalf of the landowners. Its most famous acquisition was to be granted the selling rights of Château Pétrus in 1945 from the owner, Madame Loubat. On her death in 1961, Jean-Pierre was able to purchase a half-share of the property, in partnership with Madame Loubat's niece, Madame Lacoste-Loubat. Today Château Pétrus is the biggest star in the constellation of vineyards that the family either owns, controls, manages or represents. Christian Moueix has run the firm since the retirement of his father.

I was taken by Nathalie, a representative of Établissements Jean-Pierre Moueix, to the vineyard of Pétrus. I instantly understood one of the reasons for the high prices of the Pétrus wines: the vineyard is tiny, covering only the top of a hill on the Pomerol plateau. Its soil is almost pure clay; dark, dense and with a strange blue tinge. The French call the top of the hill the *mamelon* (nipple), and its geographical position offers perfect drainage in a quite compact soil that can only absorb a certain amount of water. This helps in the concentration of the flavour in the grape.

The *encépagement* (type of vine planting) here is quite unique, as it is nearly 100 per cent Merlot. The vineyard itself only comprises 1.5 hectares (over half an acre) and the vines are exceptionally old, being on average over forty years of age and some of them having root stock over eighty years old. Madame Loubat refused to replant after the great frost of 1956, preferring to *recépage* (graft) instead, a process not attempted in the region before. Success was slow, but no one can fault the result.

At the time of my visit the vineyard was perfectly ploughed, but in winter, Nathalie explained, they plant a weed between the rows of vines to dry the soil. Once ploughed in, the weed will naturally fertilise the soil and provide extra nutrients for the vines. In winter a severe pruning is done and in summer a heavy crop-thinning is executed to reduce the grape bunches by between 30 and 50 per cent. This lowers the yield to a maximum of 45 hectolitres per hectare, or three tons per acre of grapes.

If an old vine finally gives up it will not be replaced immediately, ostensibly to allow the soil a well-deserved rest, though I suspect the real reason is to permit a certain mourning period.

Harvest is a time of frenetic activity. It lasts for only ten or twelve hours, and is mostly carried out in the afternoons by a team of 180 people, led by the aristocratic Christian Moueix, a farmer for the day. The pickers await his command before the harvest can commence. He judges when sufficient dew has evaporated and when the berries are warm enough to have elevated the alcohol level in the grapes.

The grapes are crushed and fermented in concrete tanks, monitored by computerised thermo-regulation. The maceration of skin, with a small proportion of stem of up to 30 per cent, lasts eighteen to twenty-five days. After the blending the wine is transferred to new oak barrels.

In Pomerol few buildings are of grand construction, and Pétrus was no exception. The building was of a thoroughly practical design, but the tasting salon, by contrast, was furnished exquisitely. Nathalie was proud to show me the *chai* (ageing room), but first had to contend with an impressive digital alarm system. Luckily she succeeded in entering the correct digits. Here I was, in the quiet confines of the barrel ageing room, with the total Pétrus production of 1996 of only 400 barrels. So many of my friends would have envied my position at that moment. More envious still would they have been of the barrel tasting to come.

Nathalie carefully filled my glass directly from the barrel and, standing back, waited for my assessment and appreciation. The wine was silky and incredibly concentrated in fruit due to the heavy pruning and lowering of the yield it had received. It had power without the expected heavy tannin, the wine being so full of flavour and fruit that it overpowered the small amount of oak imparted by that time; it left me with a profound appreciation of the early complexity of one of the greatest wines in the world.

FOOD OF THE GODS

We left Bordeaux to head south to some of the most fascinating regions of France: Périgord and Quercy. While these regions are famous for *foie gras*, goat cheese, wine and walnut oil, I decided to learn what I could about two very special products that are closely identified with this part of France: wild mushrooms and the incomparable truffle.

My first encounter in Australia with an edible wild mushroom was at the Sydney Wholesale Market, many years ago. While browsing in the rows of the growers' market, I came across an older man crouched against a wall away from the busy section. Always on the lookout for a new find, I spied two boxes of mushrooms at his feet. The mushrooms, to my excitement, were wild. The man, a Greek-Cypriot, had collected the mushrooms on a weekend picnic in the Blue Mountains near Sydney. To earn some extra cash he had brought them to the market. Although he assured me they were edible, I was still slightly suspicious.

When I arrived back in the kitchen, most of my chefs were quite unwilling to try the mushrooms. Clearly I had to be the tester. I cooked them simply and ate them with a mixture of enjoyment and apprehension. Finding myself still in good health, I immediately created a dish with pigeon. I organised for this to be printed on the evening menu.

The next day, to be doubly sure, I sent the mushrooms to a local university's research section, which confirmed that they were edible. The mushrooms came to be known by us as Blue Mountains mushrooms, or orange fly cap, but the correct name is lactaire or saffron milkcap. It took only one speech from me at the local cooking school for young students to start collecting mushrooms. Over the next few weeks I was deluged with students showing up at the hotel with car boots full of mushrooms, which I felt I had no choice but to purchase and distribute around town to my overjoyed colleagues. With time, cèpe and morel mushrooms were found and collected for the many enthusiastic chefs of Australia.

One of my purveyors was quite keen to import mushrooms from France. Having once met a mushroom seller by the name of Jean-Claude Monteil in Sydney, and knowing him to be one of the best-regarded suppliers of these delicacies in France, I passed on the name of his firm. When Yvette and I were planning our trip to France, I suggested we take a first-hand look at Jean-Claude's mushroom-sorting operation. Yvette readily agreed.

We arrived late in the afternoon after a long drive and met Jean-Claude at his factory. He had just arrived from Portugal, where he had been organising the pickers for the coming season. He drove us to our hotel for the night, apologising in advance for its shabbiness. After our long drive, all we wished for was something modest and clean. However, beautifully manicured lawns and perfectly groomed trees suddenly announced the building at the centre of the park: an incredible château with turrets and gardens. It was a dream hideaway.

For over three generations the Monteil family has specialised in the provision of wild mushrooms. When the company was formed in 1920, Antoine Monteil restricted himself to the collection and sales of cèpes, a most exceptional mushroom growing in the heart of the woody country around Brive in the Corrèze region, where the Monteil family has its roots. Antoine's son, Jean, expanded the range to include chanterelle, morel, trumpet and wood hedgehog when he took over the firm in 1950.

These days the Monteil family prides itself on being able to deliver its mushrooms to any place in the world within forty-eight hours of picking. Freshness is the main concern, as it means full flavour. Over thirty wild mushroom types are now collected and sold by Jean's sons, Jean-Claude and Michel.

Wild mushrooms, by simple definition, cannot be cultivated. Thus they have to be harvested by an army of pickers who swell to up 6000 during the peak of the season. At Monteil the forty-five employees who specialise in the identification of the edible mushrooms can be increased to 200 during the critical October and November months, the height of the season.

Hunting and picking methods have not changed in more than seventy years. The pickers still go armed with nothing more than a wooden basket fashioned from chestnut, a hazelwood stick, a pocket knife, a pair of warm, durable boots and, most important of all, a well-developed sense of orientation to remember exactly where the good spots are. Good spots are kept secret and their locations are handed down to the present picker's children or grandchildren. Not only are the locations handed down, but also the techniques of detection and preservation.

The pickers stroll through the woods, gently pushing and lifting ground debris until they find what they are looking for. Once located, they will almost certainly approach the site with caution, carefully brushing aside leaves, hoping that underneath hides a cèpe or chanterelle. When a single mushroom is at the feet of the picker, he will pluck it clean from the ground, tearing the mushroom from its base rather than using his knife, which could create rot in the base left behind and prevent the regrowth. He will then cradle the mushroom in one hand, scrape it delicately to remove any soil, and place it carefully into the basket, taking care not to let the mushrooms bruise each other.

After a day's gathering, the pickers meet at specified collection points. It is at these places that Monteil employees will carry out a first-level quality control and decide whether the product will be processed or sold fresh. Every night the mushrooms are collected in each area by small Monteil vehicles, to be transported to Brive and to the Monteil company based in the heart of the Corrèze region.

When Yvette and I visited the Monteil warehouse, mushrooms were arriving there from all over Europe: from Spain, Germany, Turkey. The selectors were busy grading, cleaning and packing them to be redirected to restaurants like Alain Ducasse's in Paris, where a few weeks earlier I had sampled the Monteil morels. Crates upon crates of mushrooms were piled high, with dozens of teams of workers ensuring the correct selection and sorting of the masses of mushrooms.

I saw orders being prepared for Hong Kong, Singapore, New York and Sydney. Peering into one crate I saw boxes of girolle or chanterelle, plus small *mousseron* boxes of wild asparagus (not from the asparagus family at all, but in fact wild herbs). Jean-Claude told me that this box was for Barry, my supplier back in Sydney. It was funny to think that those mushrooms might soon be landing back at my workplace in Sydney, to be cooked by my chefs. I contemplated leaving a message in the box.

Jean-Claude invited us to share a simple meal with him at a nearby restaurant. Naturally, we chose dishes in which wild mushrooms featured prominently. I needed no reminding of what a wonderful ingredient the wild mushroom is. The flavours of the cèpe and morel mushrooms I tasted were so sweet, earthy and buttery that I was almost tempted to agree with the ancient Egyptians, who thought that wild mushrooms were fit only for the gods.

Here is one of my favourite recipes for wild mushrooms— troffiette pasta filled with mushrooms that have been delicately flavoured with veal jus.

Wild Mushroom and Veal Troffiette Pasta

For the filling:

1 veal shank, boiled (see page 258—use half quantity)

60 ml (2 fl oz) olive oil

2 shallots, sliced

100 g (3½ oz) Roman brown mushrooms, finely cut into small strips

100 g (3½ oz) wild mushrooms (cèpes, chanterelle or field), finely cut into small strips

1 clove garlic, chopped

50 g (2 oz) butter

4 leaves sage, julienne

40 ml (1 fl oz) Veal Jus (see page 256–7)

Clean and shred the veal shank, keeping the pure meat.

Heat the olive oil and cook the shallots over high heat, add mushrooms and cook with the garlic until all the moisture from the mushrooms is nearly evaporated. Add butter and sage. Season and remove from the heat. Add veal jus to flavour the mushrooms. Finally, add shredded veal and combine thoroughly. Put aside in a cold place.

For the pasta:

> 1 quantity of plain pasta (see page 259)
>
> 1 egg, beaten with a splash of water, for egg wash
>
> a little semolina flour
>
> 60 ml (2 fl oz) olive oil
>
> 200 ml (7 fl oz) Veal Jus (see page 256–7)

Roll pasta into a long sheet, then cut into 10 cm x 8 cm rectangular pieces. Place a small amount of filling in the centre of each piece. Brush one side with egg wash and roll over to close the pasta. Twist each end and form into the shape of a small lolly. Arrange on a tray dusted with semolina flour. Cover with a cloth and refrigerate for 2 hours. You should have between 5 and 7 troffiettes per person.

To assemble:

When ready to serve, heat olive oil and panfry the troffiettes. When well coloured, add half the veal jus to glaze.

Serve on a warm plate with remaining jus and accompany with a rocket salad.

(Serves 4 as a main)

Returning to Jean-Claude's office at the conclusion of our meal, we gained a sense of the complexity of his operation. Airline schedules, delivery times and operating hours—the essential tools to ensure that the pickers' harvest makes its way to customers worldwide—were pinned up on the walls. The Monteil family and their team of workers guarantee satisfaction to their customers the world over.

Yvette and I certainly had nothing to complain about at the end of our visit.

Caviar has a decadent attraction, *foie gras* is exceptional, but there is probably no other food in the world with the mystique of the black truffle of Périgord. In its fresh form it has an entirely unexpected aroma which alone merits its special place in the pantheon of gastronomy.

Like most non-French people, I was always very sceptical of the value of truffles. My first contact with a real truffle was at my cooking school, where the only thing the whole class could talk about was the price of the tin itself. We forgot to consider the contents. When the time came to taste it, the aroma was non-existent and its taste so unimpressive that I concluded, like many of my schoolmates, that the whole truffle story was just a big con by the French peasants.

My very first contact with a whole truffle was on my first trip to France where, at Le Moulin de Mougins in the south of France, Roger Vergé organised a *menu dégustation* for me which included his famous zucchini flower stuffed with a whole truffle. The dish did not move me. It was almost cold and the sauce was thick and unrefined.

Considering that the French truffle season is in winter, and that I had never visited France at that cold time of the year, I had never sampled a fresh Périgord truffle. The first truffle feast I ever tasted was at Simon Johnson's eclectic food shop in Sydney. He had brought the first shipment to Australia of Pébeyre truffles. Neil Perry cooked them in Simon's shop for a gathering of gourmands. His dish of steamed corn-fed chicken with truffle under the skin was a triumph. It impressed me as much as it did the assembled chefs and food writers. My opinion of the truffle was changed forever.

I first met Jacques Pébeyre in Sydney where he came to share his knowledge and wisdom about truffles. Jacques's grandfather, Pierre Pébeyre, started the family business in La Chapelle Mareuil on the Dordogne River in Périgord. In 1897 he became a distributor of food products. At first he distributed fresh fruit and vegetables, asparagus, walnuts, cherries, cèpes, stone fruit, *foie gras* and truffles. Over the years, the fruit and vegetables were eliminated from the trading due to their poor return. Pierre's son, Alain, whom he struggled to send to Switzerland to study, took over the firm in 1922 and eventually rationalised its line of products to only *foie gras* and truffles after moving the enterprise to Cahors for its better distribution network. By 1925 the only product sold by the enterprise was the truffle. In Alain's mind, it was better to trade in one strong product than in ten weak ones. Alain's education provided him with the means of improving the company's profitability by improving work methods. He had the foresight to purchase an automatic truffle-brushing machine, which helped reduce his man-, or, more accurately, his woman-power.

Despite two world wars and a decline in the consumption of truffles throughout Europe, Alain oversaw a golden era of truffle production. He was succeeded by Jacques, who nowadays crisscrosses France to visit his traders and the chefs who purchase his truffles. Today, Pierre-Jean, Jacques's son, runs the enterprise and works extremely efficiently at maintaining the quality of his products in a very different market. The few days Yvette and I spent with Pierre-Jean in Cahors were enlightening.

We met Pierre-Jean and drove with him to a secret location to the south of Cahors. Not being French residents, we were spared the indignity of being blindfolded for part of the drive. (In France, as in Italy, the truffle fields are jealously guarded.) Arriving at Pierre-Jean's location, we were greeted by Pierre Sourzat and his two Labradors, Darius and Indy. As it was summer we would be hunting for the little brother of the aristocratic *Tuber Melanosporum*, the *Tuber Aestivum*, or summer truffle. The chosen field was well looked after, with branches well trimmed, since truffles will not grow past the shadow of the tree foliage.

Pierre set Darius and Indy on their search with great shouts of 'Allez, allez! Cherchez, cherchez!'.

A definite sense of excitement permeated the whole group, all except for Darius and Indy, who were more interested in running around scratching the ground and piddling than looking for smelly subterranean fungi. Upon the presentation of a piece of chicken, however, they obviously decided that it was a fair trade and began their task with gusto.

Indy, being only four years old—half the age of Darius—was the less experienced dog. Pierre wanted to give him the chance to hunt on his own so Darius was kept on the leash for a while. We were rewarded with the first find by Indy: a small, black summer truffle. In the presence of the more experienced Darius, however, Indy soon lost his confidence. A change of role saw Darius find several more truffles, which deepened Indy's depression. Pierre-Jean thought that Pierre should become a dog psychologist instead of a truffle hunter, such was his vivid description of the feelings of each dog throughout the hunt.

Eventually Darius was replaced by Mioux, a mongrel but a true hunter, and we quickly saw the efficiency of a professional truffle hunter. Dogs are preferred to pigs, given the latter's tendency to eat all the best samples. In winter you can often see the truffle hunters driving around in small cars loaded with dogs, but on occasion you can still catch sight of the odd French peasant with his favourite sow.

Unhealthy-looking trees were singled out for extra attention in the search, as were areas of scorched earth surrounding a tree, as these were possible indications of where a truffle might be located. Truffles, which are really a type of fungi, form symbiotic associations with trees, feeding themselves via mycorrhiza and producing fruit (truffles) after a period of ten or more years. The symbiosis between the truffle and the tree often works to the detriment of the tree's health, as the mycelium (the mass of branching filaments making up the body of the fungi) is a voracious vandal, drawing away the organic substances and nutrients synthesised by the tree and giving back very little apart from some mineral salts on the death of the truffle, and only then if it is not scooped out of the ground beforehand by a hungry wild boar or a keen truffle hunter.

Pierre-Jean informed us that at the beginning of this century over 1000 tonnes (985 tons) of truffles were collected annually, in contrast to today's 30 tonnes (29.5 tons), with only 2 tonnes (1.97 tons) coming from the traditional region of Périgord. He attributed this decline to several factors, principal amongst them the move over the last fifty years of the rural population to the villages. With the urban shift came a loss of knowledge about the upkeep of the *truffières* and how to forage for them, and a general apathy concerning the products of the land. Traditionally, truffles were collected by the grazers of sheep and goats. They knew the good areas for truffles and had the expertise to encourage the fungi's growth. Another reason for today's decline in production, Pierre-Jean suggested, is that many of the oak trees on which truffles depend have come to the end of their productive life for truffle growing, which starts at fifteen years of age and lasts for up to thirty years. New trees to replace the old have not been planted.

Truffles do in fact grow in other parts of Europe, and even in China, America and most recently New Zealand and Australia. Italy produces a great amount of so-called 'Périgord truffles' from the Umbria and Marche regions, exporting them to France and other countries. The same applies to Spain, which is in fact the biggest constant producer of 'Périgord truffles'. Considering the jealousy and secrecy surrounding the search for truffles and the tribalism of the people selling them, it is not surprising to find that the French will not acknowledge the quality of truffles from outside of the traditional regions of production in France, or that the Spanish will only acknowledge and recognise their own truffles and those of nobody else, and that the Italians treat the French and Spanish truffles with contempt.

With a respectable number of truffles lining the bottom of Pierre-Jean's tin pail, we left the hunting grounds and headed back to Cahors to observe the processing operation at the Pébeyre family's factory.

The truffles that the Pébeyres handle are purchased from the local markets of the region, which number about ten. In a good year, between 20 and 25 kilograms (44 and 55 pounds) of truffles are collected by every hunter and taken to these markets. Brokers examine the truffles, offers are made and deals sealed. At the end of the trading the truffles are weighed and delivered to the merchants of the regions.

Once delivered to the Pébeyres in Cahors, the truffles are immediately sorted and washed. Jacques and Pierre-Jean are always there for the sorting, looking for the best truffles to be sold fresh. Each chef in France who buys from the Pébeyres will have a specific demand as to size, shape and weight, and it is essential to provide the likes of Ducasse, Haeberlin and Passat with their exact requirements—a standard that the Pébeyres are proud to maintain, even in the face of a small harvest. While we were there, fresh truffles were being put in the small chestnut baskets that are the signature of the firm. They would be delivered, Pierre-Jean assured us, to Paris on the very same day.

Those truffles that are not sold fresh by the Pébeyres are canned. Attempts at preserving the truffle go back to Apicius, a gourmet of the first century AD, who recommended the layering of the truffles with sawdust in an earthenware jar and keeping it in a cool place. This method would certainly not have preserved the truffles for a long period, but it might have helped somewhat to extend their fresh life. At the end of last century, when truffle production was at its peak, the fungi were kept in brine, oil or fat in barrels of up to 500 kilograms (1100 pounds). This method of preservation was fairly rudimentary and meant that the distribution of the truffles was limited.

In the factory we saw experienced workers preparing to transfer truffles from the large sterilisation containers to the smaller retail versions. A second sterilisation was then necessary. This, we learned, was usually done at the end of the busy winter season. These tins of truffles would then find their way onto the shelves of fine food stores around the world.

Pierre-Jean had invited us to his home for dinner with his wife, Elizabeth. I was right in presuming that truffles would be present in at least one of the dishes. Elizabeth was going to prepare her specialty: *Asperge au beurre de truffe* (asparagus in truffle sauce). If you did not come from France and were not part of a truffle house, this dish would be considered extremely decadent, but in one of the great truffle regions of France, with one of the grandest truffle families in the world, what could be better suited to a dinner?

We watched Elizabeth as she prepared the meal. The secret of her recipe was in the truffle sauce. A whole tin of *brisures* (chopped truffle peel) was combined with a full pound of fresh butter. Elizabeth proceeded to heat the now puréed *brisures*, adding more and more butter to the truffle base to produce a rich, glossy black sauce that she smothered over the asparagus at the table. Yvette could not believe the amount of butter used in the sauce. Being a chef I knew better, having provided rich butter sauces in the past to unsuspecting customers. They always found the sauces delicious.

There are foods that go perfectly with truffles. These include eggs, potatoes, asparagus and pasta. Elizabeth served us a simple dish of golden egg noodles doused in the remaining sauce. If we did not think we had sampled enough truffle on the first course we certainly thought otherwise after the pasta. We decided, on our return to our hotel, that we had literally died and gone to heaven.

Anyone who has the chance to come into contact with a fresh Périgord truffle in its prime is fortunate indeed. We learned so much over those few days but, in particular, I learned to respect the best product of the region, *la truffe noire du Périgord*. Its radical and mystical look, its exotic scent and its ability to enhance so many dishes makes the black Périgord truffle the ultimate product for any chef and gourmet.

GLAMOUR ON THE MEDITERRANEAN

*O*ur entrance to Monaco was not gracious; I missed the exit we wanted, probably due to driving at a speed only tolerated on European autoroutes, and nearly had to go to the Italian border before I could turn around. I was certainly more conservative, and successful, on my second attempt. In the future, I told myself, I would take the drive along the coastal Moyenne Corniche, which is judged to be one of the most scenic drives in the world.

The steep drive down to Monte Carlo, which is the part of the city where the famous casino stands, was stunning. The number of apartments built in precarious positions could not fail to impress, but I am afraid of heights, and as I reflected upon the fact that our place of residence for the next three days was in one of the tallest buildings in the principality, I began to feel nervous.

The principality of Monaco was purchased in 1297 by the House of Grimaldi, a rich family from Genoa. Following the French revolution it was annexed to France and then became a protectorate of the Kingdom of Sardinia in 1815. After this tumultuous period it was returned to the Grimaldi family under the guardianship of France in 1861. Monaco is now an oasis of high living. The reign of the Grimaldi family has created an affluence for the residents unrivalled in the world, and this tax haven has become a retreat for the old wealth of yesterday and the entrepreneurs of today.

We were to stay with an old friend, Max, who used to live in Sydney. Keys were left with the concierge of Max's apartment building, our pied-à-terre for the next few days. On seeing his view through the floor-to-ceiling windows I realised it was the nightmare I had feared: the drop was sheer, and the towering apartment building seemed to cling precariously to the steep cliff. Monaco, to my mind, was the Hong Kong of Europe.

I was to meet Max in one of the most famous spots in the world: on the terrace of the Café de Paris, next to the Monte Carlo Grand Casino and opposite the magnificent Hôtel de Paris, housing Le Louis XV, Alain Ducasse's ritzy and super-sophisticated Monaco restaurant. The Hôtel de Paris register of the nineteenth and twentieth centuries is a roll call of leaders of the world: General Grant, King Gustav V of Sweden, the Grand Dukes of Russia, the Duke and Duchess of Windsor, Winston Churchill, Guiseppe Verdi, Jules Verne, Alexander Dumas and other luminaries.

Max made his way on foot from his office. In the glorious afternoon sun we had a drink on the famous terrace and took the time to admire the Ferraris, Porsches and Rolls Royces that passed us by on the place de Casino, each more polished and immaculate than the one before. Around us people were having expensive drinks or luscious ice-creams from the kitchen of the famous café. We admired the beautiful people of Monaco, or what we presumed to be the people of Monaco, as only a fifth of its 30 000 inhabitants are true Monégasque with the privileges of citizenship.

Monaco can be fairly sleepy at night-time, and this has never really helped the restaurant trade. Even if the restaurants are full for lunch, few people venture outside in the evening except during the tourist season. Max took us to his regular haunt, a French restaurant with a name that reminded me of the past grandeur of Monaco: La Maison du Caviar. Owned by the Dacosta family, the restaurant used to showcase the caviar it imported. These days, caviar is more likely to be eaten in the privacy of the luxury yachts anchored in Monaco Harbour, owned by a vast array of high-flying entrepreneurs.

We started with a simple deep-fried zucchini flower—my first hint of Mediterranean-style cooking since leaving the very rustic food of Périgord. For good measure, and as an encouragement, we shared a portion of Oscietra caviar on a superb *blini* with *crème fraîche*. Max then selected a *Salade gourmande*, consisting of green beans and *foie gras*. I chose a *Salade d'artichaud au parmesan*, an artichoke and parmesan salad drizzled with virgin olive oil and fresh lemon juice.

I then selected the *Confit de canard* and Max chose the *Poulet curry*, a classic dish that owes its origins to the British occupation of India. I was able, for a relatively good price, to enjoy a 1994 Antonin Rodet Meursault and a surprisingly affordable 1991 Vosne-Romanée by the same winemaker.

During the meal I met Jean-Pierre Dacosta, the young and talented chef, and we were served by his shy mother, Monique. Jean-Pierre's father, of Chinese and Portuguese heritage, makes the marriage an unusual blend. Even though Jean-Pierre was born in Monaco, he is not considered a citizen. Only about thirty naturalisations are granted by the Prince in any given year. Jean-Pierre, knowing I came from Quebec, introduced me to one of his more regular clients, Jacques Villeneuve, the famous French–Canadian Formula One car driver.

Yvette and I spent the next few days in Monaco, driving around the magnificent coast, viewing the surrounding villages, learning the quickest route to Cannes and the food markets of Nice, and walking on La Croisette and on La Promenade des Anglais. I made a return visit to Juan-les-Pins, where I lodged on my first stay on the Côte d'Azur, and Antibes that houses the Musée Picasso, a former residence of the Grimaldi family.

Everything we saw and tasted confirmed just how from northern France we were, and how much season, history and lifestyle could affect a cuisine. We had loved France and the rich food it produced, but now that we were in Monaco we were revelling in the lighter and sunnier cuisine of the Mediterranean.

Just one more evening remained to us in this tiny sovereign state. Tomorrow we would be in Italy, immersed in a new language, a new culture and experiencing a new approach to food. But before then we would enjoy a meal in one of Europe's most exceptional restaurants, sampling dishes that had their roots in both France and the Mediterranean. A meal from the kitchen of Alain Ducasse was to be the perfect *adieu* to France and *buongiorno* to Italy.

Alain Ducasse arrived in 1987 at the prestigious Hôtel de Paris in Monaco, having been lured there by the board of the Société des Bains de Mer, the managing arm of Prince Rainier's holdings in Monte Carlo, from the Michelin two-star restaurant La Terrase in Hôtel Juana in Juan-les-Pins. Alain's experience in working in a hotel environment and his steadily growing reputation for creating superb food made him an ideal candidate to refresh the food operation at the Hôtel de Paris. Alain was thus offered the running of all the restaurants of this prestigious establishment, with a newly renovated kitchen equipped to the best possible standards. The Hôtel de Paris employs more than ninety cooks, who staff the restaurants, provide sophisticated room service and cater for functions of up to 400 people in one of the most gorgeous ballrooms of Europe.

Yvette and I decided to have a drink with Max at the American Bar of the Hôtel de Paris before being met by Lucas, Alain's assistant. We were escorted by the formal *garçon* to plush seats with silver ornaments littering the table. When we noticed the clientele present, we soon realised that we were in a rarefied world. It would not have been surprising to see Pierce Brosnan stroll in to have a martini as he did in his role as James Bond in one of the famous series of films, which was filmed next door at the Monte Carlo Grand Casino.

Alain Ducasse had organised for us to eat in a small alcove directly facing the kitchen. To eat here was an enormous privilege. As in the tradition of the past, *La table du chef* is reserved for the chef's friends and the food press, or is the site for regular menu tastings assisted by the chef's key staff. On the night of our visit it was to be the base for my foray into the cuisine of the south, as interpreted by the great Alain Ducasse.

Entering Le Louis XV in the hour preceding its opening, we were afforded a glimpse of the attention given to setting the room. Silver was polished to a high sheen by white-gloved waiters, Swiss-woven tablecloths were ironed onto the table to remove any possible creases, silver gilt underplates were positioned precisely on table mats by the waiters, captains and *chefs de rang* (head waiters), while the *premiers sommeliers* and the *maître d'hôtel* surveyed the room with eagle eyes to ensure that all was in impeccable order.

The standards of Le Louis XV are such that if you leave the table at any point, all of your drinking glasses will be replaced, as well as your napkin. Customised ashtrays match the style and patterns of the china, so when you move from your main course to dessert you will see the ashtray replaced to accord with the new crockery. A baby ottoman is positioned beside each female guest, providing a place for her handbag.

Lucas introduced us to *le directeur du restaurant* and took us through the large mechanical doors to the lower basement where the grand kitchens are situated. I was introduced to Franck Cerruti, Alain's *chef de cuisine* for Le Louis XV. Franck had a warmth that made me feel immediately at ease in this challenging environment. He took the time to show me through the kitchen, which was much bigger than I could have imagined. Alain Ducasse is now only concentrating on Le Louis XV, having left the running of the food operation of the rest of the Hôtel de Paris to a capable team.

The kitchen of the restaurant was linked to another kitchen that catered for functions. There were large preparation areas for fish, meat, pastry and baking. The washing area was stacked high with gleaming copper pots carrying Le Louis XV insignia. The store where the cutlery is kept was amazing: there were rows of silver dishes that could hold sugar, boiled eggs, coffee or caviar, decorative silver platters, rows of plates and glasses, even spoons made of horn for the caviar service. I felt I had gone back a hundred years into the past to the era of Auguste Escoffier, one of the greatest hotel chefs the world has ever seen.

We returned to *La table du chef* (aptly named 'the fish bowl' by the *garçons*) for our first course. We were offered a glass of champagne and some Wattwiller mineral water from the Vosges mountains in Alsace. Franck came and sat with us in the lull just before the start of the service to exchange histories. It turned out that he had been the *chef de cuisine* for Annie Feolde at the Enoteca Pincchiori in Florence a few years earlier. She is a great friend of mine and I told Franck we would be visiting her in the next few weeks. He was delighted.

I could see the *garçons* pacing outside our private recess, waiting for the service to start. In the meantime we were served a stunning little *canapé*, a *Barquette d'anchois frite à la fondue de tomate aux olives confites et au basilique* (a long pastry shell of fried boned anchovies with a tomato fondue with pitted olives and fried basil), so small, so elegant and so delicious. This was followed by the most stunning bread basket one could ever see. I pride myself on my bread basket, but this surpassed the realm of competency; this was pure artistry. Franck explained that two bakers work full-time to produce this range. There were crispy *grissini*, superb mini *baguettes*, *feuillantines* that opened up like fans, *Fougasse au lard de campagne* (olive oil bread) and the incredible five-cereal bread which forms a central part of the bread trolleys in the dining room.

The first order arrived from the dining room. Franck was off to his position, and I moved to the back of the kitchen, ready to observe. Franck called the first order loudly: '*Une primeur, deux langoustines, un foie gras, à la suite, un turbot, un saint-pierre, un pigeon et un confit.*' Everyone in the kitchen acknowledged him: '*Oui chef!*' The coordination between sections was to be essential over the next hour or two. Tension was high.

I saw the *potager* section where the soups, *veloutés* and *consommés* were simmering gently. The *rôtisserie* at the back of the kitchen was amazing; there was tuna steak cooking on a wood charcoal grill, and a small *gigot d'agneau* (leg of lamb) was being roasted on an open vertical spit. Pigeon was being seared on hot coals and a truffled *poulette jaune des Landes* (a corn-fed Landes young chicken) was roasting gently on a rotating spit. It was an amazing feast of cooking that reflected and respected the methods of the past.

Behind the *rôtisserie*, through an open door, I visited the *garde-manger* (pantry), where all the merchandise arrives. Here all the foodstuffs are cleaned and stored, ready to be used for functions or restaurant *mise-en-place*. *Buffets* and *canapés* are prepared in this cool area, and the cleaning of fish is carried out too. A huge tank filled with seawater was full of Brittany lobsters, dark and lively, whose fate would depend on the whims of the guests.

From the back I could see the fish section, the section of the *chef poissonier*. An amazing modern fish *rôtisserie* was situated here, and *tronçons* (fillets) of turbot or John Dory could be cooked very slowly under the gentle electric heat of an infra-red reflector.

Towards the front was the *entremetier* section, responsible for all the vegetable *garnitures* and pasta. As in every section, it was lead by a *chef de partie* followed by a *demi chef*, first assistant, second assistant and several apprentices and trainees from all over the world. It was an intensive section, requiring a great deal of cutting and peeling for the *mise-en-place*, and a great number of pots and pans to cook and heat up the garnishes. All vegetables, ravioli, spaghettini, gnocchi and risotto were prepared on the command of Franck.

Fronting the line was the *saucier* section. Here, in any large restaurant, is where the more experienced cooks position themselves, and where others aspire to be. It is technically a very demanding section where the sophistication of the chef's cuisine will become apparent. The most refined of Monsieur Ducasse's dishes came from here, prepared at the hands of the intense young chefs. The base of each sauce had been prepared earlier in the day so that it would be in a perfect state just before the service began. I was shown some of the recipes; they ran to several pages for a single sauce, with several processes in the making—a true sign of the precise dedication of Alain and his team.

I made a full circle of the kitchen, arriving back in front of the service pass which backed on to the cellar, where there were over 250 000 bottles of 621 wines, thirty-seven *grands et rares millésimes* (rare and old vintages), and eighteen *belles et rarissimes bouteilles* (very beautiful and extremely rare bottles).

After experiencing the delights of the kitchen, I agreed to select a bottle of wine. I insisted on something humble and requested a local wine: a Château de Bellet 'Cuvée du Baron' 1990, from the commune of Nice. I always think it is a good idea to ask for a wine from the surrounding region; in most cases they are unknown, of quite good quality and do not cost a fortune.

Our first course was served: *Légumes des jardins de Provence, mijotés à la truffe noire râpée, un filet d'huile d'olive de Ligurie, aceto balsamico et gros sel gris.* A mouthful to say, but an even better mouthful to taste. The specially selected tiny vegetables comprised radish, beans, carrot, baby fennel, miniature leek, squash, broad beans, turnip, artichoke, baby zucchini, Swiss chard, zucchini with flowers, diced and sliced truffle, all slowly braised in Provence olive oil, finished with aged balsamic vinegar and the beautiful grey salt of the French marshes. A memory to savour for a lifetime.

After a small rest, and having observed the pace of the service, I returned for my next course: *Poitrine de pigeonneau des Alpes de Haute-Provence, foie gras de canard et pommes de terre de montagne sur la braise, jus goûteux aux abats et aux herbes.* This was a magnificent dish of roast breast of squab from the high Provence Alps, with slices of potato cooked on hot coals, topped with melting duck *foie gras* and a sauce of giblets and liver. The attention to detail in the cooking of each ingredient of this dish was exquisite.

After more observation of the service from the pass, I returned for a cheese course: a fresh goat cheese topped with raw broad beans, doused with virgin olive oil and balsamic vinegar and a touch of freshly cracked pepper. A very simple and effective cheese course—light, full of tang and the crispy texture that represents the Mediterranean side of Monsieur Ducasse's cuisine.

To avert any more food being served, I visited the now very active *pâtisserie*. Frédérick, the pastry chef, leads an incredible team of talented young pastry chefs. His desserts are a study in refinement of high French technique. He insisted we sample one of his new desserts. We returned to the fish bowl with Franck and tasted a *Fraises des bois dans leur jus tiède, sorbet au mascarpone* (an infusion of wild strawberries with vanilla, served warm with a sorbet of mascarpone). This was quickly followed by a beautiful Limoges porcelain box containing freshly baked *madeleines*, macaroons and four types of superb chocolate.

Yvette ordered a tea from Mariage Frères, which could have been an excuse for the *garçons* to serve a second set of *mignardises* (delicacies) on a silver stand, comprising *mini tuiles, fourées au chocolat au baies, tartlettes au pamplemousse, mini barquette au amande et au pêche* and another *petit four*. I felt lucky that I was not sitting in the dining room, as I certainly would have been tempted by the ice-cream and sorbet trolley or the colourful *liqueurs digestives*.

Every decade or so a particular restaurant makes its mark on the culinary world. It is a restaurant that sets new standards of quality, service and innovation, one that will have a lasting influence, and one that will set all the gourmands and chefs of rival establishments buzzing as they contemplate a new level of gastronomic standards. Le Louis XV is such a restaurant. With Le Louis XV having now achieved the crowning glory of its third Michelin star, Alain Ducasse can claim the distinction of being the first chef ever to run two three-star establishments at the same time, a feat never achieved by anyone. It is a true reflection of his talent.

A PLACE IN THE SUN

Early in the morning we left Monaco to drive to the Ligurian seaside resort of Portofino on the Italian Riviera. The journey took us through one of the most prolific vegetable-growing regions of northern Italy, where, because there is little fertile land, crops are grown in glasshouses perched high on the steep coastal cliffs. We saw thousands and thousands of the glasshouses, some of them bursting with colour. There were plump tomatoes, eggplants, zucchini, cucumbers, basil, salad leaves and a huge range of other products for the markets of northern Italy and the adjacent countries. Here was also where they grew the carnations which figured so poignantly in the French movie *Jean de Florette*.

The drive along the *autostrada*, which links all the coastal villages of northern Italy to the border of France, was fast and picturesque. The wide highway, carved directly through the granite mountains and spanning deep ravines, passed through numerous tunnels, dangerous for their sudden darkness.

We wove our way through Rapallo, a busy and prosperous seaside town, and then along a perilously narrow and windy road carved into the rocky hillsides of the Portofino peninsula. It was breathtakingly pretty. The road eventually led to the small village of Portofino.

I had made a reservation at the Hotel Splendido, which we found perched high on the hill facing the harbour of Portofino.

Our history books told us that back in the sixteenth century this old monastery was attacked so frequently by Saracen pirates that it was eventually abandoned. Baron Baratta refurbished the ruins some 300 years later, however, and the summer house was converted into one of the best hotels in Italy.

The Splendido was indeed a majestic hotel, but we immediately recognised that its grandeur was tempered by a pleasing Riviera informality. Our room was small but stylishly appointed. We had a romantic balcony, tiled in ocean green and covered with an ancient wisteria that provided a natural canopy. The view over the clifftops to Castle Brown, the structure rebuilt from a medieval fort by the British consul Timothy Yeats Brown in the 1840s, was dazzling, and from our vantage point we could monitor the entry into the harbour of flotillas of luxury vessels. A bottle of French champagne was awaiting us on the balcony, along with some tiny Ligurian olives. We savoured the champagne, took in the view and celebrated our arrival in Italy.

A magnificent Riviera sunset announced that it was time for a late Italian dinner. In the foyer I spotted Fausto Allegri, the concierge, and father of my friend Luca from Alain Ducasse's restaurant in Paris. Fausto was darting around the lobby instructing porters in sharp Italian. He looked the picture of confidence: tall, tanned and stylish in red-framed bifocals. I introduced myself to him and mentioned my friendship with his son. Content with news of Luca he spoke to me in French (as opposed to Italian, which I speak poorly, or English, which he also spoke) and gave me the advantage of his vast experience of this part of Italy.

Yvette and I took a romantic stroll down through the Splendido gardens and along its private path to the village. It soon became apparent that Portofino at night is a playground for grown-ups. Bars lined the harbour, bustling trattorias and restaurants spread their tables on the stone piazza, and majestic yachts, crews at the ready, awaited their evening guests. Life in the fast lane was ready to enjoy the unique charms of this gracious old fishing village.

Fausto had directed us away from the more touristy restaurants overlooking the harbour and recommended a trattoria in which the locals ate and where the food was both good and inexpensive. The unpretentious Trattoria la Concordia faced the local garage, yet we were not going to let the view deter us from eating there. Despite it being nine o'clock at night, the place was quiet; apparently its patrons had not yet ventured out of their homes and up the cobblestone street.

Mentioning Fausto elicited a large smile from Piero, the patriarch of the Manuela family. He explained that his wife, Georgina, did the cooking, that his son, Stephano, made the pasta, and his daughter, Gian, provided the service. We were in good hands, secure in the knowledge that the critical role of chef was filled by an Italian matriarch—the very best kind of cook.

The menu gave us an idea of the regional favourites: there was *Mozzarella e pomodoro* (mozzarella and tomato), *Insalata d'acciughe* (anchovy salad), *Spaghetti con olive* (spaghetti with olives) and a *Frittura di pesce* (a selection of fried fish). I followed Gian's recommendations, which she gave in faltering English. She suggested the appetisers of the day served in three courses. I selected a Pinot Grigio 1995 to accompany the meal.

The first dish comprised a stylishly simple deep-fried zucchini blossom, a small crushed potato and parsley croquette, similarly fried to a golden colour, and a crispy prawn on a stick. The simplicity of each of the ingredients, their unusual juxtaposition and the true flavours made this a wonderful starter. The second course also comprised three elements: a raw marinated anchovy with lemon, a salted anchovy fillet on a slice of roasted capsicum, and a stuffed sardine filled with a mixture of pine nuts, onions, raisins and soft bread, sprinkled with fennel seeds, fried and marinated overnight with white wine and olive oil. It was a delicious introduction to a prized local fish prepared with a keen eye and respect for flavour. Thinking it was the last of the appetisers, I was surprised to see the arrival of a plate of poached calamari mixed with diced boiled potato, tomato and chopped parsley. It certainly was different from what we in Australia understand to be *antipasto*.

I visited the kitchen, which was crowded with members of the extended family. I was introduced to all of them, and also to Roberto, the only professional cook in the trattoria (or as professional as one can be, smoking a cigar while cooking!) and Piero's wife, Georgina, who worked while keeping one eye on an Italian variety show on a black-and-white television set.

Unlike in French kitchens, there was no one here to impose discipline—all workers were equal and anarchically independent. I returned to the table when my next course was due. It was a spaghetti served with tiny crabs, all cooked in a reduced shellfish stock—the perfect *al dente* pasta, simple but superb. Yvette had the traditional dish of the region, a *Trenette al pesto* (a pasta dish in a sauce of nuts, garlic and basil) which redefined what pesto should be.

We were pleasantly surprised when Piero came to sit with us, bringing with him a well-worn red box containing photographs of Portofino as it was in decades past. The shots of Portofino and Santa Margherita in the 1930s were particularly intriguing. We saw pictures of fishing boats and the men who worked them; they wore canvas caps and traditional striped T-shirts. The absence of windows demonstrated the poverty of the inhabitants of the village at that time and was a total contrast to the ritzy shops and restaurants of the present-day village. We felt privileged to have been given a brief glimpse of the family's history and the heritage of this tiny fishing village.

We finished our evening at Trattoria la Concordia with an exceptional dessert: a *Crema di Portofino*, a fragile version of *crème caramel*, doused with coffee but silky and powerful. It was accompanied by a red muscat offered to us by Piero. It made for a memorable meal which taught us a lesson in simplicity and what true Ligurian cuisine is all about.

One of the most well-known products of Liguria is its olives, which are small, tasty and unique to the region. Olive groves are spread high on the hillsides along the coast and have to contend with frosts, rocky soils and the steep terrain, factors which are not conducive to high yields. Not long ago, Liguria was the largest producer of olive oil in Italy, but replacement crops of flowers and garden vegetables cut the production back in the early 1900s. Today there is a return to planting varieties like Lavagnina and Taggiasca, which are low yielding but provide a refined, light and very fragrant oil.

Wines, too, are difficult to produce in Liguria. The region's steep hills, difficult aspect and broken roads make access from valley to valley problematic which has created a patchwork of over a hundred grape varieties. These are used to produce the local wines. Although there is strong competition from Tuscany and Piedmont to the south, many small Ligurian wine producers thrive regardless. There are four areas where quality wines are produced: Dolceacqua near the French border, which produces a red wine called Rossese di Dolceacqua, or 'Sweet Water'; the provinces of Savona and Imperia, which produce some of the better wines of Liguria, including Riviera Ligure di Ponente; the area near the border of Tuscany and Emilia-Romagna, which produces Colli di Luni; and the coast near La Spezia, which produces some of the most unique wines of Liguria.

The five villages of Cinque Terre—Monterosso al Mare, Vernazza, Corniglia, Manarola and Riomaggiore—are all linked by *sentieri*, or bush tracks, that wind through the olive groves, vineyards and gardens of the area. Many outdoors activities are carried out in the cooler months of the year, and during the harvest season in September, men and women can still be seen with donkeys collecting and carrying great baskets of ripe grapes to be pressed. The white wines they produce include the crisp Bianco Dell Cinque Terre, which uses the Albarola, Bosco and Vermentino grapes. If one is fortunate enough to arrive by water from Rapallo to one of the five villages of Cinque Terre, the sampling of the wines after the journey can make for a unique experience.

I can recommend no finer meal to eat with one of the wines of the Cinque Terre than a seared fillet of rouget (better known in Australia as barbougnia or red mullet) with anchovy custard and tapenade—made, of course, from Ligurian olives. The following recipe requires a number of steps and processes, but is worth the effort for a truly delicious Italian experience. Try this dish with a Cinque Terre Costa de Sera, a crisp, flinty white wine that pairs ideally with the fish.

Seared Fillet of Rouget with Anchovy Custard and Tapenade

For the chlorophyll:

1 bunch English spinach, washed and patted dry

Put English spinach through a juicer, then pass through a fine sieve. Place in a pan on the stove and cook over a low heat until tepid (blood temperature); make sure you do not overheat. Remove immediately from the stove and pour the liquid into a sieve double-lined with wet cheesecloth. Place the sieve over a bowl and leave in the fridge overnight to drain the excess water. Scrape off the chlorophyll—this should give you about 20 ml or ½ fl oz—and store in a covered bowl.

For the anchovy custard:

160 ml (5 fl oz) cream
95 ml (3 fl oz) milk
6 anchovy fillets, patted dry and finely chopped
2 eggs
2 egg yolks
salt and pepper

Spray 6 demitasse cups lightly with non-stick spray. Place in a deep baking tray. In a small pan heat the cream and milk to blood temperature, then add the anchovies. Allow to infuse for 15 minutes. Beat in the eggs and seasoning, strain. Pour mixture into the cups, filling two-thirds. Allow to rest for 20 minutes. Preheat oven to 130°C (260°F).

Pour boiling water into the tray, up to the level of the filling in the cups. Cover with greased foil and press firmly onto the tops of the cups. Allow to stand for 5 minutes. Place the tray in the oven and cook for 45 minutes.

Test with a wooden skewer to check when set. If not set, return to oven and check every 10 minutes. Remove from oven and allow to rest for 1 hour. Reheat lightly when needed with the oven on very low.

For the sauce:

3 basil stems

200 ml (7 fl oz) White Wine Cream Sauce (see page 260)

Infuse the basil stems in the White Wine Sauce for 4 minutes, strain and add 20 ml (½ fl oz) of the chlorophyll to the sauce at the last minute to give it a bright green colour. Keep warm.

For the rouget:

6 fillets rouget

cornflour to dust

salt and pepper

a little olive oil

Tapenade (see page 256)

handful of mâche, or other small leaves

Make sure rouget is well trimmed and clean of any bones. When ready to serve, dust with a touch of cornflour, salt and pepper. Using very little oil, sear fish in a non-stick pan or a heavy pan on high heat, skin down first. As soon as you put the fish in the pan, press with a fish spatula to ensure the fillet does not curl. Turn over after 1 minute and sear the other side without pressing; remove and put aside. Keep warm.

To assemble:

On a warm plate arrange an anchovy custard and a fillet of rouget. Garnish with mâche leaves or other small leaves dressed with a touch of olive oil, top the rouget with a spoonful of Tapenade and drizzle lightly with sauce.

(Serves 6 as an entrée)

Yvette and I did not make it to the Cinque Terre, but we did visit the village of San Fruttuoso. Fausto, our concierge at the Splendido, recommended a simple lunch at San Fruttuoso and advised us that the village could be reached by either a two-hour walk or a fifteen-minute boat ride. We took the boat ride. The very steep granite hills of the coast made the site of the village, and of the eleventh-century abbey which dominated it, quite extraordinary. One could imagine the difficulties involved in building an abbey in such an inaccessible place, not to mention the fear the inhabitants must have felt of being attacked by Saracen pirates, living as they did in such a vulnerable position. As we approached the abbey by sea we saw dozens of curious divers trying to locate the underwater bronze statue of Christ or *Cristo degli Abissi*, which sits upon the sea floor and is revered by the sailors of the region.

After swimming and relaxing on the beach we were ready for lunch in one of the smallest restaurants I have ever seen. Giorgio is wedged into a hole in the cliff face; it houses a tiny open kitchen and as few as eight tables. Its clientele consists of regulars from past years and new customers not afraid of the steep prices charged for a simple meal. Personally, I would prefer to pay more for a spectacular simple meal than for a mediocre elaborate one.

Simplicity is one of the most difficult feats to accomplish when preparing food.

The menu listed a small selection of regional foods, like an anchovy salad consisting of ripe garden tomatoes with salted anchovies strewn on top and splashed with Ligurian olive oil. Yvette opted for the seafood soup; it was simple, fresh and slightly spiked with chilli. This was followed by a classic *Trenette al pesto*, and for me, a *Spaghetti alla marinara*, full of diced seafood stewed in a stock of shellfish and fresh parsley. The crisp Gavi la Giustiniana 1996, coming from Rovereto di Gavi in nearby Piedmont, was light and perfectly suited the meal and the location. Without our ordering it, Giorgio brought us a large platter of *Frittura di mare*, a stunning selection of lightly floured and deep-fried prawn, scampi, calamari and fish. The view across the water, the sun on our faces, the quiet, casual manner of the staff, the friendly nature of the Italian customers and the fresh food made this restaurant unforgettable.

A beautiful cruiser made its way into the bay and who else could it be calling and waving to us from behind the wheel but a tanned Fausto, taking his daily afternoon break from the hotel on one of the prettiest beaches on the Italian Riviera. A great lifestyle for a dedicated Riviera lover, we reflected.

Back at the hotel we spent the afternoon reading books on regional food. The beautiful small fishing boats bobbed in the harbour below us. I asked Fausto to find me a fisherman who could take me fishing but received the sad response that the fish stocks of former years had been severely depleted. It was only up the coast, in a village like Camogli, that fishermen were still able to catch the fresh seafood that attracts such high prices and is so loved by the Italians.

A saying from Genoa came to mind: 'Barren hills, fishless seas, shameless women'. These days, seeing the verdant hills of Liguria producing exorbitantly priced wine and virgin olive oil, and observing the women dressed in incomparable fashions, the only part of the complaint I could agree with was about the fishless seas.

It was arranged that I would meet Carmine Giuliani, the *chef di cucina* of the Hotel Splendido. During siesta, while most of the guests at the hotel were resting, Carmine received me in his kitchen and proudly showed me some of the local produce he had purchased: small eggplants, artichokes, incredibly shaped radicchio, as well as mussels and fresh fish from the Genoa market. We were to dine that night in the restaurant and I resisted the temptation to ask him questions about the dishes he had planned for the evening. Most of the team was preparing for the elaborate wedding of a Genoese belle and their energy was palpably focused on producing a magnificent buffet of Italian specialities.

In the afternoon Yvette and I decided to walk down to the village to work up an appetite. On our way we admired the superb villas of the area. I noticed a beautiful ship anchored at Portofino harbour and recognised it as the *Crystal Harmony*, a sister boat to the *Crystal Symphony* which I joined as part of a promotion cruise a year ago, sailing from Australia to Bali.

To our eyes, one of the most fascinating aspects of Portofino was its *trompe l'oeil* designs painted on the stucco facades of buildings. Even if the Italians did not invent this art of visual deception, they certainly used it with gusto and to great effect. The false shutters looked almost real, as did the balconies and columns. The artistry of some of the painters in conjuring a sense of space and architectural detail that the architecture itself had not permitted was nothing short of spectacular.

We walked like Italian lovers on the promenade, admiring the uniformed yacht crews and the sailors resting in this most improbable harbour. Beautifully attired diners were arriving to take their prize positions in the restaurants lining the piazza. Few cars are allowed into the piazza, so most Italians arrived on foot or by scooter at this buzzing Friday night spot.

Returning to the hotel we discovered that dinner was to be served on the romantic terrace at the Splendido. The smell of the jasmine, the gentle breeze and the candlelit tables overlooking the garden that sloped down towards the water made it a glamorous setting. The menu reflected the old traditions of the hotel, being built around classics of yesterday like the *Frisceau di verdure e focaccine alla Genovese* (an assortment of marinated and fried vegetables and cheese dumplings), and the *Fegato alla Genovese con purè di zucchine* (sautéed veal liver with onion and a zucchini purée). We enjoyed a languorous evening and a traditional Genoese meal—a sophisticated finale to our stay in Portofino, the jewel of Liguria.

CITY OF STYLE

austo's last piece of advice to us before we left Portofino for **F** Milan was not to attempt to drive on our own in that metropolis. The traffic, he said, was chaotic, and we would be well advised to hire a taxi and follow it to our destination. I decided to make it to the Four Seasons Milan on our own. Despite the tangle of one-way streets and streets designated for buses and taxis only (directions which I duly ignored), I finally spotted some street names which I had memorised from the map: corso Vittorio Emanuele, via Monte Napoleone and finally the tiny street where the hotel was situated, via Gesù. The porter inquired how we had got to the hotel, given that we were obviously tourists, and when I said we had driven directly from Portofino he looked suitably impressed.

As we entered the foyer of the Four Seasons Hotel the serenity was immediate. This was probably due as much to the fact of having escaped the traffic and turmoil of the streets as it was to us just having entered a church—the old Convento Santa Maria del Gesù.

Over the course of its life, all the original frescoes in this fifteenth-century convent were either destroyed or plastered over. As well, the columns were bricked up and the rooms enlarged, and ultimately the building was transformed into an aristocratic residence. In 1983 the whole convent was purchased to be converted into a luxury hotel. Eighteen months later, with the preparation and restoration of significant artistic and historical features achieved, the convent was transformed into a unique modern facility.

It was clear that the architects and interior decorators of this hotel had respected the character of the original building. Our room had very high ceilings and heavy, polished woodwork. It was pristine, elegant and exuded an air of luxury.

The advantage of the hotel, we soon discovered, was its proximity to places like Galleria Vittorio Emanuele II, the nineteenth-century shopping arcade aptly named 'Il Salotto di Milano' (Milan's drawing room); La Scala, the famous opera house built in 1778; the Duomo, the incredibly imposing Gothic cathedral with its distinctive spires and white marble facade; and the Pinacoteca di Brera, Milan's finest art collection, which is housed in the seventeenth-century palazzo.

As usual, though, food was foremost in our minds. Our first dinner in Milan was at Bagutta Trattoria Toscana, a very typical Milanese restaurant. Established in 1924, it used to be the favourite meeting place for artists and writers and today is still the seat of Italy's oldest literary association, 'Il Bagutta'. Bagutta is one of those restaurants which amazes non-Europeans; thousands of appreciative patrons frequenting it over seven decades have given it a lived-in, worn look. We were taken through a succession of old rooms leading to a pleasant garden where groups of business people and Milanese families were having dinner.

The menu, we were told, was printed daily. I counted as many as seventy dishes and quietly observed that it was as large as could safely be offered. Fortunately for the kitchen, many of the items on the menu were pasta dishes and simple-to-prepare fish dishes.

Yvette selected the *antipasto*, which she served herself from the stunning display facing the ancient open kitchen (probably very radical when it was established). I received my first course of *Ravioli di carne al ragù*, a meat-filled ravioli served with a small quantity of hand-diced, red-wine-stewed beef that went perfectly with my Barbaresco Vigneto Roche Dei 7 Fratelli 1990, a Piedmont wine of immense body that was also totally suitable for my following course, *Coniglio al forno con patate*, a rich rabbit stew with potato.

The restaurant was extremely traditional and the waiters' manner and attitude rather formal, and one felt that neither the food nor the decor would ever change. Still, I enjoyed the restaurant and its distinctive character.

The next morning I decided to have a quick coffee and breakfast on the run as the Milanese do—but in great style at Peck Ristorante. This eatery is next to the Gastronomia Peck food stores. I savoured my *panino* filled with mortadella and Bel Paese cheese of Lombardy, then headed across the street to the rustic Garbagnati bakery, which was full of superb crusty bread, strudels and pastries. I admired the *gelati* and handmade chocolates nearby at Giovanni Galli, a speciality shop stocked full with *marroni*, *canditi* and *fondenti*, glazed marrons, bonbons and confit fruit, typical of the Renaissance skills of the confectionery trade. They were so beautiful in their small boxes that I purchased a few to give to my Italian friends.

Being forewarned about Peck's food shop still did not prepare me for the reality: it was food elevated to sculptural heights. Each display was more stunning than the one before it. There were oranges, eggplants, strawberries, all in perfect condition and deftly stacked in purpose-built spaces. The prosciutto section was a reminder of what perfectly cured and aged ham should be. Salami, mortadella, terrine, fresh pork, Tuscan and Lombardian beef, white veal, Italian corn-fed chicken and every imaginable catering product was here, alongside displays of beef in pastry crust, lobster in *gelée* and decorated salmon. It was fresh, clean and gleaming, and very impressive. I thought to myself that if ever a chef lacked inspiration, a visit here would be enough to renew his or her creativity for years.

The kitchen used for preparing all this fresh food and for handling the infinite stock was amazing. Using the latest Italian equipment were professional chefs, busy blanching asparagus, making *foie gras* terrine, preparing platters of stuffed artichokes and producing *antipasto* and *canapés* for the display. I did wonder who bought all this food, but the sheer quantity on display left me in no doubt as to its popularity.

I made my way to Peck's wine store and was amazed by the quality of the selection. There was an incredible range of DOC and DOCG, the *Denominazione di Origine Controllata* and *Denominazione di Origine Controllata e Garantita*, which represent some of the better wines of Italy. If the Italian wines were not enough, the French wines were equally impressive. There were magnums of Château Margaux, Latour and other renowned wines like Ausone, Romanée Conti and Château d'Yquem. Luckily for most shoppers, Peck also stocks very affordable Italian and French wines for everyday drinking.

I left impressed, thinking that if a city which has fewer than two million residents can have a shop like this one, then the citizens of Sydney and many other similarly sized cities in the world can still look forward to seeing such a store established—if, that is, they commit themselves to buying quality food.

Despite the patriotic belief of the Romans that no good food is cooked in Milan (except, obviously, by resident Roman chefs), there is a definite style of cooking which is typical of Milan. The food of the north tends to be richer than that of the south, owing to its proximity to France and the Germanic countries which have instilled in it a love of butter, cream and cheese. The province also has good pastures for the production of dairy products.

Yvette and I sampled some of the traditional food of Milan at La Veranda, the all-day restaurant of the Four Seasons Hotel that services the stylish fashion clientele of the Milan couture precinct. I ordered a typical *Costoletta alla Milanese*, a very thin cutlet of white veal, crumbed and cooked in butter. Yvette selected the classic *Risotto alla Milanese*, rich with saffron, Parmigiano-Reggiano and butter instead of the more usual olive oil. Risotto is a very popular dish in Milan. The nearby Po Valley is one of the greatest areas to grow rice, and this is naturally showcased profusely on the menus of the restaurants. *Pasta fresca* (fresh pasta) also features on menus and is eaten more often than the *pasta secca* or dried pasta. Other dishes found in Milan include *Osso Bucco*, a succulent veal shank braised in wine and stock and served with a *gremolata* (dry garnish) of grated lemon, parsley, garlic and occasionally a touch of anchovies. It is served with saffron risotto. *Gnocchi di patate* is also prized, especially if prepared with Gorgonzola, the blue-vein cheese originally produced near Milan.

One of my best friends, Annie Feolde of Florence, owner of the famous Enoteca Pinchiorri Restaurant, had organised for one of her best friends to show Yvette and I around Milan. We were to meet Elisabetta Bastianello, a public relations dynamo, in the hotel foyer at 8.00 pm to go to Elisabetta's favourite Milanese trattoria. When we went down we found the foyer bustling with the beautiful people of Milan. Elisabetta arrived, stylishly dressed and excited to meet us on behalf of our mutual friend.

Elisabetta wanted us to have a special meal, one which in normal circumstances we would not have the chance to experience. She explained that Trattoria Masuelli San Marco, which is run by the Masuelli family, was an authentic eatery that we would enjoy. On our trip there I watched the poor taxi driver manoeuvring his way through the tiny streets to get out of central Milan. I tried to memorise the route, as I knew I would need all the help I could get when the time came for me to leave.

We arrived at the small, unpretentious trattoria and were warmly welcomed by Pino, the father of the family. That night the restaurant's patrons were in a state of anxious excitement as the final of the European Cup was being played in Germany. Elisabetta's soccer-fan husband, Tony, had flown there to support the Italian team. As we sat down the announcement came from the waiter, who was listening to the radio in the kitchen, that the match had started.

Pino came to our table to announce the evening menu in his beautiful baritone voice, sure of his knowledge and completely versed in the evening's preparations. I was awed by his descriptions of the food; his love of each product was so apparent. Elisabetta ordered our food, impressed by my proclamation that I would eat everything, the more exotic the better. We started with the *antipasto*: homemade salami, lard with rosemary, pickled pork head, anchovies, herrings in milk, hot tiny peppers and marinated eggplant in olive oil made for a complete taste sensation that left me a convert to rustic Italian food. Unfortunately I also realised that many of these products would never become popular or acceptable to the general populace because of the amount of fat in them and the difficulty of handling products like pigs' heads.

The next course was more conservative than the last. We started with a *garganelli* pasta with vegetables, a vegetable soup, a plate of *agnolotti* with a beef ragù, and zucchini flowers stuffed with ricotta and spinach. Giuseppe's daughter came in and announced that after nine minutes of play Italy was down 1–0. Elisabetta immediately called Tony in Germany on her mobile phone and commiserated with him in Italian. On finishing she said in a subdued voice, 'Oh my poor, poor husband; 1–0.' We were about to start our third course when the proprietor's daughter returned and said '2–0!' We sat in silence for a moment to respect Elisabetta's disappointment.

I was on my own for the next course, as Elisabetta and Yvette had eaten enough. My rabbit had been cooked very slowly in olive oil until it acquired the texture of tuna. There was also a poached beef tongue with a green sauce made of parsley, anchovies, garlic and spinach, which was beautiful and much appreciated. We finished the Bianco Cortese del Monferrato, a crisp elegant wine for a Ruché di Castagnole.

Before the next course arrived there was a further announcement from the kitchen that Germany had scored a third goal. This news plunged the other diners into even deeper depression. Elisabetta got on the phone again and in a very soft voice tried to soothe her suicidal husband. We sampled a few desserts: a Piedmont baked cream, which was custard-like and delicious, a rustic apple pie and a whipped mascarpone cream. It was extraordinarily fresh and simply exquisite.

Delighted that I could keep eating, Giuseppe brought three cheeses for me to sample: a blue Moncenisio, a mountain goat cheese and a dry Chevrin.

As we prepared to leave I heard that Italy had scored a goal in the dying minutes of the game. Despite this consolation goal, Italy had lost the final in bad fashion. While the Italian guests began vigorously to drown their sorrows, I could do nothing but revel in the blissful state brought on by the completion of a beautiful meal.

THE MAGIC OF LAKE COMO

The *legendary Villa d'Este is a grand hotel which has had a* tumultuous and glamorous history. It is set in a marvellous location and offers an old-world style of aristocratic refinement. For many decades Australians have been staying at the Villa d'Este on the banks of Lake Como, lured there by a unique quality of serenity. It was inevitable, then, that this magical hotel was to be one of our choices.

Como is a rich city with a beautiful vista built on the most romantic lake in the world. The hotel is situated about three miles north of Como, in the small village of Cernobbio, where some streets are so narrow that there is only one-way traffic. The enchanting drive through the wooded park prepares you for one of the grandest hotels ever built.

In 1568 Cardinal Tolomeo Gallio commissioned one of the best architects of the day, Pellegrino Pellegrini, to build several villas around the lake. His favourite became Villa Garrovo, the present Villa d'Este, which became a meeting place for the elite. On his death, the Cardinal's family continued to embellish the house, turning it into a villa that was the talk of Europe.

Over the following centuries several residents and owners dedicated themselves to redecorating the villa. One of them was Princess Caroline of Brunswick, the wife of King George IV, who escaped England after his rejection of her in 1814 and developed a love for the villa. It was at this time that Caroline changed the name to Villa d'Este. The villa changed hands many times over the centuries and eventually was taken over in 1873 by a group of ingenious businessmen who wanted to transform the residence into a luxury hotel. During the following decades additions and renovations were made, elevating the hotel to one of the best resorts in the world.

One of the reasons so many world travellers return to the Villa d'Este time and time again is Jean Salvadore. After over thirty years, Jean is still the director of public relations and a resident of the hotel; her charm and intelligence have contributed so much to the hotel's reputation. Jean has written two acclaimed books on the food of the Villa d'Este, and more recently a third one on its history, recording significant events (and the odd scandal) in the life of the hotel.

Jean welcomed us warmly, like old friends, even though it was our first visit. The many friends she has in Australia, and a visit she once made to Sydney, have made her a devotee of the Australian way of life. Many years ago she used to welcome the visits of Leo Schofield, the respected art and food critic of Sydney, who led eager groups of gourmets ready to learn the secrets of the cuisine of Luciano Parolari, the talented executive chef of the hotel. We were invited to join Jean as her guests for dinner in the Ristorante Veranda and for drinks at sunset. A gracious evening lay ahead.

In the meantime, however, we went to explore the eighteenth-century park. The manicured gardens were graced with a multitude of artistic features. There were superb mosaic walls, an Italian national monument, a long stone staircase with cascading water on each side, and several small grottoes for reflection.

The further we walked, the more treasures were revealed: beautiful statues, a 500-year-old plane tree, a cypress alley, the superb views over Lake Como.

We returned to prepare for the evening dinner (jacket required). Before meeting Jean on the terrace, which was enveloped by blooming jasmine, I was introduced to Luciano, the chef who, according to Jean, was 'so handsome, women watch him boil water in cooking class and they applaud'. We walked into the cavernous kitchens of the hotel and at the front of the pass (where I would spend the following night) Luciano greeted me. Strong, calm and in charge, he exuded a tranquil air, no doubt developed over his twenty-five years of working in the kitchen of the Villa d'Este.

Sipping a glass of champagne in the tranquillity of an Italian sunset, looking out at the lake in the company of a host as delightful and knowledgeable as Jean, made us feel privileged to be guests at this hotel.

The dining room was large and very beautiful. The style of the guests was equally impressive; there were distinguished Italian men with grey hair accompanied by young, glamorously dressed daughters (or women I *presumed* to be their daughters). The service staff were omnipresent.

On Jean's recommendation I ordered the *Antipasto Villa d'Este*, a selection of lobster, *foie gras* and smoked salmon—not so Italian but very Villa d'Este. Jean ordered a *Spaghetti all'olio* and Yvette a *Scampi e capesante all'olio e aceto balsamico*, a salad of scampi and scallops with virgin olive oil and balsamic vinegar. This was followed by a fillet of turbot cooked with champagne, a sea bass *carpaccio* with olives, basil and sesame seeds, and a *Costoletta de vitello in crosta di carciofi e patate*, a veal cutlet with a potato and artichoke crust. For dessert we all selected the

Biscotto croccante alla crema e fragole, a crunchy biscuit with fresh cream and fragrant strawberry fondant. The food was a reflection of the hotel: classic, well tried and capable each time of satisfying the most demanding guest.

We retired to the piano bar for a liqueur and to listen to an exceptionally talented soprano singer who enthralled the guests with her repertoire. The bartenders and waiters ensured everyone was well stocked with their favourite tea or digestive. This was a grand evening, crowned by the comfort of knowing that our room was only a very short walk away.

We woke up to a sunny morning and had a swim in the pool before eating a delicious buffet breakfast. We had a free day ahead of us, my only appointment being to meet Luciano in the evening. I read the day's activities on the concierge's noticeboard; his recommendation of 'A Gastronomic Tour of Lake Como' caught my eye. It described a day of boating around the lake with lunch on the only island, Isola Comacina. I was hooked. I made my way back to the concierge to make my booking for eleven o'clock—just enough time to tidy up some work and get ready for a ride on this blue-green lake.

The boat was waiting for us in front of the hotel, tied up to the pier with several other superb motor boats. Sylvio, our skipper, was all smiles as he helped us on board for our adventure. The gleaming teak surface of the boat did not disclose its age; it was clear that Sylvio took great care of his craft. I was surprised that there was no one else on our boat until I realised that the booking the concierge had made for us was for a private tour of the lake.

The departure from the Villa d'Este is superb, enabling a close look from the water at the Reine d'Anglettere pavilion and its boat marina. We headed north, starting at the base of the lake near Como. Sylvio was already pointing out some of the grand villas on the lake, beginning next door to the Villa d'Este at the house of Gianni Versace (who was killed tragically a few weeks after our return to Australia, and whose ashes were scattered on the lake), Mussolini's former residence, and Winston Churchill's favourite rented villa, now owned by the Dongale family of Milan. We sailed by the small village of Moltrasio, which boasts the former house of Bellini, the nineteenth-century composer.

We crisscrossed the lake, seeing more beautiful villas, some abandoned, like the sixteenth-century Villa Pliniana at Torno. We went to the gorge at Nesso, where we eased our boat into a river that ended in a beautiful waterfall, and we returned passing under an ancient Roman stone bridge. We disembarked at Bellagio to view the famous garden of Villa Melzi where rare vegetable species are cultivated. Then we were off across the lake to inspect the gardens of Villa Carlotta in Tremezzo, an eighteenth-century summer house ablaze with rhododendrons, camellias and azaleas in full bloom. Our last stop was in Bellano, a small village set hard against the hills, full of summer restaurants and shops selling the famous silk products that are manufactured around the lake.

Admiring the distant high peaks of Switzerland and the beautiful cruisers plying their trade on the lake, we made our way to our lunch destination, the small Isola Comacina. Many other small boats were headed in the same direction, with couples or groups of friends ready to enjoy a lunch at L'Oste della Locanda dell'Isola Comacina.

Benvenuto Puricelli, the host and proprietor, received us at the door of this large, unpretentious, open-plan restaurant. Once seated we were immediately given, without asking, a large loaf of crusty bread, whole and unsliced, to break and share amongst the table. A bottle of crisp Soave Paesagi from the Verona region and a large bottle of mineral water were also brought to the table. There were no explanations—just a set meal to be enjoyed. The fixed menu at L'Oste della Locanda has apparently remained in place since the inception of the restaurant in 1947, which is a lesson to be learned about offering food you believe in and which you know will satisfy an eager market.

Benvenuto worked in St Moritz in his formative years and then in London as an executive chef. I could see he had used his experience to create dishes out of local products.

The first course was a dish typical of the region: a ripe half-tomato topped with a paper-thin slice of lemon and a touch of dried oregano and drizzled with local olive oil. The sharpness of the lemon contrasted with the acidity of the tomato. It was an unusual combination that teased the tastebuds and created a hearty appetite.

A service table was set beside us and a vegetable *antipasto* was served in handcrafted painted bowls. The preparation was simple and the flavours so intense that I admired the audacity of serving them in such a simple form in a restaurant. Individual bowls of blanched cauliflower, sliced carrot, beetroot and slightly peeled and steamed zucchini were dressed in a touch of olive oil and pepper; roasted celery heart and sautéed lardon were also served, along with blanched beans dressed with some garlic and oil. The bowls were left beside the table so you could replenish your plate at will from this delicious selection. Wisely, at some point the vegetables were cleared away, as it would have been difficult to stop feasting on them. A single baked onion was brought to each of us, its caramelised and earthy aroma all-pervasive. It was left in its crispy husk, its inside still soft, juicy and absolutely delicious. Such elementary ingredients prepared in an uncompromisingly simple manner renewed my faith in the existence of *Cucina Povera*, the cuisine of the peasant population of rural Italy, based on simple ingredients and very little meat.

Our waiter came back to the table with a platter of thinly sliced air-dried beef—*Bresaola*—which he drizzled with the juice of one lemon and some local virgin olive oil. This theme of lemon and olive oil was becoming quite apparent in many of the meals we had enjoyed in Italy. We finished this dish with relish, then Benvenuto came to the table with a whole poached Praga ham on the bone and proceeded to carve with an incredibly deft hand thick slices for Yvette and myself. First the skin came off, then some of the fat and finally he cut a magic slice of moist, slightly smoked ham—one of the best hams I have ever tasted.

We observed a customer beside us, who tried to refuse the next course, a golden river trout, in order to save himself for the course to follow, a roast chicken. The waiter looked him straight in the eye and said, in English, 'First you get the trout, then you get the chicken.' The admonition was not meant harshly; it was just a simple directive that he should taste the trout. Clearly the waiters were in control in this restaurant. The speed and expertise with which they carried out their duties was inspiring to watch and was obviously the result of serving endless lunches and dinners over many years. Guests could do nothing but surrender themselves to their expertise and enjoy their meals.

Our trout arrived on a platter. It was a large, crispy, whole lake trout, probably farmed in the region. We ate it in the typical northern Italian manner. Our waiter deftly removed the head, sliced the skin off the spine, removed the top skin in one quick rolling movement, scooped the flesh onto a plate (taking care not to have the bone come off with it) and turned the remaining fillet over to undergo the same process. Two succulent, moist, pink fillets were set on the plate. A lemon was produced, a fork was stabbed into its flesh and a great squeeze doused the flesh, the plate, the table and part of the floor. Then olive oil, pepper and sea salt were liberally applied over both the fillets and the immediate vicinity once again. This was quite an effective sideshow and produced one of the best trout I have ever eaten.

I was starting to feel the combined weight of the many dishes we had already consumed, but seeing the other guests eating a deliciously plump piece of chicken, I prepared myself for the next course. The large chickens served at L'Oste della Locanda are roasted before the start of the service to give them a chance to rest and become tender. They are then cut up into large pieces and quickly fried before being served, accompanied by a piece of lemon and a green leaf salad. This superb chicken is similar to my favourite Chinese crispy chicken dish which I eat in Sydney in Chinatown. I wondered if the oriental influence on Venice had affected the cuisine of Lake Como.

No meal would be complete without a piece of cheese, and Benvenuto visited all the tables with a great half wheel of Grana Padano, or Parmesan, and a solid knife with which to cut it. From the end of his knife he presented slices of the delicious cheese to all takers. It was a perfect way to finish the bread and the wine, both of which had been replenished on request during the course of the meal.

If we were not already impressed with the floor skills of the staff, the presentation of dessert would have overawed us. A whole orange was pricked with a fork and the skin was spiralled away from the flesh at great speed with a small steak knife. The clean fruit was then put on our plates, quickly sliced and garnished with a large scoop of ice-cream, and the whole plate doused in Crema de San Giovanni, a pear and banana liqueur. It would have been impossible to leave the table hungry.

While people were relaxing, Benvenuto prepared himself for the final ritual of the day. In front of all the patrons of the restaurant he heated up a rich brew of dark coffee in a copper cauldron and, while recounting the history of Isola Comacina, he added sugar and brandy to his concoction. The result was a strong finish to a memorable meal.

That evening, our last at Villa D'Este, I went to observe the service in Luciano Parolari's kitchen. This estimable chef was born in the local village of Arco above Lake Garda. Like me, he had a butcher in his family: for him it was his father (for me, my grandfather). He started in the kitchen at Villa d'Este when he was thirteen years old. Like most young chefs of the region he did his classic training at school in the winter and in summer worked at the busy resorts of the region to gain experience. During his nearly thirty years at the Villa d'Este he rose through the ranks to be promoted to executive chef in 1978. Slowly Luciano introduced new dishes on to the hotel's menu. Interestingly enough, pasta was not a common dish of the region fifteen years ago; risotto was much preferred, and still this classic dish cannot be taken off the menu for fear of upsetting the regulars.

I stood at the pass to view the service and the various preparation methods. The kitchen is so large that a microphone is used so that orders are audible in all sections—not quite the high-tech setup of the bank of televisions in Alain Ducasse's kitchen in

Monaco, but a step up from most kitchens. The classics made their way out of the kitchen: *Fiori di zucchina farciti* (stuffed zucchini flowers), *Involtini di salmone* (pillow of smoked salmon with crabmeat), *Cannelloni Villa d'Este* (stuffed cannelloni of veal, pork and sweetbreads in a tomato cream sauce) and *Petto di faraona con pinoli e prosciutto, salsa tartufata* (breast of guinea-hen, stuffed with pine nuts and ham, with a truffle sauce). I quickly sensed that in Luciano's kitchen there was a well-drilled team, producing dishes designed by a great chef who understood the wisdom of respecting traditions and the value of satisfying the regulars of a place with so grand a reputation as the Villa d'Este.

LAND OF MILK AND STURGEON

We were to meet Elisabetta, our new friend from Milan, in Desenzano di Garda, a resort town at the southern end of Lake Garda. Elisabetta and her husband Tony had a house on the lake and, like many Milanese, loved to escape the fast pace of Milan on weekends. Elisabetta was to take us to the Grana Padano factory of the Medeghini family and the sturgeon farm Agroittica Lombarda, the food conglomerates she represents.

After dropping our baggage at the Park Hotel, a superbly located small hotel on the side of the magnificent lake, we headed towards Brescia via the *autostrada*. It was typical of Elisabetta that she talked on her hand-held phone while driving at high speeds. The drive revealed how productive the region was: factory after factory was spread on each side of the highway, producing everything from furniture to bakery ovens to telephone equipment.

Our first destination was Villa Cortine di Mazzano where we were to visit the Medeghini factory, which produces dairy food delicacies.

Elisabetta's friend and employer, Paola Medeghini, received us in the old mansion. Paola, who was as vivacious as Elisabetta, gave us a brief marketing outline before we visited the Medeghini factory. The firm, she told us, produced a range of dairy products but specialised in the making of the five DOC (*Denominatione di Origine*

Controllata) cheeses: Grana Padano, Gorgonzola, Provolone, Taleggio and Quartirolo, a young version of Taleggio.

The cheese I was most interested in was the Grana Padano, a form of Parmesan produced around Brescia. I wanted to understand the difference between the Grana Padano and the Parmigiano-Reggiano. Paola obliged me with an explanation. In Italy, she said, all hard grating cheeses are known as Grana; Parmesan is just a generic term used for the unsophisticated export market. The unfortunate effect of this terminology for non-Italians is the lack of understanding it leads to in differentiating Grana cheeses, and the subsequent loss of the opportunity of purchasing some of the better cheeses of Italy.

We entered the cheese factory and I was overawed by the scale of the production. The amount of milk used was enormous— more than 9000 dairy farmers supplied the unpasteurised raw product—and when I considered that one of the requirements for the making of Grana Padano is that the cows are free to graze in fields or on green alfalfa rather than on dry cattle fodder, then the undertaking seemed staggering. Yvette and I toured the large factory with great interest, fascinated by each stage in the preparation of one of the oldest cheeses of Italy.

First the surface cream was skimmed off the evening milk before being mixed with the morning milk and a touch of whey from a previous batch to start the natural fermentation necessary to raise the acidity level of the cheese. The milk was then heated to a mild 33 degrees Celsius (91 degrees Fahrenheit) in large copper vats. Rennet, the enzyme from a cow's stomach, was mixed into the milk to curdle it. When this had occurred, the curd was cut into pieces with a *spino* (a long whisk cutter) to the size of risotto rice and cooked very slowly to 45 degrees Celsius (110 degrees

Fahrenheit), then briskly to 55 degrees Celsius (130 degrees Fahrenheit), and finally recooked. Once the heating process was completed and the grain mass had fallen to the bottom of the deep vat, it was retrieved with a wooden pole, scooped into a cheese cloth and hung up for the whey to drain away. This solid grainy mass was cut into two, each piece put into a special mould, pressed with a heavy weight to remove any residual whey, then remoulded and stamped with the Parmigiano-Reggiano ensignia. Thus a cheese was born. It would thereafter be turned several times to ensure a flat surface and to allow it to form a crust, then bathed for twenty days in a saline solution.

Paola kept the pride of the firm for last: the ageing vault or 'cathedral' of the Grana Padano. Ageing vaults are like Swiss banks, the producers like to say, because so much of value is held in these incredible stores. There were over 120 000 wheels, worth a staggering 500 000 000 000 lire, in the vault we saw. All cheeses here are aged for at least a year, and in some cases three. *Fresco* (fresh) cheeses are left to age for up to eighteen months, *vecchio* (mature) ones for twenty-four months, and *stravecchio* (very mature) Parmigiano-Reggianos for up to thirty-six months. The temperature and humidity are constantly controlled. The cheeses used to be brushed by hand to keep them free of any unwanted fungal growth that would affect their preservation. Fortunately, they now have machines that pick up whole wheels and gently sand and polish them. We saw these machines patrolling and working the alleys two storeys high to ensure that the Parmesan was maintained in perfect condition. In one area I surveyed a specialist testing cheeses with a little hammer to determine by sound whether proper maturation had been achieved.

By this point we were keen to taste some Grana Padano. Paola took us to the packing room where we saw whole wheels being cut in half by modern machines, then cored and cut into wedges. Elisabetta, Paola, Yvette and I each had a piece of Grana Padano. The nutty taste of the cheese, with its sharp, aromatic, sweet and salty undertones and its crunchy texture, confirmed what a great traditional cheese it is.

Parmesan has in common with Swiss Gruyère and Emmental cheeses the 'cooked' method of production, whereby temperatures exceeding 48 degrees Celsius (118 degrees Fahrenheit) are used to heat the milk and produce a curd which is then pressed and matured. These cheeses have the lowest moisture content of all cheeses and keep for the longest time.

A cheese custard using Fontina and Parmesan makes a flavoursome entrée. Fontina is an ideal cheese for cooking as it melts easily and has a beautiful hazelnut aroma. It is quite similar to Gruyère cheese, which you could use as a substitute in this recipe. Accompany the cheese custard with small leaves tossed in a mild vinaigrette, a slice of prosciutto ham, an oven-roasted tomato and a piece of roasted wood-fired bread.

Fontina Cheese Custard

75 ml (2½ fl oz) milk
300 ml (9½ fl oz) cream
150 g (5 oz) Fontina cheese, grated
salt and white pepper
4 eggs
3 egg yolks
50 g (2 oz) Fontina cheese, for gratinée
50 g (2 oz) Parmesan cheese, for gratinée

Combine the milk, cream and Fontina cheese in a pot and slowly heat until the cheese is melted and well combined. Add salt and pepper to taste and strain through a fine chinois (or sieve) and cheesecloth. Chill well. Beat the eggs and yolks into the chilled mixture. Strain again.

Preheat the oven to 170°C (340°F).

Pour mixture into small cups lightly coated with an oil spray. Place cups in a bain marie (water bath) and bake for 55 minutes or until set. Remove and either allow to cool for 5 minutes before unmoulding or sprinkle with the Fontina and Parmesan cheese then place under a grill to gratinée the top of the custard. Carefully run a small knife down around the edge of the cup to unmould. If serving gratinée, place with the top side uppermost; if not, turn the custard over to serve.

To serve:
Place the custard on a plate and accompany with a salad and bread. Alternatively, serve with some baked onions cooked on a bed of rock salt in an oven set at 140°C (275°F) for 1 hour.

(Makes 10 small cups)

Elisabetta was very pleased with herself, as she could see I was intrigued by the fact that we were going to visit a sturgeon farm—in *Italy*. People are right in thinking that sturgeon generally comes from the Caspian Sea; overfishing and the pollution of the last few decades have decimated the established sturgeon populations in most other places. However, even the sturgeon population in the Caspian has had to come under strict controls in order to enhance its chances of survival. In Lombardy a farm has been set up to breed this fish.

On arriving at Agroittica, Elisabetta introduced us to the enterprising owner of this farm, Patricia, who led us to the breeding tanks for the trout, eel, salmon and sturgeon. These were situated in old converted warehouses serving as hatcheries. We saw tank after tank full of fish thriving in the warm water. Elisabetta explained that the reason for the success of the farm, and the reason nobody else had so far been successful in farming sturgeon, was that Patricia had access to plenty of fresh water from the deep artesian wells beneath them, and access to hot water in abundance due to the generosity of the steelworks next-door, which discharged the warmed-up water used to cool the steel. This hot water was perfect for the hatchery, as a water temperature of 20 to 22 degrees Celsius (68 to 72 degrees Fahrenheit) is required to provide an ideal growing environment for the fish.

I was intrigued by the large outside ponds that contained the first live sturgeon I had ever encountered. I studied the water and suddenly I saw one, then two, incredibly large sturgeon. It was fascinating to come face to face with such a prehistoric fish, one that few people outside of Russia have ever seen.

After visiting the filleting and smokehouse operation, Yvette and I left contented with a small gift for dinner—a tin of fresh Italian caviar and some smoked sturgeon. For me, Agroittica Lombarda was a fascinating insight into the highly specialised world of fish farming.

As a finale to the day, Elisabetta had organised a dinner at one of her favourite restaurants in the region, Ristorante al Bersagliere, run by Roberto Ferrari, a member of the prestigious Ferrari family.

Roberto proved to be a great *sommelier* and raconteur, and his interest in wine went very well with Tony's second passion (after football)—food—which he writes about for a living. The evening was to be an interesting mix of good food provided with an insight into the history of the dishes.

The meal was an experience in traditional dishes like *Tortellini di zucca alla Montovana* (sweet pumpkin tortellini), *Anatroccolo al forno con aceto e miele* (roast duckling with honey and vinegar) and *Capretto di latte al forno* (slow-cooked milk-fed goat). A good evening was had by all.

Leaving the restaurant, we encountered dozens of young girls walking along the road in revealing dresses and showing a disconcerting abundance of stockings and garter belts. Tony, sensing my confusion, told me that one of the main industries of the region was pantyhose manufacturing, and that the girls were on their way to the biggest disco in Europe, which was close by, and were promoting the local fashion.

We parted from our generous hosts of the day. The next morning it was time to leave Lombardy and head towards our next destinations: the cities of Verona and Venice in the Veneto region, one of the most historically powerful and gastronomically diverse regions of northern Italy.

FRIENDS OLD AND NEW

*O*ur *original destination in Verona was to have been the* Possessioni di Serègo Alighieri. This historical estate, located outside the city and surrounded by vineyards and orchards, was where Dante's first son, Pietro Alighieri, lived in the fourteenth century. The Possessioni house and estate is currently owned by Count Pieralvise Serègo Alighieri, a direct descendant of Dante. Like the past twenty generations of the family, he still lives in the original house.

On our visit to this famous house we found it to be fully occupied by a group of Australian students under the tutelage of Joanne Weir, a friend of mine and an author and chef consultant based in California who has a keen Australian following. Joanne's group was in Veneto on a week-long study trip to learn about the products of the region and its food and wine traditions. So Yvette and I stayed nearby in one of my favourite Italian cities, Verona. We would be seeing Joanne that same evening to join her in watching Gabriele Ferron cook for the visiting group of Australians. But first we had a rice mill to visit.

Many years ago I made a great friend in Gabriele Ferron when he visited Sydney for a promotion at the time of the growing popularity of risotto. Gabriele comes from a long line of rice millers situated at Isola della Scala, a small agricultural village south of Verona. The rice mill where Gabriele lives has been in the family for generations, making him a great spokesman for the unique rice that is grown and milled in this region.

Rice has its origins in Asia. The Persians and Mesopotamians came into contact with rice from China around the fifth century BC. It then reached Syria and Egypt in the third century, whence it eventually crossed the Mediterranean Sea to Spain. It took until the thirteenth century, however, before the Visconti Dukes of Milan, a powerful and wise family, took a personal interest in the growing of rice. The real pioneers, following the attempt by the Dukes, were their successors, Galeazzo Sforza and his brother Ludovico Moro, who brought rice to what was to become the most prolific rice-growing region of Europe: the Po Delta.

The rice produced in Italy is of the short-grain variety. In recent times cross-breeding has made the rice more resistant to rot, and the shortening of the stems has reduced the tendency of the rice to bend over once the grain begins to form, which can lead to spoilage by moisture absorption and increased risk of pest infestation. Rice harvests in many locations can be achieved several times a year. The stalks can grow to one metre (around three and a half feet) and will have six stamens and a solitary pistil. The fruit, produced at the top of the stalk, is a grain, not dissimilar to oats in that it is surrounded by a brown husk and has a layer of bran enclosing the white endosperm rice.

The ancient Pila Vecia, the rice mill at Isola della Scala, was built in 1656. Gabriele's father is considered the guardian of the mill, which is still operated by a giant paddlewheel moved by the waters of the Zenobia Canal that run directly underneath.

Gabriele is like a brother to me; we do not see each other often but his love of Australia and my love of Italy make our mutual visits a gastronomic delight. It was with eagerness, therefore, that I made my way from Verona to visit him. Yvette too was keen to meet this talented, knowledgeable and good-looking man once again.

As we approached the Pila Vecia by car, tall corn fields and green pastures provided a perfect frame for the small family mill. The land was flat, fertile and crisscrossed by irrigation canals that have flowed for centuries. We arrived at Isola Della Scala and noticed that the old mill, which we had visited two years ago, had a new skin of plastered cement on the outside. Gabriele was there and what a joy it was to see him again. He was thrilled to see Yvette and me.

Gabriele was wearing his chef's uniform. He had just captured some carp from a tank beside the canal and was in the process of filleting them—observed closely by a one-eyed cat—to serve as deep-fried *goujonettes* (polenta-crumbed fish fritters) for the Australian group that night. This regional dish was sure to be appreciated for its flavour and freshness.

These days, few parts of the original mill remain, except the very old *pila*, the pink granite hub where the water-driven arms pound the rice to remove the husk and skin and thus produce the grain so prized by the local Veronese. Gabriele disappeared to complete some preparations for the dinner, and while he was gone his father, Maurizio, who had just finished a batch at the Pila Vecia, showed me and Yvette the next stage of preparation. The rice was scooped out of the granite hub and put into a large circular sieve to remove the powdered husk and bran that had been produced by the pounding. The rice grain, being harder, had survived intact and attained a smooth, clean appearance; it was now ready to be bagged into the distinctive Ferron packaging in the tiny room near the paddlewheel chamber.

Gabriele returned to show us his pride and joy. The last time I was here he had talked about building a restaurant on the property. Now his dream had been realised. We walked up to the top floor of the new structure, built next to the mill in the same architectural style, and entered the dining room which had been built on a scale to accommodate the large groups of guests who come to study the rice growing of Verona. If the building was his pride, the kitchen was his joy. Gabriele had been dreaming of this kitchen for years. That night he would be able to show off his talent with the perfect operation of gleaming stainless-steel gas cookers.

Risotto is very popular in Lombardy and around Verona, where it is sometimes cooked in a unique way. The absorption of a slowly simmering stock is the more common method, but Gabriele's way, which is typical of the area, involves cooking the rice in an oven after stirring in its flavouring ingredients. Gabriele explained to me that the traditional way to make risotto by this method is to start cooking the rice on a fire and then to cover the pot, wrap it in an old potato cloth bag and allow it to continue cooking on its own. In the old days, ovens were not so common in houses, so after the village baker had finished baking, the housewives would load his oven with their pots, leaving their dishes to stew there slowly; thus cooking the rice in the pilaf way became a regional technique.

That night Gabriele would be preparing several risottos and rice dishes for his guests: tiny olive-shaped rice balls, deep-fried and flavoured with an olive paste; fingers of fresh carp, crumbed in polenta and shallow-fried in olive oil; rice and vegetable salad; rice with veal and spices, heavily scented with cinnamon; and another unusual rice dish for dessert, a strawberry risotto.

The last time I visited Verona, Gabriele took me to a special regional dinner and served me a banquet of twelve courses, all based on the rice of the region. I can still remember the difficulty I had at the sixth course, knowing we were only halfway through the meal. I reminded Gabriele of that famous dinner and he laughed. I am sure he learned a lesson that night: do not overload your guests or the subtlety and finesse of your dishes will be lost on them.

Joanne Weir arrived with her group of enthusiastic gourmets and, after introductions had been made, Gabriele started his dazzling display of cooking, teaching and guiding the students with great laughter. On an occasion like this it was apparent to me that the language of cooking does not need words so much as a palate to enjoy great food. The night was still young when Yvette and I departed, leaving a group of gourmets to enjoy the talents of a great friend.

That night we were to eat in one of Verona's most rustic restaurants, Bottega del Vino. Established in 1890 in the central quarter on via Scudo Di Francia, the restaurant specialises in traditional dishes of the area and, in particular, the light white polenta dishes so central to Verona's culinary culture.

The food of Verona is heavily influenced by Venice. Many Venetian products have made their way into its cuisine, like the *baccalà* (dried cod) and the famous *fegato di vitello* (veal liver), but the cuisine of the surrounding area of Verona is still based heavily on risotto and very little on pasta. Polenta is now a great staple and an integral part of *Cucina Povera*, and there are many dishes that make use of this poor-man's food. Radicchio is also found in many forms in the region and there are even restaurants totally dedicated to the preparation of this Italian variety of chicory. There are many types of radicchio, ranging from the round, tight Di Chioggia radicchio to the long and elegant La Trevisana with its wiry red and green leaves.

I was reminded of an unusual dish I sometimes made back in Sydney—braised lamb shanks with soft polenta and radicchio braised in a white wine and cream sauce. It occurred to me how appropriate this dish was to the Veneto region, using, as it did, two of its favourite ingredients: radicchio and polenta.

Braised Lamb Shanks with Soft Polenta and Radicchio

For the lamb:
   100 ml (3 fl oz) olive oil
   8 lamb shanks, chined
   salt and pepper
   1 carrot, peeled and diced
   1 onion, peeled and diced
   1 stalk celery, diced
   2 cloves garlic, crushed
   thyme, bay leaf, rosemary
   250 ml (8 fl oz) red wine, reduced by half
   500 ml (16 fl oz) water
   250 ml (8 fl oz) lamb or veal stock

Heat half of the olive oil in a frying pan and brown the lamb shanks. Season and transfer to heavy pan with a close-fitting lid.

In the frying pan add remaining olive oil and sauté the vegetables and garlic until they soften (5 minutes). Add herbs and sweat for an extra minute. Sprinkle over lamb and cover with reduced red wine, water and stock. Bring to a simmer, cover and braise for 12 hours at 130°C (260°F). Remove the shanks and clean off the herbs and vegetables. Strain the sauce and reduce in a clean pot until you achieve a rich sauce, not too thick. Put aside.

For the soft polenta:
50 g (2 oz) butter
1 onion, very finely chopped
1½ L (3 pints) chicken stock
250 g (9 oz) polenta
salt and pepper
100 ml (3 fl oz) olive oil (optional)
50 g (2 oz) Parmesan cheese
50 g (2 oz) cold butter, extra

Melt the butter and cook onion on low heat until very soft but without colour. Add chicken stock and bring to the boil. Add polenta and mix well. Cook for 30 minutes, stirring continuously until smooth and thick. Taste and season as required. (Most polenta has natural salt flavour.)

Finish with olive oil for added flavour and add Parmesan cheese and butter for more richness.

For the braised radicchio:
4 heads radicchio
50 ml (1½ fl oz) olive oil
200 ml (7 fl oz) white wine
100 ml (3 oz) cream
salt and pepper

Remove outer leaves of radicchio, leaving the full firm middle. Trim and clean, then cut into quarters with the core attached. Heat oil in a frying pan then add radicchio and fry until golden brown. Add white wine and cream, season with salt and pepper. Reduce cream and wine with the radicchio by simmering until consistency is thick and radicchio is cooked.

To assemble:

Remove the shanks from the oven and allow to rest. Serve on soft polenta with braised radicchio and sauce drizzled around.

Alternatively, serve your lamb shanks with rustic potatoes, such as Pink Fir or Patrone, which have been peeled, drizzled with olive oil, garlic and rosemary then roasted. Or serve with creamy potato purée infused with garlic.

(Serves 4 as a main)

That night at Bottega del Vino I ordered a very good Veneto wine, a Cresco from Bolla 1986. The restaurant staff evidently prided themselves on their wine service, as the way they opened the bottle was as unique as it was skilful. First they made a small, round incision in the lead cover and then shaped it in such a way as to support the removed cork on the neck of the bottle. It was a nice touch.

Another fascinating attraction at the restaurant was the glassware. Manufactured in Slovenia by Severino Barzan, this glassware had been specially designed for the restaurant. For red wines there were enormous glasses like flower vases, each of which could easily have fitted two bottles of wine! The *sommelier,*

Antonoli Maurizio, poured a small amount of wine into the gigantic glass, tilted it over the second glass, slowly rotated it and gently poured the contents into the other glass. After a good swirling he inhaled the wine vapours and then, with a satisfied look, poured another quantity into each glass and swirled them to release their aroma. The only thing left to do was to sample the wine—without hitting yourself in the forehead or damaging your teeth. Once our self-consciousness disappeared and we got used to the feel of the oversized glasses, they were a joy to use.

The menu was a recitation of *piatto tipico*, or traditional dishes, which included *Pasta e fasoi* (bean soup), *Risotto al tastasal* (risotto with sausage), *Porcini trifolati con scaglie di vezzena e polenta* (truffled mushroom, Vezzena cheese and polenta) and *Pastissada de caval* (horsemeat stew with onion and amarone wine). I selected *Antipasto dell bottega*, which consisted of polenta squares topped with Gorgonzola, speck and salami. It was both tasty and filling.

I could not resist another classic, *Risotto all'amarone*, a rich, deep-red risotto with Parmesan cheese, served fairly dry. I finished my meal with a *Luganeghe e fasoi*, a small pork sausage braised with a thick bean sauce served with a very neutral soft polenta.

We had the privilege of visiting the cellar of the restaurant. The only apparent deficiency of this cellar was a lack of space. The ancient room was crammed with bottles and it looked as if it would be extremely difficult for anyone to locate a specific wine. Still, in that magical Italian way, the staff managed to find exactly what they wanted out of the chaos.

We rose early the following morning to meet with Dr Roberto Corradi, the representative of Serègo Alighieri. Before he retired, Roberto handled many posts all over the world for the airline

Alitalia. His experience in accounting, administration and marketing made him an ideal person to revive the fortunes of the old farm estates of Possessioni di Serègo Alighieri.

After being shown some of the sights of Verona by Roberto, and breakfasting on *panini* with mortadella, we drove north to the Valpolicella zone. On each side of the road were vineyards with tall wine trellises used for the red grapes of Valpolicella, like the Corvina Veronese, Rondinella and dry Molinara grape. The trellises are set high due to the low-lying humidity of the valley. Roberto explained to us that we were to have lunch with Dottore Sandro Boscaini, the president of the wine company Masi, which has been in the hands of the Boscaini family since the end of the eighteenth century. Dr Boscaini's expertise has resulted in an association with Count Pieralvise Serègo Alighieri, whom he helps to run his large agricultural estate.

We drove directly to Possessioni di Serègo Alighieri. Joanne Weir's group of Australians were performing their duties in the kitchen of the old Casal dei Ronchi. The room was filled with budding chefs and observers, happy to watch the more dextrous students performing the tasks set by Joanne. The conviviality of the Australians made my tour of the kitchen a joy, seeing the happiness created by a group of foodies.

Roberto showed me around the property. There were fruit trees everywhere: peach and cherry trees surrounded olive groves where the Leccino, Grignano, Frantoio and Casaliva varieties are grown. Around these was the vineyard. The estate still has its own vinification facilities, as well as an ageing room where the great Amarone and Recioto are laid down.

Just to ensure I had my daily dose of wine tasting, we made our way to the public cellar in one of the branches of the estate. There we tasted several wines from Serègo Alighieri. We started with a Serègo Alighieri Bianco, made in a modern manner with the traditional Gargagnega grape and Sauvignon Blanc, which comes from the southern part of the estate near the Adige River. It was a simple white wine and rather rare in this red-dominated Valpolicella region. Before we moved to the classics, we sampled the Masi which, like the Soave, is made nearly entirely of Gargagnega with a small touch of Trebbiano di Soave. Then to the more robust Bardolino Classico, made of the same grape as the Valpolicella but coming from the Zona Storica, near Lake Garda. We then ventured on to the Valpolicella Classico Superiore, a wine full of complexity that would be well matched with many dishes.

We finished with two wines, the famous Amarone and the Recioto. The Amarone is a very full, fat dry wine with no residual sugar. The making of it is an act of love. In late September or early October a group of master pickers go into the hilly vineyards with small wooden boxes and select the best clusters of grapes. These clusters are cut by hand and are laid in the boxes so as to not bruise the grapes. After transportation to the drying shed they are further examined by another group of workers, who will remove with scissors any grapes that are bruised or rotten. The perfect grapes are placed on large wooden trays and are taken to the drying shed where they are stacked on slatted platforms. There they will spend the next few months, during which time they will develop botrytis, or noble rot. By January they will weigh 25 to 40 per cent less than their original weight and will have gained a higher sugar content.

In mid-January the dried grapes are pressed, the stems removed and the juice fermented for forty days at low ambient temperatures. The wine is then put into old barrels for further ageing. Here the distinction between the Amarone and Recioto is made: while the Amarone will have a second fermentation in the large barrels, where it will be kept for up to five years before being filtered and bottled for further ageing, the Recioto will be put instead into small barrels and maintained at a low temperature to prevent a second fermentation, thus retaining a higher sugar content.

The last wine we tasted was unique to the Masi stable: the Campofiorin. It is a wine made according to the principles of a very old and almost forgotten method: a single vineyard wine of the Valpolicella Classico or Cru will be laid on top of the lees or sediments left in the cask of the Recioto or Amarone wine, which will cause a second fermentation and will increase its alcohol content by about two degrees. This gives the wine more structure, tannin and aroma. Once the fermentation is finished it will be transferred into smaller barrels for a further three to four years of ageing.

As if this tasting were not enough, we departed to join Dr Sandro Boscaini for lunch at Trattoria Due Archi in the tiny village of Gargagnano di Valpolicella, where we enjoyed a simple meal of salad and a *pappardelle* (a long flat pasta noodle) with horsemeat stew. This meal was imbued with the characteristic flavours of this classic region of the Veneto.

By this stage in our trip Yvette and I had tasted countless meals, drunk limitless bottles of wine and travelled many hundreds of kilometres in our hired car. We had been privileged to see, taste and experience things that few visitors to foreign countries have the opportunity to enjoy. There hadn't been a moment that we hadn't appreciated. All the same, we were starting to feel tired.

It was with a sense of keen anticipation, then, that we looked forward to arriving in Venice, where we would temporarily abandon our car and enter the serene haven of the Cipriani Hotel on the island of Guidecca. True, we would probably not be spared further feasts of food and wine, urged upon us by people whose hospitality seemed boundless, but at least we would be able to enjoy some time away from the hustle-bustle of mainland Italy. Venice offered itself as a haven, remote from the headlong haste of life. For a short time we would swap the fast lane for a place of timeless tranquillity.

INTERLUDE

*I*n *every lifetime a pilgrimage to Venice is a must. This was my* first visit to this mystical city and I was enraptured.

When the water taxi pulled in at the quayside of the private pier of the Cipriani Hotel, a dockmaster was there to receive us and see us safely onto this enchanted island. The short walk to the hotel, past manicured and colourful gardens, was a relaxing introduction to the days ahead. The hotel lobby, like its concierge, was grand but not intimidating, seeming less like a hotel than part of an old house—which indeed the Cipriani was until the hotel's construction in the late 1950s.

Giuseppe Cipriani, a restaurateur, established the Cipriani. As the founder of Harry's Bar on San Marco and Giudecca Island, he was a man of great ability. Cipriani dreamt of building a hotel in Venice and in 1956 he found three willing partners in the three daughters of the second Earl of Iveagh (head of the Guinness family): Viscountess Boyd of Merton, Lady Honour Svejdar and Lady Bridgit Ness. Not surprisingly, Giuseppe had a site in mind and very rapidly the hotel was built on the three-acre plot located at the tip of the island of Giudecca.

We were taken to our suite. It was large but still managed to have a cosy feel, and the decor looked as if it belonged to a past era. Its pretty balcony offered a view over the gardens of the Cipriani and the Laguna Veneta toward the long, thin island of

Lido, where the famous Palace Hotel was built in the late nineteenth century and which became one of Europe's most stylish seaside resorts.

After arranging our belongings we had a glass of Prosecco—a sparkling wine from Veneto—to celebrate our arrival in the magical city. I then met Natale Rusconi, the managing director of the Cipriani since 1977, at the Pool Bar. He invited us to have dinner that night with his assistant, Giulio Gentile, so we could sample the famous cuisine of the Cipriani.

Typical of Europe, the evening dress code offered the chance for the ladies to wear their best apparel, which certainly contributed to the sophisticated feel of the evening. We descended to the splendid bar off the San Giorgio dining room and met Giulio, an extremely urbane and worldly man. A facial scar lent him the air of a powerful Venetian sea captain, or perhaps, even, a Saracen pirate. Giulio was a mine of information about Italy and all things Italian.

We were soon joined by other dinner companions: Noelle Sonnenfield and her husband, Dr Albert Sonnenfield. They owned houses in Los Angeles and Paris, were multilingual and had an enormous knowledge of food and wine. Albert is a director of the American Institute of Food and Wine, and Noelle is a writer. She had just completed the biography of Julia Child, one of the legends of American cuisine. Every year Julia returns to the Cipriani to help produce the wonderful cooking classes that are now a feature of the hotel. The classes are held in autumn and have featured chefs like Marcella Hazan and other food ambassadors.

We were to dine in the formal dining room, renowned for its splendid Venetian glass chandeliers, its freshly cut flower displays, its Fortuny curtains and the polished service of its experienced staff.

After ordering our meal I went to the kitchens to meet Renato Piccolotto, the *chef di cucina*. Renato was fortunate in that his kitchen had been completely renovated in recent months and he was equipped with a brand-new range of stoves and cooktops, plus other modern equipment of the highest quality. We talked quickly, as the service was due to begin, and organised a rendezvous for the next morning to visit the Rialto Market.

Our selection from the menu was served. A *Carpaccio classico con salsa Cipriani* (a sliced raw beef dish with a Cipriani sauce) was all that it promised to be. A *Brodetto di pesce in crosta* was an enhanced version of the classic Venetian fish soup, but here it was topped with a puff pastry crust—à la Paul Bocuse—to capture all the seafood and saffron aroma. One appetiser we selected was a dish that had won a European competition for the best fish dish in Europe. It was a sardine and potato tart with pine nuts and raisins that expressed, by mixing sweet and sour ingredients, the allure and style of Venice.

We selected a sampling of three pastas: *Trofiette fresche con capesante vongole veraci ed asparagi* (a tiny swirl of handmade pasta tossed with scallops, harbour clams and asparagus); a *Bavettine con scampi al pomodoro ed erbe aromatiche* (tossed shelled scampi with a rough tomato sauce and aromatic herbs); and a *Pennette padellate al ragù bianco e fave* (a ragoût of white veal with dry wine and fresh broad beans with tiny penne pasta). For a sampling, the quantity of pasta proved to be more than we desired, but so classic and delicious were the flavours that we devoured all of the dishes.

Our main course provided a variety of tastes, like the extremely fresh *Trancio di rombo al limone e capperi* (a seared steak of Adriatic turbot, its white flesh enhanced by a sauce of lemon, capers and butter). Albert and myself were still willing to indulge ourselves by ordering a course of *Fegato di vitello alla veneziana con crostoni di polenta bianca*, which is the classic Venetian dish of sautéed calves' liver with onions, served with a slice of firm white polenta, brushed with butter and grilled to make the outside crisp. Giulio had selected an Arneis 1996 Ceretto Blange, a smooth and fruity Piedmont wine, to enjoy with our meal.

We eventually retired to the bar, where Yvette was brave enough to follow the barman's recommendation of a foul-smelling but supposedly therapeutic digestive, Fernet Branca, which she sipped slowly, hoping it would have the desired effect. That night the occasional cigar was appropriate and a slow dance in the Seagull Piano Bar made the atmosphere a blend of old-world sophistication and romance.

Early the next morning Yvette and I met Renato, as arranged, for a visit to the markets. He crossed the lagoon and moored the boat at the deserted piazza San Marco. We immediately negotiated the maze of small streets, crossing tiny bridges which, in the past, belonged to private owners who charged for the privilege of using them.

We made our way to the Erberia, the fresh fruit and vegetable market. Here produce was being transferred from the large floating barges that come from the market gardens on the islands of Sant' Erasmo and Le Vignole. Perfect colourful peppers were on display, along with asparagus, red radicchio from Treviso, squash, beans, wild strawberries, peaches, plums, rocket and artichokes.

We walked to the Campo della Pescheria, the piazza where a multitude of foodsellers ply their wares. We then went to the Pescheria itself, a mock-Gothic market hall where merchants and fishmongers conduct their businesses. I saw the smallest live crabs I could ever imagine. Also for sale were small baby shark, rouget, John Dory, sea snails, swordfish and fresh turbot of the Adriatic.

Next we made for the Ruga di Speziali, where we stopped at Bacari for a coffee, then visited Giacomin Vincenzo, Renato's butcher, where we saw beef tongue, smoked beef, pork cheek, prosciutto, salami, fresh liver and great quarters of beef ageing on the hook in his coldroom.

The morning was now advanced and shops were opening everywhere. We stopped at Jesurum, one of the most beautiful shops for table linen, where an extremely tempting array of serviettes was on display, but even more impressively the coloured linen tablecloths that my heart longed for but my pocket refused to buy.

We parted from Renato and wandered the piazza San Marco, an incredibly beautiful space. Cafés and shops selling the famous silk and lace of the region, as well as exquisite jewellery, lined the elegant square. I came across Florian's, the past haunt of nineteenth-century literary writers like Byron, Dickens and Proust.

After a day's sightseeing we headed off to our dinner destination, Da Ivo. We manoeuvred down the narrow streets of San Marco, trying to remember the concierge's instructions about how many turns to take and which they were. Ristorante Da Ivo was supposed to be less of a tourist haunt than most others—a difficult reputation to maintain when at any time the tourist population can render the Venetians almost invisible. We arrived, having walked in light drizzle. The restaurant was warm, rustic and already buzzing with hungry diners. Our table had a view of the rising water of the tiny Rio Fuseri canal, where gondoliers were sheltering from the increasingly heavy rain. The chef/owner saw us to our table. He was a charming man in his sixties, and though he must have witnessed it for many years he still seemed slightly taken aback by the influx of summer tourists.

Unfortunately, less prepared diners than ourselves kept entering the restaurant, hoping for a meal, but without a reservation nothing could be done and they were turned away, back into the pouring rain.

I ordered a perfect Bolla Soave Classico 1996, to be followed by a Monfalleto Barolo 1993. Then we chose from the menu board. Yvette ordered an *Insalata di gamberoni e fagole,* a typical Venetian salad of red kidney beans mixed with finely chopped mâche lettuce, sliced raw leek and freshly boiled scampi tail and served with a small dish of white polenta. I selected a braised whole baby octopus with tomato, basil and celery. It was left whole and served with a side dish of soft polenta. We followed with a small serving of the speciality of the house: a penne pasta with a sauce made of eggplant, pepper, onion, tomato, basil, olives and capers.

To finish the wine I selected another special dish, a char-grilled sea bass cooked on the charcoal of olive-tree twigs. Da Ivo is reputed to be the only restaurant in Venice to have such an open fire on which to cook its food. The danger of fire has always been great in Venice and it is probably for this reason that all glassmakers were banished to Murano island. But somehow the grill at Da Ivo escaped this fate. The fish was everything that could have been expected from such a cooking method. It was crisp on the outside but still moist on the inside, and was delicious served with sea salt and olive oil.

I followed the white wine with a great Barolo, a perfect *Osso Bucco* and another serving of polenta. On seeing my enjoyment of the wine and the food, the chef offered me a unique cheese. It was a black-truffle-scented Pecorino served with some firm pears, and I was delighted by his generosity.

Through the night mist I could see a dark and menacing gondola, draped to protect its occupant against the rain. The gondolier was almost invisible underneath his broadbrimmed hat, and I had a vision of Casanova escaping from the Doge's prison. Such is the power of illusion that Venice exercises on its visitors.

From the Veneto we had to cross Emilia-Romagna to reach Tuscany. We crossed the River Po to leave the Veneto and found the richness of the soil amazing. Skirting the town of Bologna we headed towards Modena, having been passed on the *autostrada* by a continuous parade of Ferraris (their factory, I discovered, was nearby). Our plan was to stop in that city to see the ageing rooms of the famous *aceto balsamico*.

Like most producers of balsamic vinegar, the Malpighi family produces vinegar more in the way of a cottage industry than on a commercial scale. Many producers have had their cellars full of ageing *balsamico* for many generations, primarily for their private consumption, but the popularity of the product has enticed some families to open their stocks to the ever-eager public.

The Trebbiano grape that is grown around the area is the only grape that can be used to produce the *vero balsamo* or true balsam. This syrupy concentrated liqueur used to be consumed after meals as a sort of cordial and was prescribed by doctors as a cure for many ailments.

To make balsamic vinegar, the Trebbiano, the classic grape of Modena, is pressed and its must is slowly cooked in open vessels until it is reduced to one third of its original volume. The concentrated juice is then rested in a series of casks of decreasing size that will be subjected over the years to the heat of the attic cellar and the rigours of the winter. The vinegar will spend years acidifying, ripening and ageing, and its contact with various woods like oak, mulberry, chestnut, cherry, and sometimes juniper, will impart to the vinegar its traditional characteristics.

Only after a minimum of twelve years can the vinegar be called *L'Aceto Balsamico Tradizionale di Modena*. It has to be examined and tested by a consortium appointed to monitor the quality of the product before being bottled in the approved tiny flask. The judging ensures the colour, perfume, flavour and perfect viscosity of the product. *L'Aceto Balsamico Tradizionale di Modena Extravecchio* is aged for over twenty-five years and is very expensive. Not surprisingly, it is used sparingly.

Massino Malpighi took us to the cellars located in his attic. Here the summer heat was slowly concentrating the nectar of the wine from the thirty-year-old root stock. He showed us the special juniper barrels that had been in use by his family for more than five generations. These barrels are a sort of national treasure in Italy and are protected by law. We tasted the rich reserve from the last tiny barrel. To taste this vinegar is to appreciate the fruits of time and the wisdom of man in the ageing of a product, especially in a world moving so fast outside the great iron doors of the Malpighi estate. Our understanding of 'true balsam' now made us realise that the inferior balsamic vinegar on the market is a poor imitation sold on a large scale with no regard to the old tradition of Modena.

If you can afford real *aceto balsamico*, try it with a fondue of small vegetables for a powerful taste sensation. If you can't afford the real thing, don't worry. So long as you use a balsamic vinegar that is at least five years old, you'll still be surprised by the slightly sweet, caramel taste of the vinegar.

Vegetable Fondue

100 ml (3 fl oz) virgin olive oil

4 cloves garlic, peeled

2 large prepared globe artichoke hearts, cut in 4 and dipped in lemon juice

4 cocktail onions, outer leaves peeled

4 small red onions

4 French shallots, peeled

8 tiny potatoes, washed

4 very young leeks, green portion and root trimmed

1 small fennel bulb, trimmed of outer leaves and quartered

4 young carrots, peeled or scrubbed

2 hearts of celery, trimmed and cut in half

4 small red radishes

4 small turnips, peeled

4 green baby zucchini

4 yellow baby zucchini

8 asparagus tips, trimmed

4 green baby beans, trimmed

500 g (16 oz) fresh young peas

80 g (3 oz) baby peas

50 ml (1½ fl oz) 5-year-old balsamic vinegar

1 handful fresh oregano leaves

100 g (3½ oz) cold butter, diced

40 g (1 oz) Fleur de Sel (French sea salt)

In a large copper or heavy-based pan, heat the olive oil over a very low heat. To confit the vegetables, add the garlic and the hard vegetables (artichokes, onions, potatoes, leeks, fennel and carrots). Cook, covered, over a low heat for 15 minutes.

Add the remaining vegetables, except peas, and cook for a further 10 minutes on low heat. Add peas, deglaze with the balsamic vinegar and remove from the heat. Add the oregano and cold butter and mix until butter glazes the vegetables. Sprinkle with Fleur de Sel salt and serve immediately.

(Serves 4 as a main)

THE RENAISSANCE CITY

My sense of direction proved useful while manoeuvring through the small roads of Florence to reach our hotel. However, although I'd thought I could reach the Grand Hotel Cavour on via Del Proconsolo all by myself, I had to resort to my mobile phone to call my friend Annie, who told me precisely how to find the place. The phone I had carried all the way through Europe finally proved useful.

Like most hotels in Florence, ours had no garage, so we had to leave our car at a local parking station. We arrived late in the afternoon and spent the next few hours unpacking and exploring our hotel. The hotel building dated back to the beginning of the millennium and was first a residential palace before it was converted into an abbey and then, in recent times, a hotel. The coat of arms of the Stiozzi-Ridolfi clan, carved in stone on the building's façade, impressed us with its stern beauty.

My great friend in Florence, Annie Feolde, owns, with her partner, Giorgio Pinchiorri, the outstanding Enoteca Ristorante Pinchiorri. It was just down the road from the hotel, which made it perfect for us to stroll there and spend the evening in the kitchen with them. I met Annie nearly ten years ago when she came to Sydney to cook her recipes for an admiring Australian public. To this day Annie has remained a special friend.

That night Yvette and I were received by Coco and Bandit, the

French poodles so much a part of Annie's life. After giving us the same priority treatment as all arriving guests, they led us to the back of the restaurant where Annie and Giorgio were briefing the waiters before the service started.

I was drawn to the newly renovated kitchen where the chefs were in full production mode. Here I was introduced to the *chef di cucina*, Italo Bassi, and the kitchen brigade. The brigade was a highly polished team with clear tasks for each section. The kitchen was set up in much the same way as a French kitchen, except that here an additional section was included for pasta. Interestingly enough, a young Japanese chef was in charge of the pasta production. He had come as a *stagiaire* (trainee) from Annie and Giorgio's other restaurant in Tokyo. Every year Annie travels to Japan to review the operation of this restaurant, which has received as much acclaim as the Florentine restaurant. Annie and Giorgio's love of the Orient in part explains why the restaurant is so progressive: it combines new flavours and techniques with a great respect for tradition.

I admired the handmade fresh pasta, set in its special light mesh wooden boxes and covered with damp cloths: ravioli, tortelli, spaghetti alla chitarra and the wonderful hand-shaped Trofie pasta. The presence of a Japanese chef in charge of this section brought to my mind the debate about who invented pasta. Japan has quietly claimed the credit for making the first pasta and Italy has passionately asserted that it is responsible for this great dish worldwide. If Marco Polo were still alive, maybe he could provide an answer.

The pace of the service was at its peak. Giorgio and Annie kept darting into the kitchen to check on the progress of individual meals and to look after the personal requests of some regular guests. Giorgio's son and daughter were working in the restaurant, learning the complexities of wine service.

The menu at Enoteca Ristorante Pinchiorri is very large and includes a series of set menus: the individual *à la carte*, offering more than thirty dishes; the set *Menu di Mezzogiorno*, the special lunch menu consisting of the more serious Tuscan specialties; and the challenging nine-course *Gran Menu Degustazione*.

I watched as the service in the main part of the kitchen wound down while the pace in the dessert section increased. The superbly crafted peach and fig tarts and *petit fours* were a delight to see. The *sorbetto* (sorbet), the finishing touch for all the tables, was then served in a series of little sorbet cones, supported by exclusive handcrafted silver stands.

The other area that now went at full speed was the washing-up section. This is a hot section, full of steam and sweat. Here, not only are the delicate plates and glasses expected to be washed but also the hot and very dirty pots. I have always had a great respect for the *lavapiatti* (dishwashers). In most cases they work in these sections to support themselves while they are students. I clearly remember my time spent dishwashing in Canada and the hundreds of plates and mountains of pots we had to get through every night.

We finished the night sitting together for a light dinner around midnight when all the customers had departed and the courtyard had regained a timeless peacefulness.

Annie had organised for Yvette and myself to have lunch with Allegra Antinori, the daughter of Piero Antinori of the legendary family that has substantially lifted the standard of wine production over a large part of Tuscany and Umbria. We first walked the streets of central Florence, crossing the Arno River several times over the historic Ponte Vecchio, built in 1345. Our meanderings eventually led us to the Palazzo Antinori, which has been in the hands of the family since 1506, and where I directed myself to the reception desk to ask for Allegra. She greeted us graciously and showed us to the Cantinetta Antinori, which is situated in the building on the second floor and accessed via a narrow staircase. The restaurant was already full of people talking loudly in Italian and enjoying the simple Tuscan cuisine of the kitchen.

On Allegra's recommendation we ordered a *Tonnò di coniglio* (rabbit meat cooked with olive oil and herbs), *Bruschetta pomodoro e rucola* (grilled bread with tomato and garden rocket), and *Panzanella* (soaked bread salad with tomato, garlic, basil and onion). This was followed by *Paglia e fieno al tartufo* (green and white tagliatelle with truffle sauce), *Ortaggi al forno* (baked vegetables), and for Allegra, a simple *Insalata mista* (mixed green salad). Many of the foods on the menu were from the estate of the family and this simple, rustic and inexpensive food was perfectly in keeping with the philosophy of the Antinoris.

We strolled back to our hotel, passing through the Piazza della Signoria, where we admired Michelangelo's *David*, the Neptune fountain (1575) by Ammannati, and Cellini's *Perseus* (1554). In the middle of the square stood the equestrian statue of the Grand Duke Cosimo, a chilling image of the powerful man who brought all of Tuscany under his control in 1570.

Nearby was the famous Uffizi, the oldest art gallery in the world. The architect Vasari created a new building technique with reinforced iron to produce a long glass wall and a perfectly lit gallery that Francesco I decided to use to display the Medici art treasures.

That night we dined in a hilltop trattoria on the outskirts of Florence. The taxi drive through the narrow stone-lined streets made the journey an exercise in itself. Arriving at Omero, a restaurant situated at the back of an old grocery store, we found the ceiling festooned with drying hams and cheeses, the walls lined with prosciutto, and great salamis displayed on the counter.

Once seated we realised that the trattoria windows gave an impressive view over the valley of the Ema River. The restaurant was mostly full of locals. I ordered a bottle of Il Grigio da San Felice Riserva 1993, a great red wine that would complement the house speciality of *Bistecca alla Fiorentina*, the delicious steak from the Tuscan-bred Chianina cattle. We started with an *antipasto* plate of locally made salami and the prosciutto displayed in the shop with a *crostini* of chicken liver, spleen and capers, and another with a perfect artichoke purée. Yvette's marinated vegetable plate was perfectly cooked and offered artichokes, olives and a scattering of tiny wild mushrooms marinated in peppery virgin olive oil.

We spoke to the man sitting next to us and discovered that he came to the trattoria every night for dinner. He was an antiquarian and a writer and through him we learned that Galileo, the Renaissance astronomer, had died nearby. We were offered a *limoncello* (lemon liqueur) by our fascinating dinner neighbour, who proceeded to show us his ability to write backwards like Leonardo da Vinci. It was a fascinating meal, with stimulating company in wonderful surroundings. On the way out of the restaurant I purchased a bottle of virgin olive oil to give to Annie on our return to her restaurant that same night.

We arrived after midnight at Enoteca Ristorante Pinchiorri, where there were only a few remaining diners. Annie was appreciative of my purchase and we soon got into a discussion about the value of various olive oils. This turned into a fully-fledged olive oil tasting—at one in the morning!

Annie had received a few sample bottles of olive oil, and with mine to add to the selection we began to taste and compare. The Laudemio, produced high above sea level in Tuscany, was refined, fragrant and tasted of freshly cut grass; Il Chieco, my oil, was very mild and unfiltered with no pepper and was quite fresh; the Tenuta, a Sicilian oil, was very fruity and lively with a fiery kick but a sweet finish; Il Ronco was very powerful and almost overpowering due to its multiplicity of introduced flavours, including huge pepper and an aftertaste of raw sorrel; Ciachi, a fruity, complex oil with scented pear and a chilli spice flavour, remained with you for a while and then expressed a great nutty flavour; Fubbiano, which comes from Lucca in Tuscany, was a mild oil with hazelnut and sweet apple flavours, very light in pepper and quite sweet and oily on the lips; Il Corto, from Oreve in Chianti, was a herbaceous, fruity and fragrant oil with a short pepper but strong flower bouquet. We judged the Ciachi from Tuscany the best, and Annie revealed with a large smile that it was their house olive oil—a perfect choice, confirmed by a conscientious tasting between friends. We finished with a glass of Cervaro della Sala from Antinori to cut the fat from our mouths.

Yvette and I woke up a little late the following morning, somewhat exhausted from the previous night's tasting but very much looking forward to driving to the Chianti region. Annie was to be our guide for the day. We met her at our garage and drove off into the hills.

CHIANTI COUNTRY

We left the main road, travelling along a gravel road which wound through prolific vineyards and olive groves, and arrived at Badia a Passignano. Here we were met with the vision of an imposing monastery. Records show that a religious order was started here in the ninth century, and that in the eleventh century the Vallombrosian Benedictine order was founded here. This order specialised in viticulture and forestry. Over time it became so powerful that it came to own over a quarter of Tuscany. Galileo even came here to teach mathematics to the monks as the monastery became an important centre for theological, literary and scientific studies. Following the unification of Italy, the Italian government outlawed monastic orders and appropriated their properties. In 1987 Antinori purchased the property and, while keeping the surrounding land and the cellars of the monastery, donated the monastery back to the Vallombrosian order, reuniting the monks with their mother abbey for the first time in 121 years.

We were given access to the extensive renovated cellars, where the 2653 hectolitres (5837 gallons) of stainless steel fermenting tanks were situated. We went deeper under the abbey, where more than 2500 French oak barrels were filled with the wine from the finest clones of Sangiovese and a small amount of Canaiolo, Trebbiano and Malvasia. We barrel-tasted some wine which was on its way to fourteen months of barrel ageing. It showed all the harmony and elegance that has gained this single vineyard of Badia a Passignano the appellation of *Chianti Classico Riserva DOCG*. Next door in the small public tasting room we were able to sample a larger range of the wines and also the Pèppoli extra-virgin olive oil that came from the hand-picked, cold-pressed olives from another Antinori estate nearby. Combined with the olive trees of Badia, the Antinori family has a total of 7500 trees under its care for the production of olive oil.

We next headed towards Panzano in Chianti. Annie had heard of a butcher there who researched recipes of the past. She had purchased some local lamb from him and was eager to meet the man himself.

On arrival at Panzano we quickly found the butchery: L'Antica Macelleria-Cecchini. Loud opera music was bursting out of its doors. We entered and found ourselves in another world, the world of Dario, the successor of a long line of butchers—twenty-five generations of them, in fact. The shop was amazing, more like an eccentric private kitchen than a business place. Dario proved to be one of those eternally enthusiastic personalities, and he was happy to meet Annie and spend a little time explaining some of the products. In Italy sheep are mostly kept for the milk they supply for the production of Pecorino cheese; not much thought has been given to meat production. Most lamb found in restaurants actually comes from France. Annie was therefore happy to have found a reliable local supplier of the meat.

In a glass display in Dario's butchery was a superb piece of Chianina beef, which is prized for its T-bone and eaten at great cost in Florence. It was dressed and waiting for an eager and appreciative customer. Dario was inordinately proud of the beef as it came from his own herd.

Being in Chianti country, Dario made sure that everyone who walked into the shop had a couple of glasses of Chianti wine, poured from the traditional weaved *fiasco* that he had set out on an old butcher's block. The block was also loaded with tasty slices of homemade salami and traditional pork, prune and spinach terrine, along with some superb crusty bread. Hungry by this time, we enthusiastically plunged into a great tasting. On another block was an *Arista alla Fiorentina*, two roasted and rolled loins of pork stuffed with garlic and rosemary, the skin scored in a pretty lattice pattern and served cold for anyone to taste or purchase for home. It was moist and absolutely delicious on slices of Tuscan bread.

One whole wall in the shop was dressed with hanging prosciutto, drying *piedi di maiale* (pork fat for soup, dusted with rice flour and pepper), *salame* (cured sausage) as well as *coppa* and *pancetta*, thinly wrapped in cheesecloth, and great bundles of fiery chillies. When Dario heard that I came from Sydney he became quite excited and rang up some of his neighbours, also from Australia, and told them to come to the shop immediately. He wanted us to say hello. Dario probably did not realise that, unlike in the village of Panzano, not everyone in Sydney knows one another.

We sampled a *Crema di lardo*, a cream of lard that is worked with salt, herbs and vinegar on a butcher's block until it sets into the consistency of a French *rillettes*, but without the meat. It was delicious on bread, as long as we ignored the question of calories. We tasted the *Fegatelli Sott'olio*, a whole pork liver cooked like a *foie gras* and referred to in Italian as *Chianti Foie Gras*. Washed down with more wine, we tasted a *Lingua salmistrata* (a soft and fresh beef tongue salami), a *Tacchinella con pistachio* (turkey with orange peel and pistachio) and a superb dish of *Tonnò del Chianti*, a piece of fresh pork leg, cooked very slowly with white wine, olive oil, sea salt, prosciutto strips and one or two anchovy fillets. Once preserved for a few days in its cooking oil, the meat tastes uncannily like tuna, a fish now rare in the Mediterranean Sea. It was a very addictive alternative.

The Australians arrived and they were as surprised as we were to meet in this tiny hamlet. They had left Sydney's Maroubra Beach on their honeymoon to travel a little and, five years later, still hadn't returned. They listened with us to Dario, who was now in a full tirade against the establishment, which, he believed, was interested only in mass production. He felt that the large conglomerates were against the artisans and small growers, and colluded with the government in imposing laws restricting classic production methods in the name of a sterile and hygienic product.

On leaving, Dario gave me a jar of green-tinged powder; it read 'Profumo del Chianti', with recommendations to open it only if necessary and to breathe in 'for a sudden attack of nostalgia'. I breathed it in in the car, enjoying the fragrance of rosemary and wild thyme that somehow captured the essence of Chianti.

Since we were so keen to see Tuscany and its produce, Annie availed herself of the opportunity to visit some of her suppliers whom she'd previously not met. We made our way along the tiny road to San Pancrazio, where two brothers-in-law worked their family farm.

We first visited Tillo, who focused on cheese making, and saw his herd of sheep grazing at the side of the rocky road that led to the very old farmhouse. The peacefulness and gentle pace of life was immediately apparent; it was as though the hilly countryside had a way of absorbing your soul and returning you to the time when water was drawn from old wells like the ones in Tillo's courtyard. We walked next door to his *fattoria* where his prized cheeses were draining and ageing. We selected various cheeses to take to his brother-in-law, the winemaker. I observed that Tillo was willing to experiment and develop new cheeses as he went along. In an area so full of tradition it is nice to see members of the younger generation devoted to working in an innovative manner, without being imposed upon by the patriarch of the family.

We took our purchases to the house of Aljosoha, Tillo's brother-in-law, who lived on a nearby hill. It was cool and spacious and we installed ourselves on the balcony to prepare for a cheese and wine tasting. Annie was as keen as I was to sample those wonderful sheep-milk cheeses and the wine of Aljosoha.

We started with an Aglaia, a Chardonnay of the 1996 vintage. It was a very simple wine enhanced by a half-treatment in new oak barrels. Chianti is the land of the red and does not produce great quantities of white wine, apart from the white Trebbiano, and the fast-fading Malvasia grape that is mixed with the Sangiovese to produce the regulated wines of Chianti. With the Aglaia we tasted a simple sheep ricotta, hardly salted. We moved to a Terre di Corzano 1995, a Chianti whose fruitiness was enhanced by the initially cool but ultimately sunny 1995 summer. We tasted two cheeses with this: a Morbidone, a fresh unaged cheese set long enough in a ring to produce a great salad cheese that could easily absorb many flavours, like grilled pepper, rocket and a sprinkle of the family's own pressed virgin olive oil; and a Pecorino Fresco with a soft interior, mild flavour and perfect texture, the delicate crust of which displayed the light ageing it had received.

The next wine was in the style of the super Tuscans, made outside the DOCG dictates. In Aljosoha's case, he made a blend of half Sangiovese and half Cabernet Sauvignon, producing a robust and full wine that would easily refine with some ageing. We tasted the 1994 and 1993 vintages and I saw the improvement a year of age could make, though that could have been partially the effect of better growing conditions. These wines in Italy are simply put under the category of *Vino da Tavola,* or table wine, which, despite its modest name, is normally worth much more than some of the DOC and DOCG wine.

We kept the tastiest cheeses for last. The Buccia di Rospo (meaning 'toad skin', due to the appearance of its crust) was nice and creamy with a strong flavour and a spicy tongue. Its sharp finish made it a good combination with the 1993. The last cheese was a Blù, a crusty and heavy wheel of aged blue cheese, made with the Gorgonzola *penicillium glaucum.* It is produced in spring and we were sampling the first ready cheese; it had a sharp and quite pungent smell and a white creamy interior with pronounced blue-vein columns inside.

Annie, ever open to fresh ideas, was delighted by an idea I suggested for a fennel, capsicum and basil salad which would showcase this splendid cheese. She promised to try making it one day. The recipe I make back at home uses Gorgonzola and is perfectly delicious.

Gorgonzola, Fennel, Capsicum and Basil Salad

1 large bulb of fennel
50 ml (1½ fl oz) white wine vinegar
100 ml (3 fl oz) virgin olive oil
1 red capsicum
1 green capsicum
1 yellow capsicum

200 g (7 oz) Gorgonzola cheese
1 bunch basil, leaves only
salt and pepper

Trim the fennel, removing the green leaves and any bruised pieces. Cut in half from top to bottom then slice into 2 cm (1 in) wedges, ensuring the core holds the slices together. Drizzle with the vinegar, coating each side well, then season and pack tightly in a dish and drizzle with olive oil. Marinate overnight.

Grill the capsicums over a flame to scorch and blacken each side, or panfry in olive oil over a high heat. Place in a bowl and cover with plastic wrap to allow them to sweat and soften the skin. After 10 minutes, cut in half then remove the core and liquid. Trim into large pieces and peel the skins off with a knife.

With a clean knife that has been dipped in hot water, cut Gorgonzola into wedges, allowing 2 or 3 slices per person. Place on a small tray and refrigerate to allow them to become firm.

To assemble:
Put a slice of Gorgonzola on a plate. Stack with the marinated fennel then the capsicum, another cheese slice, basil leaves and fennel again. Drizzle with the marinating juices. Delicious served with a rocket salad and toasted crusty bread.

(Serves 4 as an entrée)

The visit to San Pancrazio provided us with a wealth of knowledge about the local produce. For Annie there was the added bonus of being able to discover a few new products that she could showcase at her tables at Enoteca Pinchiorri, where she insisted we were to dine officially that night. We returned via the fast main road that joins Siena to Florence, ready for a sleep and looking forward to dinner before our departure the next day to Vagliagi, a small town north of Siena. There we planned to visit a modern food and wine speciality producer.

We arrived at nine o'clock for dinner after a pleasant walk along the Arno River and across the Ponte Vecchio. Two glasses of Dom Pérignon arrived in tall elegant flutes, compliments of Annie and Giorgio, to refresh us while we made our selections from the classically designed menu.

After much consultation we selected a menu which started with a *Lamelle di orata con Mostarda di pera, insalata di campo e aceto balsamico tradizionale* (a sliced 'daurade' fish fillet, served with a pickled mustard fruit of pear, made by preserving the fruit in a spiced syrup, and served with tiny leaves of pickled wild lettuce), and a *Rombo avvolto nelle patate croccanti con crema di crescione* (turbot wrapped in thinly sliced potato and panfried to a crisp, served on a purée of young watercress). Both dishes showed a confidence in their simplicity, focussing on the quality of the main product rather than on a multitude of ingredients.

The next dishes were pasta ones, which traditionally follow *antipasto*. My choice was the classic *I gnudi*, a fantastic ricotta and spinach dumpling, served with gently simmered lobster and cockscomb fricassee, enhanced with a fondue of summer tomato. The combination of the slightly livery combs with the sweetness of the lobster and the delicate dumpling made the dish a delicious mix of flavours. Yvette chose a lighter dish, *Crema di pomodoro fresco, piccole verdure e ravioli al pesto, con pinali tostati*. This was a ravioli of wilted greens, garnished with a mixture of lightly cooked cauliflower, asparagus and young beans, with a barely warmed raw tomato soup, deliciously flavoured with basil, topping the succulent filled pasta. We were served a Fontallo from Fattoria Di Felsina, a highly rated 1990 white wine produced in the town of Castelnuovo Berardenga near Siena.

Annie, knowing that it had been a long day, suggested light dishes for the next course. I selected a *Rotolo di coniglio alle olive nere e scalogno, con purea di pomodori seccati al sole*, a boned, rolled saddle of farmed rabbit with a black olive and shallot stuffing, served with a sun-cured tomato purée that had beautiful sweetness without the bitterness of the commercial varieties. The rabbit retained plenty of moisture due to its gentle poaching. Annie suggested to Yvette the *Scampi con zucchine marinate al timo; tritto di fiori di zucca e zabaione ai crostacei*, a succulent, evenly seared scampi, served with steamed marinated zucchini, its flower deep-fried after being dipped in a light batter and smothered with a rich shellfish-infused *sabayon* made of an egg emulsion and white wine. Our wine, a Barbaresco 1988 Angelo Gaji, was one of the highest-rated reds from Piedmont. To my delight, the pervasive bouquet of the wine (for which it is appreciated) slowly became apparent.

At this point in the evening, Giorgio invited me to inspect the restaurant's cellar, which has been hailed by American and European wine magazines as one of the best in the world. To a visitor, the organisation and storage methods appeared haphazard, but Giorgio and his cellarmaster, Allessandro Tomberli, have devised a personal cataloguing system that works for them. The wines are arranged in a descending order of popularity, starting from the cellar door and retreating to the furthest nooks and crannies where the very precious wines are to be found. In a beautiful handcrafted cabinet stood a magnificent collection of Armagnac, some of it dating back to the nineteenth century.

The dessert wine room was amazing; the Château d'Yquem went back to 1893 and 1896. Other rooms revealed numbered full collections of Romanée Conti in increasing bottle size from half bottle to magnum, jeroboam, rehoboam, methuselah or imperial.

We walked past boxes of Pétrus, Krug, Ausone and complete collections of the artist series of Mouton-Rothschild, to see full boxes of Latour 1961, 1966, 1971 and 1978, along with stock of the great 1982 vintage of Mouton-Rothschild and Château Margaux. My only wish was that some of my wine-loving friends from back home, like David Clarke and Len Evans, could have been there to enjoy the sight of wine they had drunk over the years. They could have reminisced on their great attributes in my presence.

We returned to our table to sit with Annie and sample a final dish from the kitchen of Enoteca Ristorante Pinchiorri: a delicious *Biscotto friabile farcito di mousse alla banana*, a just-baked, delicate pie crust filled with a delicious banana mousse spiked with lemon.

The sad moment of the night had arrived for us now. It was time to farewell one of our best friends, Annie, the talented and glamorous Diva of Firenze.

Yvette and I woke up mid morning, having already packed the night before in preparation for moving on to another location. We were slowly drawing ourselves south towards our final destination: Rome. First, though, we wanted to visit Fattoria

Terrabianca at Vagliagi in the middle of the Chianti countryside, where some of the food products I use in Australia are produced and bottled. These include *Pomodori assiccati* (dried tomato), *Carciofi* (artichokes, used when fresh ones are not available), *Crema alle olive* (olive paste), and many other marinated vegetables, all useful for producing *antipasti*.

We arrived at the private house belonging to Swiss-born Roberto and Maja Guldener. It was located on a hill beside some gently sloping vineyards. Maja junior received us with the perfect poise of a Swiss girl but with the warmth of her adopted Italian custom. Roberto was busy organising the final details for the transfer of the old winery and kitchen to the brand new *fattoria* at the bottom of the valley floor—a considerable investment, but typical of the driven businessman and visionary that Roberto is—so young Maja invited us to sample some of her father's wine while we waited for him to appear. We tasted the traditional Vigna della Croce, a Chianti Classico Riserva DOCG, made of Sangiovese, Canaiolo and aged for fourteen months in Slovenian oak, and a Scassino, a Chianti Classico DOC. These were both extremely well-crafted wines with lineages that had produced great vintages. We also tasted the modern version of Roberto's wine, the *Vino da Tavola Rosso*, in a Campaccio made of 70 per cent Sangiovese and 30 per cent Cabernet. This wine had been bought by British Airways and was a rich-looking, plum-coloured wine with a pungent aroma of leather and cinnamon. It was smooth and complex and illustrated why Roberto's products are so sought after by overseas markets.

Roberto arrived home, greeted us and quickly sat down with us to review his product range. Back home in Australia I had noticed and admired the sharpness and modernity of Roberto's labelling and packaging. He explained that he had had an important business in the fashion industry before moving to Italy; this explained his love of sophisticated design.

We drove to our hotel for a quick rest and dinner at the small family trattoria next door with Maja and Roberto. We tasted more of the Terrabianca wines and listened to our new friends as they extolled the virtues of having established their winery and food factory in Tuscany rather than in either California or France. Roberto and Maja saw the potential demand for the great products of Italy, having observed the renewal of the popularity of Italian cuisine during their overseas travels. Chefs, shops and catering companies were clamouring for food speciality lines, and they had proved themselves up to the challenge of sourcing the best products of Italy and devising recipes and ideal packaging to fill this small but lucrative niche market.

The next morning we visited the food factory where Terrabianca Culinaria produce is created. We entered the brand-new kitchen to find the kitchen staff busy moving various products from the old factory. Crates of *sugo*, *salsa* and *crema* (various types of sauces), *olio* (oil) and *verdure* (vegetables) were readied for labelling and packaging into their elegant wrappers. The kitchen was like a high-tech sterile laboratory, so clean and new did the equipment look. Maja told me that the steamers and kettles were in fact a few years old—impressive evidence of fastidious cleanliness of the operation.

Italy is an ideal source for the best vegetables, spices, fruit and honey that Terrabianca Culinaria requires to create its high-quality products. Roberto and Maja source tomatoes from Apulia, mushrooms from Piedmont, basil from Liguria, small white onions from Emilia-Romagna, chilli from Calabria, olives from

Sicily and artichokes from Sardinia. Tuscany produces the exquisite virgin olive oils the company sells, as well as the fresh herbs that flavour them.

On the shelves of the factory I could see the bright packages of *Melanzane* (eggplant), *Peperoni Tartufati* (pepper with truffles), *Crema di funghi porcini* (cream of wild mushrooms), *Pate Lepre* (hare pâté), *Sugo pomodoro basilico* (tomato and basil sauce), *Salsa Verde* (spicy parsley sauce), *Fichi Caramellati* (caramelised figs) and *Miele alle Arance* (honey and orange)—wonderful lines of dozens of products so practical and loved in the modern Italian family home.

We were about to leave Tuscany to join Allegra Antinori at her retreat in Umbria. With a few free moments I reflected on the strong culinary traditions of this famous region we were departing. In a world made increasingly smaller by the ease of modern travel, it seemed amazing to me that one could still find such colourful displays of regionalism, even at the village level. The Tuscans' belief in their products and local traditions was clearly strong (I heard stories of whole villages avoiding contact with neighbouring ones for fear of culinary pollution!), and that, I decided, could only be good for the preservation of regional food and wine culture.

Maybe Australians could learn a little from these passionate people.

top left: Balconies at the Hotel Splendido, Portofino.

top right: The courtyard at the Four Seasons Hotel, Milan.

bottom: The tiny Giorgio's restaurant at San Fruttuoso.

top left: Tina Masuelli of Trattoria Masuelli San Marco, Milan.

top right: Tomato, lemon and oregano is a speciality of Lago di Como.

bottom: The mosaic wall at the Villa d'Este, Lake Como.

top left: Gabriel Ferron prepares his special risotto.

top right: Maurizio Ferron and his rice at Pila Vecia.

bottom: Nowadays machines brush and polish the Grano Padano cheeses as they mature in the ageing cellars.

above: Barges unloading produce on the Grand Canal, Venice.

top left: Dario preparing meat in the lively L'Antica Macelleria-Cecchini butchery in Panzano, Chianti.

top right: Annie Feolde, co-owner of Enoteca Ristorante Pinchiorri in Florence, and her *chef di cucina*, Italo.

bottom: Balsamic vinegar undergoing the long acidifying, ripening and ageing process.

top left: Gianfranco Vissani's kitchen at his restaurant on Lake Corbara.

top right and bottom: Pasta fresh from the extruder.

above: The tranquil courtyard of the Castello della Sala.

top left: Rome's famous public market at the Campo dei Fiori.

top right: Diane Seed at work in her apartment in Rome.

bottom: The beautiful Conero Peninsula.

LA DOLCE VITA

With its *vast expanses of undulating pastures and lonely mountainous* wilderness, Umbria seems to have been forgotten by the outside world for centuries. It has been populated since ancient times by the Umbrians, a farming tribe who began to establish settlements in the eighth century BC. Today it seems as though the area, after colonisation by the Etruscans, Romans and Lombards, has left the modern world behind and returned to the peaceful ways of those earlier times.

Driving south towards Lake Trasimeno, we passed the site of one of the worst defeats ever suffered by the Romans at the hands of Hannibal, the Carthaginian general. While Umbria has often served as a battlefield for other competing powers, in more recent times it has benefited from being mostly untouched by the massive tourist invasion that its northern neighbour, Tuscany, has suffered.

Allegra Antinori had given us fairly simple instructions to reach our destination, the Castello della Sala: 'Exit at Fabro, follow the winding road through to the small town of Ficulle, first right down the hill, second driveway on the right, and park there.' I readily followed her directions through the increasingly beautiful countryside, but upon entering the gravel road and seeing the building in front of us, had to doubt that I had taken the right turns. We had arrived not at any humble Umbrian house but at one of the most beautiful medieval forts in Italy. It perched more than 530 metres (1750 feet) above sea level on a dramatically steep road overlooking the Paglia River Valley. On checking my instructions I had to conclude that this was, in fact, to be our weekend address.

If someone had been observing us from the tall tower of this medieval castle they would have found the next scene very comical. Here we were, walking around the castle, trying to find the main entrance. I could see a few cars but no sign of life. Eventually I returned to the tiny door I had first spotted. (The primary purpose of a fortress, I later realised, was to keep people out, not to allow them in.) I knocked on the thick, spiked door, hoping that someone could hear me. The door opened and a pleasant lady welcomed us. She led us through a small corridor and past a beautiful chapel to an immense courtyard, filled with sunlight and blooming wisteria vines—such a lively contrast to the forbidding exterior.

Allegra came to greet us with a smile and a new puppy. She led us to our room, recounting the history of the Castello della Sala, from its construction in 1350 to its purchase by the Antinori family in 1940. We dropped our baggage in our charmingly refurbished room. That night a group of visiting wine representatives selling Antinori's wines were also to be accommodated in this historic building. Allegra took us to the refuge tower, the final stronghold if the castle was stormed. From the giddy heights of the ramparts we had a superb view over the valley and saw the plantations of Procanico or local Trebbiano, Grechetto, Verdelho, Drupeggio and Malvasia, which produces the Orvieto Classico, as well as the more modern and popular varieties like Chardonnay and Sauvignon Blanc.

The vineyards were originally planted with the traditional grapes of Umbria, primarily Procanico and Grechetto, but the Antinoris made measurable improvements over the years, changing from a rustic style of cultivation, which inhibited quality, to one which increased the fruit flavour at the expense of volume. Grass was planted between the rows to improve drainage and secure the soil against erosion, and new single-variety vineyards were planted to offer products more in line with today's tastes, like Chardonnay and Semillon.

Leaving the castle to explore the countryside, we drove along the valley amid the flourishing vineyards, studying the grafts of improved clones of Grechetto, a noble, thick-skinned, small, dark-yellow Umbrian grape. We followed a small private road into the forests of the property, where the famous Umbrian truffles grow. In late winter, bands of truffle hunters trek these same roads with their dogs, hunting for the inherent taste of Umbria.

To get from Castello della Sala to the town of Orvieto we had to negotiate the winding roads through the valley of the Chianti River. The hilltop city, which occupies the entire space on the 300-metre-high (980 feet) plateau, was an imposing sight.

We climbed the narrow streets in our car, up the steep hills that led to the summit of the town, where we left the car to explore the cobbled streets of the city on foot. The butchers of Umbria are famous throughout Italy, and we stopped at Dai Fratelli, a superb food shop with a fabulous window display, offering wild boar products as well as fresh summer truffles, pasta, spices and the famous lentils of Castelluccio. Colourful shops selling the traditional handpainted plates and bowls of this central region caught our eyes, as well as a plenitude of wine shops, some of them linked to underground caves carved from the tufa, the soft rock on which Orvieto is built. On Viale San Gallo we observed the most incredible antique well, built in 1527 by order of Pope Clement VII. This was designed in a double helix, each spiral permitting one-way traffic down or up, to and from its incredible depth. Built out of tufa stone blocks and bricks, the well at one time afforded a constant water supply to the town in case of siege or attack.

After viewing the massive Duomo of Orvieto with its amazing thirteenth-century facade, we returned in the late afternoon to join the wine-tasting group for dinner at Castello della Sala, cooked by the resident chef of the castle in the brand-new kitchen. After a small siesta, we met in the courtyard at dusk. Everyone was relaxed and in good spirits. We were served a very stylish Marchese Antinori Brut Millesimato 1991 with some simple *bruschetta*, drizzled with Pèppoli, the extra-virgin olive oil from the Antinori estate in Tuscany. The perfect weather, the setting, the company and the Spumante wine made for a superb start to the evening. We moved to the second floor and into a 300-year-old dining room. Its tiled floor, heavy wooden beams and white chalked walls represented the classic construction of the time. In the middle of this room was a huge antique table, simply set to emphasise the rustic qualities of the Umbrian way of life.

The first course came in a soup tureen which was passed around from guest to guest. It contained a thick potato and rosemary soup enhanced with diced pieces of mature goat cheese; it made a wonderful dish when sprinkled with crispy croutons and generously drizzled with olive oil. The thickness of the soup offered a perfect starter for a group of ravenous guests. A Castello della Sala Orvieto Classico DOC was the perfect accompanying wine, possessing a good structure with light refreshing fruit. We followed with another Umbrian dish of *Spezzatino di vitello alla salvia*, a simmered veal stew with garlic, herbs and tomato, reduced to a thick sauce. A Fattoria La Braccesca 1996 a Rosso di Montepulciano was served with the stew. This robust wine came from the southern part of Tuscany, the nearest classic red wine area to the Castello della Sala.

A selection of goat cheeses produced on the Antinori estate was then offered. One was flavoured with pepper, one with herbs and another was well aged. To challenge our palates Allegra served two wines with the cheese. She served another Montepulciano from La Braccesca, but this time it was a Vino Nobile di Montepulciano, a better wine than the previous red, its superiority achieved through longer barrel-ageing. It had a rich, amazingly concentrated collection of berry juices with soft tannin but a thick texture. The wine she particularly wanted to show us, and especially the Italian dealers and restaurateurs, was an Atlas Peak, Sangiovese 1994, produced on their estate in the Napa Valley and made with the typical grape of Chianti: Sangiovese. A lively discussion ensued in the typical Italian fashion, but no consensus could be reached as to which was the best wine.

We finished with a bowl of fresh fruit and one of the wines that the buyers wanted extra stock of: the late-picked Muffato della Sala. This rich and velvety dessert wine made of the Sauvignon Blanc, Grechetto, Traminer and Riesling grapes was very much a product of its environment: the morning mists of the area created '*Botrytis cinerea*', or noble rot, which concentrated the juice of the grapes and raised its sugar content. The wine was so fresh and drinkable that the only complaint raised about it by those at the table was that it would be difficult to procure sufficient stock. Fuelled by *grappa*, the evening became a delight. However, when conversations in slurred Italian became difficult to follow, we retired discreetly for the night.

After a farewell breakfast with the incomparable Allegra, we visited the renovated medieval cellars of the Castello, which were stacked with small French oak barrels for the production of Castello della Sala Orvieto Classico DOC, Sauvignon Blanc-based Borro della Sala and Chardonnay-based Cervaro della Sala dry white table wines. We then headed north-east, along the narrow country roads to Perugia, the capital of Umbria. The countryside of Umbria was like a 200-year-old canvas, depicting wheat fields, dense forests, hilltop villas, quiet villages and fortress towns.

We arrived in Perugia late in the morning and searched for the Hotel Brufani. Somehow I had assumed it would be located near the fortified town centre, on top of the hill. I was right. Eventually, after driving through the twisting, winding roads, which at times were lined by ramparts and straddled by large stone gates, I saw a sign directing us to our desired destination. We arrived on a busy piazza. On the hillside, the grand old hotel stood like a guardian of the past.

We were ushered into the immense Queen Victoria suite, the magnificent bedroom of which overlooked the steep hill of Perugia and the flat plains way below.

We quickly set out to explore Perugia's historic centre and soon discovered its incredible maze of medieval streets, partly covered by overhead bridges linking houses. The town centre winds around each side of the hilltop to create a web of alleyways, perhaps more beautiful today than in centuries past, with their weathered stone walls, thick wooden doors and mysterious narrow staircases leading to the dark corner dwellings.

In the city centre, the large corso Vannuci links the city from all directions, and at the top of the corso stands San Pietro, the tenth-century church rebuilt in the fifteenth century in extravagant style, with superb painting and carving and a breathtaking wooden choir decorated in striking gold. I walked the corso to face a most imposing building, the Palazzo dei Priori, Italy's finest public building, born out of the necessity to rival Siena in grandeur and opulence. This thirteenth-century building, decorated over the next two hundred years to depict the civil activities of the town, also housed the important guilds of the city. Today it houses the Galleria Nazionale dell'Umbria, where the town's most famous painters from the thirteenth to the eighteenth centuries are displayed, including works by Perugino, Luca Signorelli and Raphael.

In front of the Galleria on corso Vannucci is the famous shop of Sandri, established in 1860 by a Swiss baker. Today it represents all that is good in gastronomy in Umbria. Apart from the display of delicious-looking pastries, cakes, bread and cookies, the old rooms also serve as a simple *caffè*. Starving after our walk through the old town, we decided that this was a perfect place for us to have lunch.

The decor of Sandri could not have changed since the time of its inception. Apart from the new display fridges, everything seemed frozen in time. The walnut shelves were loaded with classic wines that, by now, would have been undrinkable but made for an impressive display. The vaulted ceiling and its subtly painted walls were untouched. We sat at the white marble counter and chose from a selection of hot food, displayed in a warm cabinet. The range boasted frittata, potato croquette, horse stew, baked garlic tomato, veal involtini stuffed with prosciutto, chicken breast with mushroom, schnitzel, veal parmigiano, bean and spinach stew and a fantastic long, thick pasta like a large finger filled with a veal stuffing and covered with a striking spinach sauce the colour of pesto. While we were eating, a steady stream of people came in to purchase the superb cakes, which were boxed in elegant red paper and tied with a gold ribbon. I myself couldn't resist a delicious pastry to finish my meal.

Feeling energetic after lunch and a walk, we headed off in our car towards Terni, in the south of Umbria, where we were to meet Maria Possenti, the producer of a wonderful Umbrian olive oil I purchase in Sydney. The trip on the *superstrada* took us within reach of two of Umbria's most famous towns: Assisi and Spoleto. Assisi is the Lourdes of Italy, full of nuns and monks, not to mention tourists. It is a city immortalised in the mind of Catholics, being the burial place of St Francis. Spoleto, the other famous town, is known not so much for its Umbrian origins or its Roman settlement but more for its famous Festival dei Due Mondi, the art festival held in June and July with days and nights full of such entertainments as ballet, theatre, concerts and art exhibitions.

But neither of these towns was our destination today; we were off to Terni. Allied bombing during World War II mostly destroyed this town, requiring it to be almost completely rebuilt. It is now an industrial city of metallurgy and car manufacture. Maria had told me not to attempt to find her building, as Terni is difficult to navigate. Her instructions were to phone her once we were in town and she would come and pick us up. I ignored her instructions for as long as I could and miraculously ended up not two hundred metres from her house before giving up and calling her.

We drove in tandem to her house, or more appropriately *palazzo*, and with great difficulty manoeuvred through the narrow streets—one of the few remaining features of old Terni. The *palazzo* was built in the 1600s by joining two towers dating from 1100. Once I had succeeded in fitting our car through the old horse tunnel we arrived in an amazing *cortile* or courtyard, four levels high and masked on all sides by an amazing vine which reached as high as the tall parapet of the building. Seeing the huge terracotta jars, called *orci*, that used to contain fresh, cold-pressed oil, I was transported back in time. The jars reminded me of Roman vats I have seen in books, jars that held this same precious food product all those centuries ago.

Maria had organised an olive oil tasting and a sampling of other products sold in all corners of the world to people in search of the pure taste of yesterday. Maria's extra-virgin olive oil is made from a blend of olives from old and new trees. This produces a highly rated oil which has a strong, fruity aroma with a taste of green grass and sweet salad leaves and a perfect medium hint of pepper on the back of the tongue. It is a refined and elegant oil. Maria also has a great range of flavoured oil. She uses pure and natural ingredients like tarragon and mushrooms to infuse into the olive oil. She produces a superb olive paste, an asparagus and artichoke paste, ready to be tossed into a bowl of warm pasta, as well as the famous Midnight and Devil's Sauce (made from dried tomatoes, red-hot peppers, vinegar, salt and olive oil) that has taken London by storm. To finish, we tasted a new addition from an old recipe of the Possenti Estate: a Clementine marmalade made from a concentration of tiny mandarin-like citrus fruit.

Maria then took us up to the second level of the *palazzo* via an imposing stone staircase to her private quarters. She told us that the *palazzo*, which contains over one hundred rooms, was progressively boarded up over the years as the family declined in numbers and members increasingly chose to live elsewhere.

Production fell drastically. Then Maria and her partner, Mario, set about rescuing the family heritage and securing this historic asset. They embarked on a mission to develop quality products from the productive olive groves, and with perseverance and vision were able to ward off collapse. The business is now in a state of expansion and new lines of food products have been launched, ensuring an adequate level of revenue to sustain the running and renovation of the *palazzo*.

Following a fascinating inspection of the ancient cellars, Maria took us on a tour of the region around Terni. Once again we manoeuvred our way out of the tall, narrow opening, more suitable for a cart than Mario's four-wheel drive. Getting quickly out of town we drove to the hillside groves near Rocca San Zenone to see hundred-year-old olive trees. Sheep were grazing under the trees; Maria explained that a family who lived nearby owned the sheep, and that the husband, Luigi de Feincenzoni, was a Pecorino cheese maker. We decided to visit them.

The Feincenzonis received us enthusiastically into their home, where Natalina had a whole chicken roasting on an electric spit in the style of a wood fire. Maria organised for me to sample some cheese and also to observe a demonstration of one of the techniques of making *pasta alla chitarra*. This special pasta is made with fresh eggs, water and wine and is rolled over a Chitarra—a guitar made of wire strings. Once pressed through, it produces long spaghetti, ready to be dropped in boiling water and served with a simple tomato sauce or, as we sampled the next day, a sauce made of walnut and truffle.

Maria's plan for dinner was to dine in one of the tiny hilltop villages of Umbria. We wound up the narrow strees and arrived at the walled village of Portaria. We toured the few streets and marvelled at the age and beauty of the place. Maria reminded me that although today it appeared a romantic town, in the olden days villages like this used to be besieged by bandits and bands of mercenaries, making life within the walls perilous. From that point on, the picturesque fortress villages took on a different meaning for me.

In the town square we sat down at one of the set tables. Young children and adults were playing around us, as if they were in their own living rooms. In such a tiny place no secrets could be kept and it was quickly apparent that tourists were uncommon here. However, Maria knew that the quality of the food we were to eat was worth our journey. She ordered a range of typical Umbrian food for us to sample. More so than Tuscany, Umbria is proud of its rustic peasant food tradition and most families in these parts cook their food over a wood fire in the age-old fashion.

We started with a plate of little pork sausages and tiny lamb cutlets, grilled over the amber ashes of the fire. Served with this was superb *torta al testo* (flat bread) baked directly on the brushed stone where the embers were. This *focaccia* proved to be one of the most delicious breads of the entire trip. We were next served a large bowl of *Spinaci saltati con patate*, a mixture of crushed potato and boiled spinach drizzled liberally with lemon juice and olive oil. We all agreed it was as perfect as anybody could ever have wished.

The next course was stunning; its simple cooking was above reproach. It was a *Piccione arrosto*, a platter of roasted wood pigeon, marinated in olive oil with garlic and herbs and slowly roasted over hot coals on a rotating spit. The insides were stuffed with the bird's liver, finely chopped with onion and bread, and the skin was regularly basted with lemon juice and olive oil over the two hours of cooking. The resulting dish was superb; the bread and liver filling had absorbed the meat juices and the slow cooking and constant basting had made the meat extremely tender. I was delighted to sample the true *Cucina Povera* in such a perfect setting.

We returned to Terni for what promised to be a special evening. That night we enjoyed a theatre festival, combining the famous theatre troops of various Umbrian towns like Assisi and Spoleto. Maria hung the family's medieval silk banner over their street balcony, as tradition demanded. Below, enthusiastic art students dressed in medieval costumes were making their way to the small square beneath the *palazzo* where the plays were to be performed. Burning torches made for an eerie pageant, situated in the oldest part of forgotten Terni. We moved further down to the main *piazza* in front of the thirteenth-century church, where the principal show was to be acted. The ensuing play involved the seasons, harvesting and the spirits, and clearly renewed the links to the past for both young and old.

Afterwards, we mingled with the crowds, finding the idea of a late-night ice-cream enticing. We walked to Genni on via Roma, where Maria introduced me to two of the best ice-cream makers of Italy, the owner brothers Paolo and Leo. She even managed to organise a tour through their manufacturing room where, despite the lateness of the hour, gelato was still being made. Judging by the large crowd queued ten deep in front of the shop, we were not the only people to enjoy this delectable creamy ice-cream.

We departed late in the night, promising to return to visit Maria and Mario in a few years on Maria's fiftieth birthday and to celebrate the completion of the renovation of the Possenti Castelli.

OFF THE BEATEN TRACK

The next day we were to meet Carlo and Carla Latini, the manufacturers of the magnificent pasta which bears their name, at one of the best restaurants of Italy, the controversial Vissani.

Vissani is situated in Civitella del Lago on Lake Corbara. As the lake is used to irrigate surrounding pastures, its level rises and falls according to the demands made upon it. This means that its banks are not attractive all year round. Regardless of this, I was surprised to see that the restaurant did not make the best of what view it had. Carlo explained that Gianfranco, the chef-owner, does not want his customers to be distracted by the view, preferring the focus to remain on his food.

Gianfranco Vissani came to say hello to Carlo and Carla, whom he knew as expert pasta producers. Gianfranco is a huge man, both in stature and intellect. I was looking forward to sampling his dishes and seeing whether his strong opinions translated into meaningful food. He offered to prepare a menu for us and we gladly agreed. What followed was a surprisingly light and delicious lunch.

We started with a *Grazzetto di cozze con tortino di finferli, juliennes di zucchine* (an omelette of tiny mussels, cooked in a light Japanese style, served with chanterelle mushrooms and a slightly pickled zucchini salad). This was followed by a *Trancio di spigola con ovolo salsa, acqua di tartufi e sedano da taglio* (a steamed slice of sea bass in a fish stock perfumed with truffle and served with a melting of 'Caesar mushroom' and a julienne of softened celery-like noodles). Next came an *Astice con risotto ai cetrioli, salsa di fiori di zucca* (lobster and cucumber risotto enriched with butter and topped with a sauce made of young zucchini flowers).

We then had a *Cannolicchi di fagiolini con galinella, salsa di foie gras e Madeira*, a dish of tiny pasta with green beans topped with guinea fowl and served with some seared *foie gras* and a sauce enhanced with Madeira. The dish was small and quite light, even though the ingredients were so rich, so we were able to follow with the *Anatra con caponatina di zucca gialla, salsa di anatra capperi e rosmarino* (a perfectly roasted breast of game duck with a caponata of yellow zucchini and a sauce perfumed with rosemary and capers).

Gianfranco's robust character had led me to expect heavy and hearty dishes, but the food he served us was a model of the best of the products of Italy prepared with French cooking techniques. We felt that Vissani certainly deserved the accolades it receives from regular customers and food critics.

After the meal, Carlo and Carla led us to their village in the Marches. Le Marche, as it is known locally, is one of the least known and appreciated regions of Italy, suffering from the neglect of both Italians and tourists. Situated on the Adriatic coast, the region is separated from Umbria by the Apennines mountain range, which accounts for its relative isolation. Yvette and I drove east from Perugia, following Carlo through flat valleys and across steep mountain peaks on our way to the town of Osimo near

Ancona. The mountains finally gave way to the hilly terrain that constitutes the majority of the Marches. We passed through Jesi, the town that made Verdicchio wine famous in 1960, with its distinctive amphora-shaped bottles.

Vast wheat fields came into view, confirming this region's ideal climate for the cultivation of Italy's most important crop. The Marches, like the rest of the Adriatic coast, is a sheep-grazing region and a producer of great Pecorino cheese. One of the most famous and appreciated cheeses is the Formaggio di Fossa, a sheep's-milk cheese found in abundance from here to Puglia. The creation of Formaggio di Fossa came about centuries ago when the shepherds sought to hide their precious cheese during the many hostile invasions the country suffered. After covering the cheeses with leaves, they hid them in the moist tufa caves of the mountains, or in deep ditches. These conditions eventually started a second fermentation and caused a transformation in the cheese. The end result was a unique cheese that has remained popular to this day.

We drove up to the historic centre of Osimo, a small agricultural town with a concentration of government services and some beautiful churches. The town will never be listed as a tourist destination but we were happy to spend a couple of days in the area with Carlo and Carla Latini. Carlo was keen to show us his experimental wheat field, where he grows more than a hundred types of wheat, assessing their performance to see if he can improve the quality of wheat for making his premium pasta. The Latinis have always been wheat growers, but when their efforts in growing quality wheat went unacknowledged and unappreciated by the millers, they decided to create their own *pastificio* (pasta factory). For Carlo and Carla, developing their own brand was a milestone in raising the general standard of dried pasta (*pasta secca*) that was commonly found on the Italian market.

Italians came to produce what we know as dried pasta around 1400. They milled durum wheat to a granular flour and mixed it with water, producing a dough that needed a great amount of work to bind it and make it malleable. Men were employed to tread barefoot on the dough for a whole day so it could be extruded through a screw press powered by two strong men or a horse. The resulting long strands of vermicelli, shaped by the pierced die of the press (like the grille of a meat mincer), thus became the first durum pasta. After a slow drying period, it was found that the pasta could be kept for a long time.

The durum wheat preferred to produce dried pasta has been around for a long time. The name comes from the Latin word *durum*, meaning hard, because of the hardness of the grain compared to other varieties. Today the ancestral species have been improved to make them drought and disease resistant, high in protein and with an improved yield. The Mediterranean countries, in particular Italy, are amongst the best for growing durum wheat. Parts of Canada are also suitable.

We arrived at Carlo's field in the late afternoon and watched the sunset change the wheat field from gold to aubergine. There were over one hundred different types of wheat here. Some were short-stemmed and strong; others were long and fine, bending precariously in the wind. Carlo, with the help of an agronomist, was cross-pollinating selected varieties to develop better strains. All over the field we could see small paper envelopes attached to the stems of wheat. These contained the grains of a different species to see if the resulting cross-breed produced an improved wheat. It was a painstakingly slow and long-term project and a measure of Carlo's commitment and dedication.

Carlo was keen to develop a pasta made of a single variety of durum wheat, and to do this he chose Senator Cappeli, which he planted in 1991. This produced his first *cru* pasta, which is similar to a wine in that it can be recognised by taste. The Senator Cappeli wheat is an old variety which was widely grown at the beginning of the century. Carlo found a low-yielding but perfect grain with a superb aroma and taste. He marketed this single variety under the brand name of *'Senatore Cappelli' Raccolto 1996*, the year denoting the year of harvesting in the same way as the vintage of a wine. His challenge now was to improve the yield of the wheat to make the pasta economically viable.

Carlo took us to the nearby flour mill where the wheat is processed. Here the mill foreman showed us the various steps necessary to produce the semolina (the large, hard grains of wheat left after the flour has been sifted) that Carlo would take to his *pastificio*, mix with a little water and transform into a quality pasta. The wheat has to be cleaned and conditioned to separate the bran (husks) from the endosperm (the tissue of the seed). In most circumstances the objective is to produce a flour made of pure endosperm. Further grinding in separate machines, and careful sifting, eventually produces semolina and white flour.

We were to have dinner on the beach at Portonovo, a beach resort on the Conero Peninsula near Ancona. It sounded tempting, despite the succession of lunches and dinners we had eaten over the last few months. Gianfranco Vissani was to join us there with a couple of friends. On the way to the coast we stopped at the Latinis' warehouse where boxes and boxes of pasta were stored, ready to be dispatched to all corners of the world: Japan, America, Asia, Australia. The range was impressive. There were long pastas like taglierini, trenette, bucatini, tagliolini, and short varieties like penne, maccheroncini, strozzapreti, penette, fusilli, conchigliette and the tiny minestrone for soups. It is a sign of the Latinis' success that the famous Parisian food emporium, Fauchon, was their first customer.

We arrived at the coast, and from high on the clifftop looked along the shoreline at the famous white cliffs and beaches where the first Greek settlers had landed. We drove down the steep road to reach the tiny seaside resort of Portonovo with its perfect turquoise water. Arriving there, we walked to the white stony beach where several open-air restaurants were scattered. The sun was setting, taking with it the oppressive heat of the day, and the ocean breeze was a welcome relief.

The restaurant we were to dine at was typical of coastal Italy, serving mostly seafood. Like most others in Portonovo, it had simple, unpretentious decor. These restaurants are perfect for the short summer season, offering uncomplicated pasta and seafood menus. The Marches is the third highest seafood-producing region in Italy and its offerings are very fresh.

Gianfranco was able to join us at Ristorante il Laghetto as his restaurant, Vissani, is closed on Sunday for dinner. We laughed at the unexpected opportunity to have dinner together so far away from Umbria, especially as we had not hoped to see each other again so soon. We were served a local Verdicchio, a Casal di Serra 1995, which prepared us for the dinner soon to come. The last rays of sun on the ocean made a perfect setting for a seafood dinner.

We started with an *Antipasto caldo*, a warm shellfish selection which included scampi split in two and sauced with warmed-up cherry tomatoes and Ligurian olives, *cozze* (black mussels in tomato sauce), *lumace di mare* (sea winkles), and a local shellfish only found in the waters around the peninsula and collected by divers by hand. These *fasolari* were simply prepared by steaming them with a touch of white wine. The dish was served with a salad of wild grasses and dressed with salted anchovies and olive oil.

Gianfranco was in fine form, contradicting everyone, questioning the validity of every gastronomic creation and generally being both entertaining and objectionable. Here, at least, was someone eager to provoke a discussion, all the better if it was with a journalist as the hapless guest sitting beside me turned out to be.

The next course was served steaming from a large pan. It was a *Spaghetti alle vongole*, a perfect clam spaghetti tossed in the reduction of the cooking liquid of the clams and enhanced with a dry white wine. The spaghetti used was made by the Latinis and Gianfranco was at it again, disputing with the owner about the amount of water the chef had used to cook the pasta. His feeling was that the water had reduced too much to cook the pasta perfectly. To me it seemed pretty good.

A perfect fish arrived at the table on a platter: a *Branzino alla griglia* (grilled sea bass) sprinkled with sea salt and olive oil but no lemon. This was a change from the Riviera, where nearly all seafood was served with a squeeze of lemon. The fish was perfectly moist and, in the manner customary in Italy, fully cooked through.

We finished with a *Ciambellone* (a form of *panettone* with grapes) and a fig parfait topped with caramelised figs. Here is my adaptation of this to-die-for dessert.

Fig Parfait with Caramelised Figs and Pistachio Wafer

For the fig parfait:

1 L (1 pint) cream

150 ml (5 fl oz) water

200 g (7 oz) caster sugar

4 eggs

2 egg yolks

250 g (9 oz) fresh figs, chopped

75 ml (2½ fl oz) orange juice

Whip the cream until it just forms soft peaks. Refrigerate.

Place the water and caster sugar in a copper saucepan, and stir over moderate heat until sugar dissolves. Boil, without stirring, until the mixture caramelises and is cooked to soft-ball stage (116°C, 245°F, on a candy thermometer). Use a small brush dipped in cold water to clean sugar off the sides of the saucepan if necessary.

Meanwhile, whisk eggs and yolks on top speed for 3 minutes. Reduce the speed and slowly pour the syrup over the eggs. Whisk until golden and allow to cool.

In a small bowl, mix the chopped figs with a quarter of the whipped cream. Add to the egg mixture. Mix in the rest of the cream and the orange juice.

Pour the parfait mixture into 2 square cake pans that are lined with plastic wrap for easy removal. The mixture should be 4 cm (1½ in) high. Freeze overnight.

For the caramelised figs:

1.5 kg (3 lb) caster sugar
1300 ml (44 fl oz) water
200 ml (7 fl oz) hot water
20 fresh figs

Place the caster sugar and water in a saucepan, and stir over a moderate heat until sugar dissolves. Boil without stirring until the mixture caramelises and is dark golden in colour. Immediately pour in the hot water and stir to dissolve caramel. Pour this syrup over the figs and allow to cool.

For the pistachio wafer:

120 ml (4 fl oz) egg whites (approx. 3)
130 g (4½ oz) icing sugar
130 g (4½ oz) plain flour
130 g (4½ oz) butter, melted
vanilla essence
pistachio nuts, chopped

Combine the egg whites, icing sugar and flour, add the melted butter and a drop of vanilla essence and mix well. Refrigerate until cold.

Preheat the oven to 170°C (340°F). Spread the mixture thinly onto a buttered baking tray. Sprinkle with chopped pistachio nuts and bake until golden. While still warm and soft, use a knife to cut out 11 x 7 cm (4½ x 3 in) rectangles. Allow to cool.

To assemble:

Just before serving, cut the caramelised figs in half and sprinkle caster sugar on each one. Using a blow-torch (or a very hot grill), caramelise the sugar until golden brown in colour. Remove the *parfait from the freezer, cut a 10 x 6 cm (4 x 2½ in) rectangle, set on a biscuit base and top with another.*

Place on a dessert plate and place a fig on top. Serve straight away, accompanied with a sauce made from fig pulp and syrup.

(Makes 2 terrines, 10 portions each)

The next morning Carlo thought we were ready for a short period of waterside relaxation. By this stage of the trip neither Yvette nor I were keen to get into bathing suits, but the blue water, the superb sun and Carlo's carefree attitude towards his own considerable pasta-induced stomach convinced us that we should let go and enjoy a day on the water. Carlo rented a speedboat and we made our way south around the incredible rocky cliff of the peninsula to a secluded cove, where we swam in the warm waters of the Adriatic. On our return we followed the coast and, from the water, observed one of the oldest standing churches of Italy, the Chiesa Romanica di Santa Maria di Portonova, dating back to 1034. Portonovo's isolated location, protected as it was by the steep green cliffs of the peninsula, and the availability of fresh water induced the French to build a great sea fort there, the Fortino Napoleonico, in 1812. Carlo knew the manager of the establishment, now a superb hotel, and he organised for us to have lunch on its roof-terrace restaurant.

We left Portonovo lightly tanned, relaxed and definitely heavier.

There is a certain harshness to the landscape of Molise: its hills are parched and dry, its coast is flat and featureless, and long sandy beaches offer no protection from the wind. Not much seems to turn green here, apart from a few olive trees. This is an area which is mostly unknown to Italians, and even less known to tourists.

Molise is a deeply religious region with pagan rhythms. The character of this region has been formed by long struggles for survival, not against armies, but against hunger and the harshness of the unforgiving landscape. Not surprisingly, the principal activity of the past was sheep herding, which necessitated the annual *transumanza*, the walk south by the shepherds and their flocks to the market of Foggia. While this journey is no longer undertaken, Molise is still considered one of the Italian regions most reluctant to embrace the new way of life in Italy.

Our drive was to lead us to Termoli, a coastal town popular in summer with holidaying southerners escaping from the dried and sweltering interior of Italy. Most of Termoli was destroyed by heavy bombardment during World War II, though luckily the historic walled seaside quarter was spared.

We made our way to the clifftop, where some hotels were situated, and selected the first one in sight. I was later to learn it was the best in town. I could only agree—if, that is, I ignored the ineffective air-conditioning unit, the leaking shower, the dim lights and the noisy fan.

That night, Yvette and I wandered the streets of Termoli in search of a small restaurant serving simple, uncomplicated food that would represent the style of Molise. Walking past a terrace restaurant I spied through the open door of the kitchen three older women carrying out last-minute preparations for the coming dinner service. There were no men in the kitchen; that seemed to me to be a very good sign, as the food, I knew, would be cooked with love. I decided that this would be our dinner choice.

The menu was very simple: a few antipastos, some pasta and risotto, and a small number of fish dishes. It sounded perfect. I started with a *Frittelle di pesciolini*, a cake of small minnows mixed with garlic, herbs and egg, fried to a crisp golden colour. Yvette had a *Risotto ai frutti* and I selected a *Spaghetti alle vongole*, made with the fresh small clams collected on the Adriatic coast. Yvette's risotto was a very fresh selection of tiny shellfish, barely cooked in the risotto. The risotto, as well as my pasta, was deliciously cooked to order. The next course was the famous Adriatic '*Brodetto*', a selection of whole fish simmered in a tomato sauce. This was a classic dish which benefited from the infinite variety of seafood that could be found along the coast. The rich, deep-red tomato sauce was prepared with a lot of onion, softened in olive oil and used to flavour a great amount of peeled crushed tomato, and cooked for so long that the sauce had a glistening shine and sweetness I had rarely encountered before. Five local fish were gutted, but were otherwise left whole, set in this tomato sauce and braised in the oven until the fish was cooked through. The dish was brought to the table still bubbling, with great slabs of crusty bread. The flesh of the fish had received the rare treatment of a slow starting temperature that gently penetrated the fish to its backbone without destroying the structure of the flesh or altering its principal taste. The skin helped to retain all the moisture in the flesh and the sauce was a perfect enhancement. With a glass of local Bombino Bianco it proved to be an outstanding meal in a forgotten part of Italy—perfect before heading inland to visit Marina Colonna at her property in Ururi.

Surprisingly, one of the best olive oils I purchase does not come from Tuscany—reputedly the best place for olive oil—but from the estate of the Colonna family in Molise. The oil produced here is an aristocratic one, very flavoursome, fresh and spicy, with a crisp green colour.

This was to be my first visit to Marina's estate and I was eagerly looking forward to staying at her farmhouse. The Colonna family is directly descended from the Counts of Tusculum, taking their name from the castle of Colonna in the Albans hills. The family's history is a vivid one, with members boasting such ranks and occupations as Grand Constables of Naples, warriors of Ravenna, officials for the Spanish service during the occupation of the southern part of Italy, admirals and even a pope—Oddo Colonna (Pope Martin V). After generations of loyal service to the Church, the family was rewarded with a royal ranking. Today we were to meet Princess Marina Colonna, who took over the running of the family's country estate after the death of her father, Prince Francesco Colonna, a few years previously.

The drive through the countryside leading to the estate was very telling of Molise—hot, hilly, and with a visibly slow pace of life. We arrived at San Martino, near Marina's property, and saw all around us fields of olive trees, wheat and hardy vegetables.

The estate was unpretentious. This was evidently a working farm; its principal buildings were the warehouse, factory and press house. The villa was tucked away at the back, facing a shaded garden. Our arrival was announced by the customary bark of the villa dogs and Marina was there to greet us. She is young, has perfect English and the sharp manner of the Romans. Her welcome was warm, and over cooling drinks in the garden we planned our day ahead. We wanted to visit not only the olive groves but also the wheat and sweet beetroot fields, the sheep-milking facilities and the *frantoio*, where Marina's olives are pressed.

The principal residence of the Colonna family is in Rome, where the family was established and rose to prominence over many centuries, but the importance of this property makes it necessary for Marina and other members of the family to spend a great deal of time running and developing it. Marina described the amazing difficulty she had had in taking over the agriculture business from her father. Like many men of his era, he had conducted his business secretively, intuitively and based on personal relationships built up over years. Promises that lasted a lifetime were made over the years and agreements were struck with a handshake. Not surprisingly, the difficulty of sorting out all this without legal documents was onerous. It would have been easy for Marina to leave the management to the previous farm manager, as he had been appointed heir apparent of all the properties, but Marina's rebellious nature and her determination to improve the image and running of the estates compelled her to take on the task herself. Ultimately Marina prevailed, transforming the estate into a professionally run business. Her skills in marketing quickly led her to identify the advantages of bypassing the large food conglomerates and establishing her own brand of olive oil, knowing full well that the estate produced some of the best oils of Italy.

We climbed into Marina's heavy four-wheel drive and headed off to inspect the milking facilities on the property. A large barn with sophisticated milking equipment was filled with more than 500 sheep. The automatic rotating milking platform could be run by two men capable of handling hundreds of sheep per hour. At the time of my visit, the milk was being sold to a local cheese factory to produce Pecorino, but I could detect a glint in Marina's eyes at the possibility of producing her own cheese—another day, another battle, her look seemed to say.

Marina also showed us a grove of incredibly old and beautiful olive trees on the estate. Some were as old as 300 years and yet still yielded fruit. Olive trees can live for centuries if prolonged frosts do not kill them, and it is not unusual to find trees 500 or even 1000 years old. The varieties Marina preferred were Coratina, Nocellara, Peranzana, the eating variety Ascolano, and the great Leccino and Frantoio, typically used to make Tuscan oil.

Only about 10 per cent of the world's olive oil is classified as extra virgin. In Italy, because of the favourable climate and expertise of the growers, nearly 50 per cent is classified as extra virgin. To produce extra-virgin olive oil it is very important first of all to avoid bruising the olives, and secondly to get them to the press as quickly as possible. The time of harvesting is also critical, as picking too early will create a very bitter oil and picking too late, when the fruit is overripe, will create an oil that will not last and will oxidise quickly. In Tuscany, where they like their oil peppery, the olives are harvested in October and November. In the south the harvest starts at this time but continues way into December or even January.

For centuries the method of harvesting was to hand pick the olives. The recent invention of the tree shaker, which grabs the trunk of the tree and, through a constant low vibration, makes the tree drop its fruit on to the matting set under its branches, has speeded up the harvesting process. Using the traditional method, a good picker can collect up to 40 kilograms (88 pounds) per day, or about 20 000 olives, which could, depending on ripeness and the time of the year, yield between 5 and 10 litres (8 to 16 pints) of oil. Marina uses both methods, but a good quantity of olives from her estate is collected by hand.

Once the olives have been collected they are quickly taken to the *frantoio*, where they are cleaned of branches and leaves by a blast of compressed air and then either put through a mincer or, much better, crushed to a pulp by rotating stone wheels. The whole fruit, stone and all, is processed in this manner. Each variety is kept in a separate stainless steel tank, thus creating a spectrum of quality oil which, when blended by an expert, will produce a superb oil of perfect refinement, consistent in style from one year to the next.

We tasted the range of oils Marina produces, keeping for last the citrus-flavoured oil that has made her famous in England. Originally this oil, called Grandverde, was the preserve of the family but now it has been made available to the public. It is an oil enhanced by lemons, oranges or mandarins. These oils are exceptional, flavoured by adding cut pieces of citrus fruits (which are organically grown on the property) into the olive paste. After a centrifugal spinning the juice is extracted, leaving the natural citrus oil behind. This is blended with the olive oil to produce an unparalleled oil, perfect for grilling fish, for dressing salads or for grilled vegetables.

We retired at last to the coolness of the old villa, which was furnished with intriguing antique pieces which have belonged to the house for as long as anyone could remember. Once the harsh sun had faded we enjoyed a glass of Northern Spumanti on the terrace, and ate a simple meal. This consisted of preserved vegetables in olive oil (made under the supervision of Marina) and a bowl of traditional orecchiette pasta tossed in her delicious *Pâté d'olive nere piccante*, a flavoursome tapenade of olives. It was a delicious meal that made for the end of an informative day spent with a woman determined to revive the fortunes of her family's estate.

ALL ROADS LEAD TO ROME

We left *Marina Colonna's property early in the morning and drove west towards Rome.* This was to be our last destination before returning to Sydney, and it was with a mixture of regret and relief that we made our way towards this chaotic, wonderful city for a final few days of gastronomic and social indulgence.

We arrived by taxi in the late afternoon, having dropped our car at Fiumicino airport. We were sad to see it go, as not only had it been our mode of transport for the last two months, it had also served as our retreat and comfort zone in the varied and unfamiliar places we had travelled through.

In Rome we were to meet Diane Seed, the popular English cook–author who has made such a dramatic impact on the way non-Italians see food. On her recommendation we had booked a room at the Albergo Santa Chiara, which was quite close to her residence as well as to the awe-inspiring Pantheon.

Diane met us at our hotel in her seldom-used car and we launched ourselves into the traffic of Rome and the activities of the day. First we drove up to have lunch at Ristorante Cecilia Metellan, a shady restaurant on via Appia Antica, an old Roman road lined with ancient tombs and mausoleums. We had plenty of planning to do, as on my return to Australia I was to hold a promotion with Diane in Sydney to launch her new book, *Diane Seed's Roman Kitchen*.

At the restaurant we were seated outside under green vines, which provided the coolness we needed. It was a beautiful setting for a simple meal.

We enjoyed a *Fave e Pecorino* (a spring salad of tender fava beans sprinkled with Pecorino cheese) and *Carciofi fritti* (fried young artichokes), followed by a *Bucatini all'Amatriciana* (the hollow spaghetti-type pasta served with bacon, tomatoes, garlic, onion and hard Pecorino cheese) and *Zite al Prosciutto* (a fresh pasta sheet tossed with butter and prosciutto). This last pasta dish was a difficult one to handle—the tablecloth and my shirt bore evidence of my lack of dexterity.

On the completion of our meal we decided to meet later that night to have dinner at Checchino, a historically significant Roman restaurant. To fill the hours before we were all to meet again, Yvette and I went to visit one of the most interesting public markets of Rome: the Campo dei Fiori.

Campo dei Fiori literally means 'field of flowers', though the cafés and bars surrounding this historic area struck us as being very far removed from its name. Merchants were moving their stock while chanting songs and haranguing the passers-by. Good prices were to be had at the end of the day, and many local restaurateurs and chefs were searching the stores for quality products at bargain prices. At one end of the market we saw a freshwater fountain, dating back to the times of the ancient Roman aqueduct system and still in operation, being used to cool large watermelons. These were sliced to order and eagerly bought by thirsty customers.

Evening arrived and with it our renewed appetites. It was time to rejoin Diane at one of the most traditional restaurants Rome has to offer.

I had heard of Checchino from a friend in Australia who loves restaurants which are true reflections of the past. He recommended this eating place, which is situated near the old meat market. The menu at Checchino has evolved from the use of the *quinto quarto*, the fifth quarter of the animal which had no value to the butcher and consisted of the discarded offal and offcuts left over after the slaughtering of the beast. These portions of meat were given to the workers as part payment in lieu of wages, and were often exchanged for meals in the local trattorias. Traditional Roman cuisine makes great use of mint, onion and vinegar, as these were originally needed to neutralise the smell and taste of many of these less-than-fresh cuts.

Checchino is built, or more appropriately carved, into the Monte de' Cocci, the hill made up of hundreds and thousands of the broken amphoras or urns used to carry wine and oil. An ancient dictate proscribed their stacking in this location that is known as the seventh hill of Rome.

As it was a warm evening we decided to dine outside. Diane chose our wine with the help of the *sommelier*, who was the son of the owner, Ninetta Mariani. We resolved to try the house specialities and they selected a Bricco Maiolica 1993, Nebbiolo d'Alba, to accompany them, a deep-red wine made in the Barbaresco style from Piedmont. It was still young but quite delicious and reasonably priced.

We ordered apprehensively, Yvette selecting a safe *Crostini ai porcini* (a roasted slice of bread topped with sautéed porcini mushroom and fresh herbs enhanced with a touch of garlic). Diane ordered a *Crostini misti con calice di Spumante* (a selection of crostini with toppings of tuna and goat cheese, artichoke pâté and rendered pig's cheek). I selected the *Insalata di Zampi* (a trotter salad made of boiled calves' feet, boned and served with a bean salad in a green sauce made of parsley, basil, onion, anchovies and olive oil).

The next course for Yvette was a delicious if conservative *Spaghetti casio e pepe* (a spaghetti tossed with Pecorino cheese and black pepper). Diane selected the light *Stracciatella* (a soup made of fresh eggs whisked in a soup with some semolina and Parmesan). By this point I was very much looking forward to my *Arrosto misto di animelle fegato, pajata, schienali e granelli* (a mixed roast of calves' entrails consisting of sweetbread, liver, small intestine, spinal marrow and testicles). Offal can often be transformed into something almost unidentifiable from the original organs. This was not the case in this instance, but I still enjoyed the dish, the restaurant and Diane's company.

We made plans for the next day to visit the Testaccio market and to purchase some ingredients for dinner at Diane's home in the fabulous Palazzo Doria Pamphilj.

We met up with Diane at her home on via del Plebiscito. Our plan was to purchase the ingredients for four dishes for dinner that evening. I was looking forward to cooking, having eaten restaurant meals almost every day for the previous two months. Taking Diane's car we manoeuvred out of the impressive courtyard of the *palazzo* and drove to the Aventine section of the city, a largely residential area bordered on two sides by the river Tiber and to the north by the ancient Circus Maximus, which used to be Rome's largest stadium and, at its peak, could hold up to 250 000 spectators. Today only the grassy shape of the stadium remains; its enormous stone construction was pillaged long ago for other building projects.

The market, which covers the whole of the piazza Testaccio, has been entirely covered to provide shade and shelter. Where the Campo dei Fiori was partly a tourist market, this market was very much for the locals. The array of fruit and vegetables on offer was incredible, and despite the dim light, the colours were vibrant. Summer was certainly here—the array of fruit was at its peak. Tiny red and white currants were on display, along with yellow and red cherries, raspberries, wild mountain strawberries, tiny pineapples, mangoes and, surprisingly, limes, which are seldom used in Italian cuisine. Further along in the market I spotted superb figs, white cherries and fragrant melons.

The vegetable displays were as stunning as the fruit. There were green, red and yellow tomatoes, tiny potatoes that I would love to have in Australia, a marvellous array of beans, fresh peas, superb porcini mushrooms and a large selection of salad leaves (with one mixture comprising only wild leaves). I selected some egg-shaped and garden tomatoes, a bunch of fresh spinach leaves, young peas, zucchini flowers, basil, lettuce leaves, garlic and raspberries. I was tempted to purchase more but knew that my eyes were bigger than my stomach. Also, I knew that the secret of a good meal often resides in focusing on two or three quality ingredients treated in a simple manner.

One of the surprises Diane had for us was a visit to her favourite grocery store. Volpetti is an amazing food shop; it is not very large but the range it offers is exhaustive. The success of the store resides in the fanatical commitment Claudio Volpetti and his family have to their producers. At the shop entrance his assistant was offering a tasting from two long slabs of pizza, one with artichoke and the other with olives and pancetta. I restrained myself from purchasing too many items and bought some eating olives and some oven-dried ones. These I would use to prepare an olive crust for the fish I intended to cook that night. I also selected a packet of lentils from Umbria plus some anchovies and creamy mascarpone cheese. We departed happily, loaded with our purchases, stopping only for coffee served with a *pampepato*, a sweet bun of pine nuts, almonds and honey spiced with pepper.

After finding a parking spot we walked to Sylvio's, Diane's favourite fishmonger. I had visited the Mercati Generali, the wholesale market of Rome, on a previous trip and had not found the fish quite up to the standard of that of Paris or Sydney. For Diane, the small local shop offers a more consistent product. Supplies of fresh fish were arriving; I saw swordfish falling out of their crates before a fascinated audience of customers. I selected a young one, much smaller than the ones we have in Sydney, and Sylvio sliced me some thick steaks from it. The flesh was a perfect creamy pink and would make a delicious dish for the evening.

Diane's expertise in Mediterranean food and the enormous success of her books has naturally led to her offering cooking classes in the various cuisines of Italy. She has converted one of her apartments in the Palazzo Doria Pamphilj into a cooking school, holding classes for twelve students, each class running for a week. Due to the oppressive heat of June, July and August, her classes are held before and after summer. During summer Diane lives in the quarters of the cooking school, while in winter she uses her other apartment.

Diane's classes teach the basics of Roman and other regional cuisines. Her recipes are simple and totally uninfluenced by

Cucina Nuova. In fact, most of her dishes are based on single vegetables, like artichokes or eggplants, or other humble ingredients.

As soon as we arrived at the apartment, Diane and I got to work preparing our food for the evening meal. Diane used the ricotta to make a simple stuffing for the zucchini flowers, enhancing it with the salted anchovies we had bought at the Testaccio market. She prepared a batter of flour, yeast, egg and water, and flavoured it with some white wine and a touch of olive oil. I, meanwhile, prepared my swordfish by trimming it into thinner steaks. I then cleaned the peas and the spinach and prepared a purée flavoured with capers and butter. I washed and drained the special Castelluccio lentils and, while they cooked for ten minutes, marinated the tomatoes with some garlic, pepper, olive oil and sea salt, ready for roasting at a very low temperature for the rest of the afternoon to concentrate their flavours.

Diane selected Sicilian vine-ripened tomatoes full of aroma and bursting with colour. She then drained the *mozzarella di bufalo Campania* we had brought her as a gift. I prepared my ingredients for the dessert, washing and draining the raspberries and mixing the mascarpone cheese with a touch of fruit sugar and a few dashes of Amaretto. Our preparations finished, we parted for a few hours for a rest.

The walk to our hotel from Diane's apartment took us through the old section of Rome near the Pantheon. Many of the shops in the area supply ecclesiastical robes and clerical items to the hordes of Catholic priests and nuns who visit this most religious of cities. These costly religious artefacts contrasted strangely with Diane's warnings not to wear jewellery or carry a bag in this part of Rome, to avoid being the target of theft.

We returned to Diane's grand apartment in the evening. Diane had invited one of her best friends, Margaret, to join us for dinner. Before her arrival, however, we sipped on the last glass of champagne of our trip and celebrated the near-completion of a rich and eventful journey. On Margaret's arrival we moved to the rooftop terrace of the *palazzo* to watch the sun set over the city—a glorious sight that will be enhanced in a few years when all Rome's rooftop antennas are removed, as is the plan.

Diane went into the kitchen to split her zucchini flowers and stuff them with the prepared ricotta filling. After stirring her batter back to life she dipped and fried the stuffed flowers in hot virgin olive oil. After a light salting they proved perfect with a chilled Barolo Vigna del Gris. The next course was the classic *Mozzarella Caprese*, a salad made famous in Capri with its layers of mozzarella, tomatoes and basil, flavoured with cracked pepper and extra-virgin olive oil. The unctuosity of the *mozzarella di bufalo* made a stunning contrast to the bursting flavour of the tomatoes—a classic Italian dish.

I completed my first dish by warming up the lentils in their stock with a touch of olive oil. The green vegetables were further seasoned and finished with a spoonful of cold butter. I quickly seared the swordfish to an underdone state and assembled the dish by setting the first piece of fish on the lentils, then adding a full spoon of purée, then another layer of fish, then the tapenade I had made in the afternoon, and finally the deep-red, slightly dehydrated tomato. We enjoyed the dish with a Collio Tacai Ronco della Chiesa 1989, a superior wine from Friuli near the Slovenian border. Finally dinner came to an end with the flavoured mascarpone cheese served with lightly stewed raspberries and coffee by the moonlight on the terrace.

Here is my recipe—with slight variations—for olive-crusted swordfish with spinach purée on a ragoût of lentils. Eat it and dream of a rooftop dinner in Rome ...

Olive-crusted Swordfish with Spinach Purée on Lentil Ragoût

1 small carrot

1 clove garlic

1 stick celery

1 small onion

1 sprig thyme

1 bay leaf

1 sprig rosemary

4 x 160 g (9 oz) brown lentils (Castelluccio or any dark lentil)

a little extra-virgin olive oil

Boil all vegetables and herbs in a small pot with plenty of cold water for 5 minutes, then add the lentils. Simmer for 20 minutes, covered. Do not add more water unless the lentils become dry. Discard vegetables and herbs, season with salt and pepper, and a little extra-virgin olive oil. Put aside.

For the spinach purée:

2 bunches English spinach, leaves only, washed well

1 clove garlic, cut in two

125 ml (4 fl oz) cold water

20 g (½ oz) butter, diced

salt and pepper

Place spinach in a pot with the garlic and water, cover and cook for 5 minutes, stirring occasionally. Drain and press in a fine strainer. Discard garlic. Place in a food processor and blend into a fine purée, adding the butter. Season and put aside.

For the oven-roasted tomatoes:

4 large egg tomatoes
100 ml (3 fl oz) olive oil
2 sprigs thyme
a few stalks basil
1 clove garlic, sliced
sea salt and pepper

Cut the tomatoes in half and marinate in the remaining ingredients overnight to absorb flavour. Set cut sides of tomatoes face up on an oven rack. Sprinkle with salt and any remaining marinated herbs. Place in an oven set at 80°C (175°F) and slowly dry them for 5 hours. Remove the skins and oven-dry the tomatoes for a further hour, placing them cut sides down.

To assemble:

8 thick swordfish fillets (90 g each)
sea salt and pepper

In the remaining 20 ml (½ fl oz) olive oil, sear the seasoned swordfish fillets, leaving them slightly undercooked. Arrange in layers, starting with the lentils, then the swordfish, spinach purée, more swordfish, olive tapenade and finally the warm tomatoes.

(Serves 4 as a main)

Wanting to make the most of our last night in Rome, Diana took us to one of the most historical sections of the city, the old Jewish ghetto. The Jews were first brought to Rome from Jerusalem as slaves by Pompey the Great in AD 68. They quickly proved themselves worthy of respect for their expertise in financial and medical matters. It was not until the sixteenth century that they began to suffer authorised persecution: they were confined at night in the ghetto behind a wall constructed at the order of Pope Paul IV. This state of affairs continued until 1848, when the abolition of Jewish servitude in Italy was granted. Today, many Jews still live in the old Jewish quarter of Rome. The cuisine here has remained unchanged for centuries. Cut off for so long from external influences, the food created in the ghetto retains the true character of dishes of the Roman heritage.

It is a tradition in Rome to eat fried cod fillet. The best cod fillet, Diane assured us, was to be found in the ghetto. She guided us through the narrow streets of the old quarter, passing the many shops and restaurants that still serve traditional food, until we reached the destination of her choosing.

Dar Filettaro a Santa Barbara was located in a tiny cul-de-sac; booksellers, a small church and a few simple eating places were squeezed in close together. We were seated at a table on the uneven pavement outside Dar Filettaro. The trattoria offered a one-dimensional menu based on fried cod. We followed Diane's recommendation for a starter and selected *Giardiniera di sottaceti* (pickled vegetables), *Acciughe* (marinated sardines), *Buntarelle* (wild chicory salad) and *Filetti di Baccalà* (fried cod fillet). The food was prepared in a small open kitchen kept impeccably clean.

The meal—a simple one based on typical local products—could not have been more fitting for our last night in Italy. The food was a reflection of what Italy is, and of what it can offer to the world: simplicity, tradition and respect. It was an exceptional end to our gastronomic travels.

EPILOGUE

I have always said that food is to be enjoyed, not enshrined and worshipped, but a lot of near-religious respect has to go to the people who grow, produce and cook the magnificent foods and wines that we eat and drink. The efforts of these people have ensured that our interest in good food has not waned in this age of commodity food. Our food and wine artisans are the conscience of our society. They enrich our lives in a multitude of ways.

One of the greatest pleasures in the modern age is to travel and discover the world. More and more, food is an integral part of our travelling plans. It provides us with little rewards along the way, and teaches us to enjoy the pleasures of the table and the significance of the regions we find ourselves in. The sense of adventure that one derives from discovering an 'unknown' restaurant that provides beautifully cooked food is often reward in itself.

France and Italy provide so many opportunities to roam, explore and savour the cultures and foods of these countries that it is impossible to advise on a 'must do' list. Each individual should simply push his or her own personal boundaries and not be afraid of a different language, culture or way of life. Most locals will help and guide you if you show respect and a thirst for knowledge.

I had the opportunity to meet some extraordinary people on my travels, and I believe that *everyone* has this chance. Europe is full of merchants, growers, wine makers and chefs ready to share their products and opinions with you. Let them dazzle you, and let yourself be swept away by the flavours of what they have on offer.

APPENDIX OF RECIPES

Olive Tapenade

100 g (3½ oz) dried black olives
40 ml (1 fl oz) extra-virgin olive oil
1 clove garlic, chopped
1 French shallot, chopped
1 anchovy fillet, chopped
2 teaspoons chopped parsley

Pit the olives and cut them finely with a knife until you have a rough-textured tapenade. In 20 ml (½ fl oz) olive oil sweat the garlic, shallot and anchovy. Add to olives with the parsley and remaining olive oil. Allow the flavours to blend for 24 hours in a cool place.

Veal Jus

2 kg (4½ lbs) veal bones
100 ml (3 fl oz) olive oil
2 small carrots, diced
1 leek, diced
2 cloves garlic

1 stick celery, diced

1 medium onion, diced

1 bouquet garni (thyme, bay leaf, peppercorn, rosemary)

750 ml (24 fl oz) Shiraz or Cabernet red wine

500 ml (16 fl oz) chicken stock

250 ml (8 fl oz) verjuice

4 shallots, sliced

1 carrot, diced

a sprig each of thyme, tarragon, parsley stalk and rosemary

In a roasting pan add a little olive oil, the veal bones, carrots, leek, garlic, celery, onion and bouquet garni. Roast at 230°C (450F) for 20 minutes. Stir and cook for 10 minutes more. Deglaze with half the red wine and cook on top of the stove over moderate heat until the ingredients have nearly dried, approximately 15 minutes. Transfer to a large pot, cover with stock and simmer for 4 hours. Strain stock and reserve.

In a clean pot add the rest of your wine, verjuice, shallots and carrot, reduce to one third of the volume.

Add the reserved stock and reduce slowly, skimming regularly, until you have a perfect jus. Strain through a wet muslin cloth into a bowl and adjust the seasoning. Add the fresh herbs and cover the bowl with plastic wrap to infuse the herbs in the warm sauce for 10 minutes. Strain again.

(Serves 4)

2 medium veal shanks

1 onion, cut into quarters

2 small carrots

1 stick celery

1 sprig thyme

1 bay leaf

2 spring onions

1 tablespoon black peppercorns

1 tablespoon salt

Place veal shanks in a high-sided pot. Cover with cold water and bring to the boil, then simmer, uncovered, for 10 minutes. Drain, wash the shanks and pot and return to the pot. Cover again with water and add all the vegetables, herbs and seasoning. Cook over a low heat for 4 hours, ensuring the stock does not boil. Skim frequently.

Remove veal shanks and, while still warm, break off meat, discarding the fat and gelatinous tissues.

The bouillon can be kept aside for use as a soup base for another meal. Strain through a fine chinois or muslin. Allow to settle for 30 minutes, then skim any leftover fat and decant any impurities remaining on the bottom. Adjust the seasoning with salt and a touch of white pepper, if necessary.

Pasta Dough

300 g (10½ oz) plain flour
1 pinch salt
3 eggs
20 ml (1 fl oz) olive oil

Combine the flour and salt. On a work bench, form a mound with the salted flour and make a well in the centre. In a bowl, mix the eggs and olive oil. Pour the egg mixture into the centre of the flour and slowly incorporate the flour with your hands, a little at a time, until you form a firm dough.

Clean the bench with a scraper, incorporating the scrapings into the dough and, after dusting the bench with flour, knead the dough with the heel of your hand for 10 minutes or until it is of a homogenous consistency.

Wrap in plastic wrap and refrigerate overnight or, if using on the day, rest in the fridge for 1 hour.

Cut the dough into 100 g (3½ oz) portions. Lightly dust the board with some flour and roll each portion of dough through a pasta machine or with a rolling pin to achieve sufficient thinness; dust lightly with flour. Cut into desired shapes, stack, and wrap with plastic wrap until ready to use.

White Wine Cream Sauce

8 shallots, chopped

2 cloves garlic, chopped

60 ml (2 fl oz) olive oil

100 ml (3 fl oz) white wine

200 ml (6 fl oz) fish stock

thyme, parsley stalks, sorrel stalks

12 black peppercorns

400 ml (14 fl oz) cream

salt and pepper

Sweat shallots and garlic in olive oil without letting them change colour. Add white wine and reduce to one third of the volume. Add fish stock and reduce by one third of the volume. Add herbs and peppercorns, then add cream and reduce by half, or until you achieve a creamy sauce consistency. Season and strain.

FRANCE

Paris

RESTAURANTS
Alain Ducasse
59 avenue Raymond Poincaré
75116 Paris
Tel 01 53 65 62 00
Fax 01 53 65 62 01
One of the best restaurants of
France with quality and price to
match. Alain Ducasse's cuisine is
imbued with intelligence.

Restaurant Petrelle
34 rue Petrelle
75009 Paris
Tel 01 42 82 11 02
Fax 01 40 23 05 69
A small local restaurant with
simple yet delicious food.
Inexpensive, and enjoys the
patronage of the designer set.

Le Boeuf sur le Toit
34 rue du Colisée 75008 Paris
Tel 01 43 59 83 80
Fax 01 45 63 45 40
A typical Parisian brasserie,
renovated to its former grandeur
and catering to lovers of classic
food.

Le Grand Vefour
17 rue de Beaujolais 75001 Paris
Tel 01 42 96 56 27
Fax 01 42 86 80 71
An eighteenth-century two-star
Michelin restaurant. Its
atmosphere is redolent with
history.

Le Dauphin
167 rue St-Honoré
Place André Malraux
75001 Paris
Tel 01 42 60 40 11
Fax 01 42 60 40 11
Specialises in regional dishes.

L'Écluse
15 Place de la Madeleine
75008 Paris
Tel 01 42 65 34 69
A wine bar which offers a large
range of Bordeaux wines by the
bottle or the glass, and also light
meals if you wish to accompany
your wine with food.

FOOD SHOPS

Boulangerie Poilâne
8 rue du Cherche-Midi
75006 Paris
Tel 01 45 48 42 59
The best bread in Paris is baked and sold in this unique little bakery. A pilgrimage here is a must for any bread connoisseur.

La Fromagerie Boursault
71 avenue du Général-Leclerc
75014 Paris
Tel 01 43 27 93 30
Fax 01 45 38 59 56
A superb cheese shop which specialises in raw milk and regional cheese. Jacques Vernier is its supreme master.

L'Étoile D'Or
30 rue Fontaine 75009 Paris
Tel 01 48 74 59 55
Denise Acabo's chocolaterie–confiserie offers the finest chocolates and confectionary in all of Paris.

Fauchon
26 Place de la Madeleine
75008 Paris
Tel 01 47 42 60 11
Expanding into all corners of the Place de la Madeleine, Fauchon has to be the greatest food store in the world.

Hédiard
21 Place de la Madeleine
75008 Paris
Tel 01 42 66 44 36
Heaven for all food lovers, offering a huge range of the best French products.

E. Dehillerin
18 rue Coquillère 75001 Paris
Tel 01 42 36 53 13
Fax 01 42 36 54 80
The supreme kitchen equipment shop for the fanatical chef, E. Dehillerin sells everything from huge copper pots to the most unusual or old-fashioned kitchenware item.

MARKETS

Rungis Market
Semmaris 1, rue de la Tour
BP 316 – 94152 Rungis Cedex
Tel 01 41 80 80 80 Fax 01 41 80 81 89
The largest fresh produce market in Europe. Situated on the outskirts of Paris, the Rungis Market houses fish and seafood, meat, fruit and vegetables, dairy produce and flower markets.

Marché de la rue Lepic
rue Lepic
75018 Paris
A whole street packed with food sellers of every type, this market has enormous character.

Place de la Madeleine
75008 Paris
The best food and wine shops in Paris are found here. A delight for window shopping or small indulgences.

Champagne

HOTELS
Les Crayères
64 boulevard Henri-Vasnier
51100 Rheims
Tel 03 26 82 80 80
Fax 03 26 82 65 52
A superb retreat set in peaceful wooded surroundings.

Le Grand Hôtel des Templiers
22 rue des Templiers
51100 Rheims
Tel 03 26 88 55 08
Fax 03 26 82 65 52
A perfect alternative to the high luxury of Les Crayères, with very personal service.

HOTEL–RESTAURANTS
La Briqueterie
Route de Sézanne
Vinay, near Épernay
Tel 03 26 59 99 99 Fax 03 26 59 92 10
A restaurant and hotel located in the middle of the picturesque Champagne countryside.

L'Assiette Champenoise
40 avenue Paul Vaillant-Couturier
51100 Rheims
Tel 03 26 84 64 64 Fax 03 26 04 15 69
A small hotel–restaurant run by a chef owner and his family. Serves classic food.

RESTAURANTS
Les Crayères
64 boulevard Henri-Vasnier
51100 Rheims
Tel 03 26 82 80 80
Fax 03 26 82 65 52
Offers the most elegant dining in the whole of France.

Le Foch Restaurant
37 boulevard Foch
51100 Rheims
Tel 03 26 47 48 22
Fax 03 26 88 78 22
An up-and-coming restaurant with a young chef at the helm.

CHAMPAGNE HOUSES
Champagne Louis Roederer
21 boulevard Lundy
51100 Rheims
Tel 03 26 40 42 11
Fax 03 26 47 66 51
A leading champagne house, home of the exclusive Cristal Champagne.

Champagne Krug

5 rue Coquebert
51100 Rheims
Tel 03 26 84 44 20
Fax 03 26 84 44 49
The champagne traditionalists
and a house that has a strong
commitment to gastronomy.

Champagne Laurent-Perrier

Domaine de Tours-sur-Marne
51150 Tours-sur-Marne
Tel 03 26 59 91 22
Fax 03 26 58 95 10
A domaine located centrally
between three prestigious
growing regions.

Alsace

HOTELS
L'Hôtel des Berges

4 rue de Collonges
68970 Illhaeusern
Tel 03 89 71 87 87
Fax 03 89 71 87 88
A small, intimate, family-run
hotel linked to L'Auberge de L'Ill
restaurant.

Hôtel de Rohan

17–19 rue du Maroquin
67000 Strasbourg
Tel 03 88 32 85 11
Fax 03 88 75 65 37
A small hotel situated near the
cathedral in the old quarter
of Strasbourg.

RESTAURANTS
L'Auberge de L'Ill

Chefs: Haeberlin family
68970 Illhaeusern
Tel 03 89 71 89 00
Fax 03 89 71 86 40
One of the oldest surviving three-
star restaurants of France.

Au Pont Corbeau

2 quai Saint Nicolas
67000 Strasbourg
Tel 03 88 35 60 68
A typical *Winstub* or brasserie
which serves the traditional food
of Alsace in a rustic setting.

FACTORY
Georges Bruck Foies
Gras de Strasbourg

7 rue Friesé
67000 Strasbourg
Tel 03 88 32 62 62 Fax 03 88 32
63 00
This company has been making
the world's best *foie gras* products
since 1852.

SHOP
La Boutique du Gourmet

11 rue Mercière
67000 Strasbourg
Tel 03 88 32 00 04 Fax 03 88 32
00 04
A superb shop selling all the *foie
gras* specialities, as well as caviar
and wines.

Burgundy

HOTEL–RESTAURANTS
Lameloise
36 Place d'Armes
71150 Chagny
Tel 03 85 87 08 85
Fax 03 85 87 03 57
A superlative restaurant serving
faultless food by a humble but
magical chef.

Georges Blanc
01540 Vonnas
Ain, Bourg-en Bresse
Tel 04 74 50 90 90
Fax 04 74 50 08 80
A unique family enterprise
comprising a hotel and superb
restaurant on the Veyle River.

RESTAURANTS
Restaurant Ma Cuisine
Passage Sainte-Hélène
21200 Beaune
Tel 03 80 22 30 22
Fax 03 80 24 99 79
A small family restaurant which
serves regional dishes for the
local clientele.

J.L. Barnabet
14 quai République
Tel 03 86 51 68 88
Fax 03 86 52 96 85
A one-star Michelin restaurant
serving honest food. Its
impressive glassed-in kitchen
allows the diner to view the
quality French equipment used
to prepare the food.

VINEYARDS
Maison Louis Jadot
21 rue Eugène Spuller
21200 Beaune
Tel 03 80 22 10 57
Fax 03 80 22 56 03
One of the best *négociants* of
Burgundy with superb holdings
in quality wines.

Domain Laroche
L'Obédiencerie
22 rue Louis Bro
89800 Chablis
Tel 03 86 42 89 24
Fax 03 86 42 89 29
A superlative Domaine of Chablis
offering a range of fantastic wines.

COOPERAGE
Tonnellerie Damy Pére et Fils
21 rue des Forges
21190 Meursault
Tel 03 80 21 23 41
Fax 03 80 24 15 28
A small, quality, family barrel-
making enterprise which sells its
barrels all around the world.

MUSEUM
Musée de la Bresse
Domaine des Planons
01380 Saint-Cyr-sur-Menthon
Tel 04 85 36 31 22
Fax 04 74 32 66 53
A restored regional farm
demonstrating the traditional
farming of the famous *poulet de
Bresse.*

COOKING SCHOOL
La Varenne
Château du Feÿ
89300 Villecien
Tel 03 86 63 18 34
Fax 03 86 63 01 33
Anne Willan's exclusive cooking
school. Here, in magical settings,
one can experience the luxury of
château life.

Bordeaux

HOTEL
L'Echassier
16100 Châteaubernard Cognac
Tel 05 45 32 29 04
Fax 05 45 35 01 09
A small practical hotel near
Cognac.

HOTEL–RESTAURANT
Château de L'Yeuse
16100 Châteaubernard Cognac
Tel 05 45 36 82 60
Fax 05 45 35 06 32
A newly restored hotel–restaurant
offering a superb menu.

RESTAURANT
La Ribaudière
Place du Port
16200 Bourg Charente
Tel 05 45 81 30 54
Fax 05 45 81 28 05
A Michelin restaurant offering an
astonishing range of Cognac.

COGNAC HOUSE
Rémy Martin
20 rue de la Société Vinicole
16100 Cognac
Tel 05 45 35 76 00
Fax 05 45 35 77 98
A committed Grande Maison de
Cognac which welcomes visits
from the public.

COOPERAGE
Tonnellerie Seguin Moreau
ZI Merpins–BP94
16103 Cognac
Tel 05 45 82 62 22
Fax 05 45 82 14 28
A huge cooperage which offers
tours to the public.

HOTEL
Château de Castel Novel
19240 Varetz
Tel 05 55 85 00 01
Fax 05 55 85 09 03
A château–hotel with old-world charm in a beautiful wooded setting. A perfect base for exploring the surrounding countryside.

HOTEL–RESTAURANT
Hôtel Terminus
5 avenue Charles de Freycinet
46000 Cahors
Tel 05 65 30 01 97
Fax 05 65 22 06 40
A hotel–restaurant in the centre of Cahors with pleasant rooms and a good restaurant.

RESTAURANTS
Le Pont de l'Ouysse
46200 Lacave
Tel 05 65 37 87 04
Fax 05 65 32 77 41
Honest food in a remote and idyllic location in Périgord.

Le Gindreau
St-Médard 46150 Catus
A romantic restaurant set in the Vert valley near the town of Catus. Serves superb regional food prepared by Alexis Pélissou.

PRODUCERS
Moulin à l'Huile de Noix
MM Castagné
Route de Bretenoux
46000 Martel
Tel 05 65 37 30 69
or 05 65 37 38 39
A rustic walnut oil press house which sells its oils to the public.

Monteil, Champignons des Bois
20/22 rue Francois Labrousse
19100 Brive
Tel 05 55 88 00 73
Fax 05 55 87 14 13
An old family company which collects and sells wild mushrooms and enjoys a worldwide export market.

Pébeyre S.A. Truffles
66 rue Frédéric-Suisse
46000 Cahors
Tel 05 65 22 24 80
Fax 05 65 30 01 66
A respected family business dedicated to the promotion, enjoyment and trading of black truffles.

Rocamadour Fermier
Ferme des Champs-Bons
46200 Lachapelle-Auzac
Tel 05 65 37 82 52
A small goat's cheese factory which sells the traditional Rocamadour cheese. Well worth the detour.

MUSEUM
La Chantrerie
35 rue de la Chantrerie
46000 Cahors
Tel 05 65 23 97 32
A museum exhibiting the food
and wine products of Périgord
including Cahors' famous wines
and truffles.

Monaco

RESTAURANTS
Le Louis XV
Hôtel de Paris
Place du Casino
Monte Carlo
MC 98000 Monaco
Tel 377 92 16 30 01
Fax 377 92 16 69 21
Alain Ducasse repeats his
fabulous cuisine here with a
strong Mediterranean influence.
Stunning dining room.

Café de Paris
Place du Casino
Monte Carlo
MC 98000 Monaco
Tel 377 92 16 20 20
Fax 377 92 16 38 58
The perfect place to watch or be
watched while sipping a cocktail
or enjoying a light lunch. An
enormous nineteenth-century-
style brasserie serves classic, well-
cooked food.

La Maison du Caviar
1 avenue Saint-Charles
98000 Monaco
Tel 93 30 80 06 Fax 93 30 23 90
Affordable restaurant with well-
prepared French food. Enjoys
a regular clientele. Look out for
the superb blinis with caviar.

ITALY

Liguria

HOTELS
Hotel Splendido
Salita Baratta 13
Portofino
Tel 0185 26 95 51
Fax 0185 26 96 14
An amazing hotel set high on the
cliff above Portofino,
overlooking the beautiful
harbour.

TRATTORIAS
Trattoria La Concordia
Western end of Piazza della
Libertâ
Portofino
Tucked away in a cobblestone
street, facing the local garage, this
family-run trattoria offers simple
but fantastic Italian food.

Giorgio
San Fruttuoso
Portofino Peninsula
Tel 0185 77 17 81
Tiny seafood restaurant carved
into the cliff face. Delicious and
unique.

Lombardy

HOTELS
Four Seasons Hotel
Via Gesù 8
Milan
Tel 02 77 08 8
Fax 02 77 08 50 00
Located in a beautiful old
convent building, the Four
Seasons Hotel has to be one of
the best hotels in the world.

Villa d'Este
Cernobbio
Lake Como
Tel 031 34 81
Fax 031 34 88 44
A grand and gracious hotel on
the banks of Lake Como where
every guest is treated like royalty.

RESTAURANT
Il Teatro
Four Seasons Hotel
Via Gesù 8
Milan
Tel 02 77 08 8
A wonderful contemporary
restaurant.

L'Oste della Locanda
Isola Comacina
Lake Como
Tel 034 45 50 83 or 567 55
Fax 034 45 70 22
Situated on the only island of
Lake Como, this restaurant offers
a unique experience in the pure
flavour and style of Italy.

TRATTORIAS
Bagutta Trattoria Toscana
Via Bagutta 14–16
Milan
Tel 02 76 00 27 67
An idiosyncratic restaurant with
overflowing character and food
to satisfy everyone.

Trattoria Masuelli San Marco
Viale Umbria 80
Milan
Tel 02 55 18 41 38
A temple of northern cuisine
where the food is cooked simply
but with incredible flair.

FOOD STORES
Peck
Via Spadari 9
Milan
Tel 02 86 46 11 58
Milan's exceptional food shop—
the range is phenomenal and you
could spend hours here admiring
the displays.

Il Salumaio
Via Monte Napoleone 12
Milan
Tel 02 76 00 11 23
A small and unique food shop
that cannot but leave you
hungry.

PRODUCER
Medeghini, Industria Agricola
Via Cortine 2
Villa Cortine di Mazzano
Brescia
Tel 030 25 991
Fax 030 25 99 200
A large cheese factory run by the
Medeghini family, with an
amazing ageing vault of Grana
Padano.

Veneto

HOTEL
Hotel Victoria
Via Adua 8
Verona
Tel 045 59 05 66
A very clean and well-run hotel
in the centre of Verona with easy
access to the Arena and all the
sights of Verona.

POSSESSIONI AND VINEYARD
Possessioni di Serègo Alighieri
Gargagnago di Valpolicella
Tel 045 770 36 22
Fax 045 770 35 23
This historical estate is divided into eight apartments, making it a great base for a group of friends, or food lovers wanting to learn about Italian wine and food.

RESTAURANT
Bottega del Vino
Via Scudo di Francia 3
Verona
Tel 045 800 45 35
Fax 045 801 22 73
A rustic wine bar with a very impressive wine list. Also serves traditional food.

TRATTORIA
Trattoria Due Archi
Via Ghetto 3
Gargagnago di Valpolicella
Tel/Fax 045 770 33 00
A small and pleasant trattoria serving local specialities like horsemeat stew and risotto.

PRODUCERS
Pila Vecia
Via Saccovener 6
Isola della Scala
Tel 045 730 10 22
Fax 045 730 19 89
Gabriele Ferron's rice mill, where you can eat risotto cooked in the traditional way.

Masi Agricola
Gargagnago di Valpolicella
Tel 045 680 05 88
Fax 045 680 06 08
One of the better wineries of Valpolicella whose excellent wines are exported throughout the world.

Venice

HOTEL
Hotel Cipriani
Giudecca 10
Venice
Tel 041 520 77 44
Fax 041 520 39 30
One of the most romantic hotels in the world, situated on the island of Giudecca across the Canale di San Marco.

RESTAURANTS
Ristorante Da Ivo
Ramo dei Fuseri
San Marco 1809
Tel 041 520 58 89
That rare thing—a Venetian
restaurant that remains true to its
origin. Simple cooking but
superb seafood and a wine list to
challenge any wine lover.

Florian's
Piazza San Marco
San Marco 5659
A nineteenth-century café that
includes Dickens and Proust
amongst its famous historical
patrons.

Tuscany

HOTELS
Scandicci
Florence
Tel 055 76 85 43
Fax 055 76 85 31
A superb villa in the hills just
outside of Florence. Wonderful
personal service.

Grand Hotel Cavour
Via del Proconsolo 3
Florence
Tel 055 28 24 61
Fax 055 21 89 55
An elegant hotel in what used to
be an abbey. It has a grand
atmosphere and well-appointed
rooms.

Viva Hotel
Pitti Palace
Via Barbadori 2 Angolo Via
Guicciardini
Florence
Tel 055 239 87 11
Fax 055 239 88 67
A small hotel next to the Ponte
Vecchio.

RESTAURANTS
Enoteca Ristorante Pinchiorri
Via Ghibellina 87
Florence
Tel 055 24 27 77 or 24 27 57
Fax 055 24 49 83
A fabulous restaurant which
showcases the food of Annie
Feolde, and Giorgio Pinchiorri's
incredible wine cellar.

Cantinetta Antinori
Piazza degli Antinori 3
Florence
Tel 055 29 22 34
Fax 055 23 59 87
An inexpensive and very buzzy
wine bar serving excellent
fare which, for the most part, like
the wine, comes from
the Antinori landholding.

TRATTORIA
Omero
Via Pian dei Giullari 11
Florence
Tel 055 22 00 53
A very authentic trattoria situated
at the back of an old grocery store.

PRODUCERS
L'Antica Macelleria-Cecchini
Panzano, Chianti
Tel 055 85 20 20
Fax 055 85 27 00
A fascinating butcher's shop
operated by a dedicated butcher
who is reviving Tuscany's ancient
recipes.

Fattoria Corzano e Paterno
Localitâ San Pancrazio
San Casciano
Florence
Tel 055 824 81 78
A small, difficult-to-find cheese
factory which specialises in the
traditional cheeses of the area.

Fattoria Terrabianca
San Fedele a Paterno
Radda, Chianti
Tel 0577 73 85 44
Fax 0577 73 86 23
A superb new winery and food
factory which prepares and
exports all the Italian specialities.

Umbria

HOTEL
Hotel Brufani
Piazza Italia 12
Perugia
Tel 075 573 25 41
Fax 075 572 02 10
An old-world hotel set high on
the hilltops of Perugia,
first opened in 1884.

RESTAURANTS
Vissani
Strada Statale 448
Civitella del Lago
Lake Corbara
Tel 0744 95 03 96
A serious restaurant which can
claim to be one of the best in
Italy. Chef Gianfranco Vissani
serves precise food and uses
superb products.

Sandri
Corso Vannucci 32
Perugia
Tel 075 610 12 or 572 41 12
A caffè–pasticceria, established in
1860, which produces
spectacular cakes and pastries.
Also serves bar meals which, if
freshly made, are a delight.

Pesciaioli Roberto Bar Ristorante
Piazza G. Verdi 4
Portaria, near Acquasparta
Tel 0744 93 11 74
A bar/restaurant in a tiny fortress hill town which serves authentic Umbrian food.

SHOPS
Panetteria Ceccarini
Piazza Matteotti 16
Perugia
A specialist bread shop that also displays a range of cookies, cakes, tarts and petit fours.

Genni Bar Gelateria
Via Roma 180
Terni
A glorious ice-cream shop with a large and delicious range of the creamiest and most refreshing ice-cream or gelato. A meeting place for young and older lovers.

Dai Fratelli
Specialità Gastronomiche
Via del Duomo 11
Orvieto
Tel 0763 34 39 65
A superb food shop selling everything gastronomic from truffles to wild boar sausages. Very impressive displays.

Spezeria Bavicchi
Piazza Matteotti 32
Perugia
A shop selling beans and other essential dried goods required for Umbrian cuisine.

PRODUCER
Azienda Agricola
Conti Possenti Castelli
Via Cavour 16
Terni
Tel/Fax 0744 42 81 70
Maria Possenti's olive farm produces magnificent olive oil and other products. Tours can be arranged by prior agreement.

WINERY
Marchesi Antinori Estates
Castello della Sala
Headquarters: Piazza degli Antinori 3
Florence
Tel 055 235 95
Fax 055 235 98 84
Antinori have an immense range of wineries throughout Tuscany and Umbria. Tours can be arranged at some of them.

The Marches

HOTEL
Hotel Fortino Napoleonico
Portonovo
Ancona
Tel 071 80 14 50
Fax 071 80 14 54
A superbly situated hotel built in an old Napoleonic fort right on the Adriatic sea. Isolated and relaxing.

RESTAURANTS
Ristorante Il Laghetto
Portonovo
Ancona
Tel 071 80 11 83
A seaside restaurant which serves local seafood in a magic setting featuring views of the Conero Riviera.

La Cantina dello Squaloblù
Via de Gasperi 49
Termoli
Tel 0875 83 20 3
A simple restaurant that cooks plain dishes well.

PRODUCERS
Azienda Agraria Latini
Via di Jesi 186
Osimo
Ancona
Tel 071 78 19 768
Carlo and Carla Latini produce superb pasta with wheat grown in their own fields. A tour of the wheat fields, flour mill and the Pastificio in Francavilla can be arranged.

Colonna Estate
I 86046 Masseria Bosco Pontoni
San Martino in Pensilis
Campobasso
Tel 875 60 57 35
Fax 875 60 56 06
Marina Colonna is considered a pioneer of quality in the production of her excellent virgin olive oil and other olive products.

SHOP
Casa del Fromaggio
Piazza Mercato
Termoli
A wonderful shop for cheese, olives, bread, wine and salami. The Piazza Mercato also houses some good pasta and vegetable shops.

Rome

HOTEL
Albergo Santa Chiara
Via di Santa Chiara 21
Rome
Tel 06 687 29 79
Fax 06 687 31 44
This is only one option out of the
many hotels Rome has to offer. It
is pleasant, clean and efficiently
run and is handy to many of
Rome's attractions.

RESTAURANT
Checchino dal 1887
Via di Monte Testaccio 30
Rome
Tel 574 63 18
A historic restaurant which serves
food inspired by the culinary
style of the past century. Offal
features heavily on the menu,
but it is deliciously prepared.

COOKING SCHOOL
Diane Seed Cooking School
Via del Plebiscito 112
Rome
Tel 66 79 71 03
Fax 66 79 71 09
Diane Seed's Cooking School
offers week-long courses
in Diane's own home in the
Palazzo Doria Pamphilj.
The course includes excursions to
the markets and ends
with a typical Roman dinner.

SHOPS
Volpetti
Via Marmorata 47
Testaccio market
Rome
Superb and unique food shop,
small in size but with an
exhaustive range of products.

Trimani
Via Goito 20
Rome
Impressive wine shop which also
sells food specialities and has a
caffè attached.

Giolitti
Via Uffici del Vicario 40
Rome
A gelateria not to be missed. Mix
your favourite flavours and ...